THE

Resume Strategies for Stay at Home Moms

KAREN GURNEY

Get the free video companion course to see this book in action at

www.karengurney.com/mom

CAREER IQ LLC PUBLISHERS
CLEVELAND OH

Copyright © 2017 by Karen Gurney

All rights reserved.

ISBN: **9780999142721**
ISBN-13: **978-0-9991427-2-1**

DEDICATION

To my mom who raised three great men and a pretty ok daughter, 'managed' dad, kept the household clicking, and touched thousands of lives as a nurse. You were my first model of what it meant to be a powerful back to work mom.

Contents

MY STORY AND WHY THIS BOOK IS FOR YOU 9

B2W MOM MANIFESTO 12

CHAPTER 1: B2W MOM CORE STRATEGY 15

1.1 B2W Moms Top 15 Myths 16
1.2 B2W Mom Core Strategy 24
1.3 Meet the B2W Moms 25
1.4 The B2W Mom Strategy Summary 36
> Homework 37
Quiz 1: B2W Mom Strategy (T/F) 38

CHAPTER 2: GET RECRUITERS TO WORK FOR YOU WITH LINKEDIN 40

2.1 Nine Most Common Job Search Myths 40
2.2 The 3-Step Recruiter Process 43
2.3 Types of Recruiters and Why It Matters 48
2.4 "Leverage the Recruiters" Strategy Recap 61
> Homework 63
Quiz 2: Recruiters (T/F) 64

CHAPTER 3: YOUR CORE-3© CAREER ASSESSMENT 66

3.1 Career, Jobs, and Personality Test Myths 67
3.2 The Core-3© Career Assessment 71

3.3 FINDING YOUR DREAM JOB 79
3.4 TARGETED JOB ALERTS 81
3.5 IDENTIFYING PART-TIME & STAFFING AGENCIES 82
>HOMEWORK 84
QUIZ 3: CAREER ASSESSMENT (T/F) 85

CHAPTER 4: MARKET-BASED RESUME© TEMPLATE 87

4.1 MODERN RESUME MYTHS 89
4.2 THE 4-EASY STEPS TO A RESUME THAT GETS CALLS 98
4.3 COVER LETTERS 112
> HOMEWORK 117
QUIZ 4: RESUME & COVER LETTER (T/F) 118

CHAPTER 5: LINKEDIN AND ONLINE PROFILES THAT TAP THE HIDDEN JOB MARKET 120

5.1 LINKEDIN AND ONLINE JOB BOARD MYTHS 121
5.2 MONSTER.COM AND PROFESSIONAL CATEGORIES 123
5.3 LINKEDIN.COM PROFILE OPTIMIZATION 128
5.4 INDEED.COM AND THE TOP OF YOUR RESUME 139
5.5 OTHER JOB BOARDS & NICHE STAFFING WEBSITES 142
5.6 CHECK THE COMPETITION, BOOST RANKINGS, GET MORE CONTENT 143
>HOMEWORK 145
QUIZ 5: LINKEDIN AND ONLINE JOB PORTALS (T/F) 147

CHAPTER 6: B2W MOM CAMPAIGN KICKOFF 149

QUIZ 6: B2W MOM KICKOFF CAMPAIGN (T/F) 155

CHAPTER 7: PHONE SCREENS & INTERVIEW PREPARATION. 157

7.1 INTERVIEW MYTHS 157
7.2 PHONE SCREEN INTERVIEW 167
7.3 COMMON PHONE SCREEN & INTERVIEW QUESTIONS 174
7.4 REASON FOR EACH QUESTION AND STRATEGY 175
7.5 INTERVIEW WORKSHEET SCRIPTS 184
7.6 EXPLAINING TERMINATIONS OR DISMISSALS 191
7.7 BEHAVIORAL INTERVIEW SCRIPTING 197
7.8 QUESTIONS FOR THE EMPLOYER 206
7.9 WHAT NOT TO SAY IN AN INTERVIEW 210
7.10 INTERVIEW PORTFOLIO 214
7.11 THANK YOU LETTER 215
>HOMEWORK 218
QUIZ 7: INTERVIEWING (T/F) 219

CHAPTER 8: SALARY NEGOTIATIONS AND DESIRED SALARY QUOTING 221

8.1 SALARY NEGOTIATION MYTHS 222
8.2 WHAT TO QUOTE FOR DESIRED SALARY 227
8.3 PERFORMING A SALARY SURVEY LESSON 235
8.4 NEW HIRE SALARY NEGOTIATIONS 238
8.5 EXISTING EMPLOYEE SALARY NEGOTIATIONS LESSON 247
8.6 ALTERNATIVE NEGOTIATION ITEM QUICK REFERENCE SHEET 262
>HOMEWORK 264
QUIZ 8: SALARY NEGOTIATIONS (T/F) 265

CHAPTER 9: NETWORKING TO GET A JOB: ALTERNATIVE STRATEGIES 267

9.1 NETWORKING MYTHS 268
9.2 MAKING A LIST OF CHAMPIONS AND INFORMATIONAL INTERVIEWS 271
9.3 VOLUNTEERING 275

9.4 STAFFING AGENCIES, FREELANCE/GIGS, AND TITLE AND REFERENCE SWAP 277
>HOMEWORK 281
QUIZ 9: NETWORKING (T/F) 283

CHAPTER 10: ADVANCED LINKEDIN STRATEGIES 285

10.1 ADVANCED LINKEDIN STRATEGY MYTHS 287
10.2 LINKEDIN PREMIUM -TO BUY OR NOT TO BUY 289
10.3 NETWORKING 2.0 VIA A LINKEDIN CONNECTION CAMPAIGN 293
>HOMEWORK 298
QUIZ 10: ADVANCED LINKEDIN STRATEGIES (T/F) 299

CHAPTER 11: UNIQUE CAREER CHANGE TYPES AND STRATEGIES 301

11.1 CAREER CHANGE COMMON MYTHS 301
11.2 LATERAL MOVE LESSON 307
11.3 OVERQUALIFIED - STEP DOWN LESSON 312
11.4 MOVE FOR PROMOTION LESSON 320
11.5 RETURN TO PRIOR PROFESSION LESSON 327
11.6 NEW GRADUATE OR ENTRY-LEVEL LESSON 331
11.7 NEW INDUSTRY BUT SAME PROFESSION LESSON 339
11.8 COMPLETE CAREER CHANGE INTO A NEW PROFESSION AND INDUSTRY LESSON 341
11.9 GAPS IN EMPLOYMENT LESSON 345
11.10 GEOGRAPHIC RELOCATION LESSON 350
>HOMEWORK 352
QUIZ 11: CAREER & JOB CHANGE TYPES (T/F) 353

CHAPTER 12: TIMING AND TROUBLESHOOTING THE JOB SEARCH CAMPAIGN 355

12.1 THE 3-MONTH STACKED JOB SEARCH CHECKLIST.................... 359
12.2 TROUBLESHOOTING CHECKLISTS 361
12.3 JOB SEARCH TIMING CHECKLIST 365
>HOMEWORK 367
QUIZ 12: JOB SEARCH STRATEGY (T/F) 368

ABOUT THE AUTHOR 371

ONE LAST THING 372

My Story and Why This Book is for You

I have been working in the recruiting industry as an Executive Search Consultant and Career Coach since 2004, but in 2010 I signed a client that completely shook the foundations of my coaching business – a Back to Work (B2W) mom with a 17-year gap in employment.

My client, Marie, was going through a horrible divorce resulting in the family business going bankrupt. She had no income, spouse, or health insurance. Her child was about to enter college and she told me during a coaching session that her self-esteem was in the gutter.

Marie had no idea where to start with her job search and honestly, neither did I. How could we reasonably overcome a 17-year gap to achieve any type of meaningful job opportunity?

Before I started her job search campaign, she sent me her original resume - a jpeg snapshot of a resume from 1993. That was before MS Word 1995 and it seemed to be written before the dawn of time.

But guess what? Marie did achieve a dream-fantasy job move despite her barriers to employment and that is not the best part... she was quickly earning her professional rate, as if she had never left the workforce.

So, what is the secret? Six simple B2W mom strategies that you are about to learn in this book.

I have been crushing with my B2W mom job candidates. Once you learn this strategy, you can too.

What You Will Be Able to Do After Reading This Book:
- Get back to work.
- Get back to your full (as-if-you-never-left) income.
- Have a reliable strategy that provides more certainty.
- Quickly and happily overcome a gaping hole on your resume.
- Interview based on your great skills (not your gap.)

This book is a revised strategy specifically for my B2W mom job candidates that includes everything in my book *Stacked: Double Your Job Interviews, Leverage Recruiters, Unlock LinkedIn* but is uniquely tailored to B2W mom challenges.

The Stacked Strategy Teaches You How To:
- Have Recruiters Come Straight to You for Great Jobs.
- Get Calls for Jobs Without Applying.
- Double Your Interviews.
- Tap Unadvertised Jobs in The Hidden Job Market.

Bonus - You Also Get My Online $200 B2W Mom Class - Free!
This book works hand-in-hand with my online video class which allows Q&A for targeted personal strategy questions. With the class you get:

- Video Instruction
- B2W Mom Resume Templates
- My copyrighted 'Core-3© Career Assessment

- Fill-in-the-Blank Interview Preparation Scripts
- Salary Negotiation Scripts
- And so much more!

This strategy is specifically for B2W moms that have:

- A 1-year to 20-year gap in employment.
- A work history prior to the stay-at-home period.
- Or, a series of intermittent work experiences and gaps.

This book is not written for the moms that went straight back to work after maternity leave.

These methods have facilitated thousands of career changes, and now you can use them too!

I look forward to giving you a plan to help close the gap and change the dialogue to reach your career goals.

Sincerely,
Dr. Karen Gurney

B2W Mom Manifesto:
Back to Work (B2W) Mom Rules of Engagement

To win the game you need to know the following rules.

To get a job and advance in your career as a B2W mom, you will need to help employers overcome the level of **uncertainty** they have about your ability to:
1. Make work a priority.
2. Manage the competing demands of home and work.
3. Emotionally handle leaving 'full-time' parenting.
4. Physically handle the discipline of clocking into a job every single day.
5. Perform well on a job with out-of-date or stale skills.

To improve the employer's level of **certainty, you will need to:**
• Show evidence of a 'current' commitment to your career. (You simply cannot just tell them you are ready—you must provide evidence.)
• Offer professional explanations for your gap.

To improve your own **personal level of certainty,** you will need to:
• <u>**Plan ahead**</u> of when you want to be full-time.
• ***Begin practicing*** your commitment to your career over a 2-year re-entry period.
• **Give yourself a break.** It takes a lot of emotional, psychological and physical energy to make this shift. The good news is that you are not alone and I will give you a plan that works.

• If you are a mom that absolutely needs **full-time work** immediately, these strategies also work for you. BUT, on average, it will take 2-years to achieve the 'as-if-you-never-left' full employment title and income.

The B2W Mom Strategy
  > Increases employer certainty in your abilities.
  > Increases your confidence and certainty to manage all your 'moving parts.'
  > Pre-qualifies you for jobs.
  > Makes job changes quicker and less painful.
  > Creates easier job interviews.
  > Builds a solid foundation for salary negotiations.
  > Closes the gap and gets you back to 'full-employment' faster.

In the B2W mom strategy, you do not apologize about your status. Instead, you position yourself based on your strengths to achieve the best possible outcome.

How This Book is Organized

There are 12 chapters of B2W mom strategy with a typical chapter including:

- Myths Discussed and Debunked
- Section Exercises
- Homework
- Quizzes

Chapter 1: B2W Mom Core Strategy
Chapter 2: Get Recruiters to Work for You with LinkedIn
Chapter 3: Your Core-3© Career Assessment
Chapter 4: Market-Based Resume© Template
Chapter 5: LinkedIn and Online Profiles That Tap the Hidden Job Market
Chapter 6: B2W Mom Campaign Kickoff
Chapter 7: Phone Screens & Interview Preparation
Chapter 8: Salary Negotiations & Desired Salary Quoting
Chapter 9: Networking to Get a Job: Alternative Strategies
Chapter 10: Advanced LinkedIn Strategies
Chapter 11: Unique Career Change Types & Strategies
Chapter 12: Timing and Troubleshooting the Job Search Campaign
About the Author
One Last Thing

Chapter 1: B2W Mom Core Strategy

As a B2W mom, you intuitively know that recruiters are seeking qualified professionals that have current work experience. Common wisdom suggests that overcoming the gap in employment is the biggest issue for this segment of job candidates.

I am not going to say that your employment gap isn't a big deal. However, what if I told you that, after 7+ years of coaching B2W moms, it actually is one of the *last items* on the rather large list of issues affecting your transition?

In the next section, you will hear some of the most damaging myths that B2W moms have said to me. Every myth will not apply to you. But, chances are you will find one or two that do.

Following the myth section, I will present the six core B2W mom strategies. The online class has a further discussion of each strategy and resume templates for your use. Once we learn the B2W methods, we will also learn how to deploy them within the Stacked strategy. But first, we need to get some B2W mom housekeeping out of the way.

This chapter includes the following lessons:
1.1 – B2W Moms Top 15 Myths
1.2 – B2W Mom Core Strategy
1.3 – Meet the B2W Moms
1.4 – B2W Mom Strategy Summary

1.1 B2W Moms Top 15 Myths

Chances are, one or two of these myths apply to you. Do not pass this section. It creates an important foundation for the strategy.

Myth 1: I am ready to get back to work.

Yes and no. Yes, I find that many moms are 100% ready to be cognitively engaged with a group of professionals discussing adult issues. Moms may also be ready to start generating a solid wage or to contribute to society through the work-world in addition to raising quality human beings. So, in that sense, it is true that a mom may be ready to get back to work.

On the flip side, I often find that many moms do not fully calculate the tectonic emotional shift or resource allocation demands that will occur in a 'return-to-work' scenario. Psychologists that study the mother-child bond state that an infant can literally not separate their existence from their mother. I find the same for the mom. The link between the mother and child is so strong that a woman's self-worth can become completely tied to her success as a mom. The problem is, if your self-worth is linked to being a mom, then getting a job theoretically reduces your self-value. If you are a mom that feels this way, you are unconsciously telegraphing your concerns to the employer.

In addition to the emotional aspects of walking out that door and into the work world again, you may have chosen to stay at home because there was no acceptable child care solution. This means that your resources for child care are limited. To further compound this issue, there are the daily child care needs *and* the last-minute 'my child has the flu' requirements. Employers know that children have sick days or other issues and, when they hire a mom, they are hiring *all of those issues*. Companies do not offer enough sick time to cover mom and her children's time-off needs.

That is where this strategy coupled with your effective resource management comes into play.

Myth 2: Going back to work is scarier for me than it is for the employer.

Yes and no. Employers are fully aware that this is huge shift for stay-at-home moms and it scares the heck out of them. For an employer to hire a B2W mom, they need to know that mom is not scared or worried about making work a primary focus for a set daily schedule. The employer also needs to know that you have resources to support the daily child care and the last-minute sick days.

I want to stop here and say...the employer is not actually going to ask if you have arranged your child care resources. One of the things you will learn in this book is the fine art of 'telegraphing' the message that you have everything worked out through your resume content and interview answers.

If you view the employer as completely scared s***less about your candidacy, you will be in a good position to apply the strategy I am offering you.

What you are about to learn will help calm the employer's fears and put you in control of your career.

Myth 3: There is no one with a gap as big as mine. I must be your hardest client ever.

No. My first B2W mom had a 17-year gap and was going through divorce, bankruptcy, loss of her house, no health care, and multiple major life crises. It is rare for me to come across someone as challenging to place as Marie. However, I find a lot of moms like to start the conversation with me by stating "I must be your hardest client ever." Is it because they want to sink into a pit of despair? Do they secretly want me to say, "I can't help you?" Do they want to self-sooth over the pain of not having a robust career? Do they want to feel special by focusing on their unique challenges? Chances are, your transition is not the worst I have ever seen.

Believe me, you are special, but not due to your job transition.

Myth 4: Employers understand I need work-life balance.

No. In fact, they fear your need for work-life balance. Employers need to feel that they are your #1 priority for a set schedule per week and that you have the resources and a support system available to manage issues that arise with the family during the time you have dedicated to work.

What is one more kid? (Sigh) You can do this!

Myth 5: Employers respect that my children are #1 in my life.

Yes and no. Employers understand that children are the most important priority in virtually any parent's life. BUT, the employer is like a child and it demands your attention for a set schedule. This is even more complicated because most of your interviewers will have children. Therefore, they will have immediately gone back to work or have already gone through the process of striking this balance. The level of empathy and understanding will differ but the fact remains they need you at work on a regular schedule with extremely infrequent absences.

Your kids are #1 but for the job search, we will not be messaging that.

Myth 6: Employers should view my parenting experience like a job.

No. Unfortunately, this has not changed much over time. You and I both know being a mom is a 24/7 job with no pay, retirement, or time off. But from the employer's perspective, being a mom is not the equivalent of a professional job.

Myth 7: I am a back to work mom (even though I have actually been working).

This requires some explanation. I cannot even tell you how many moms come to me saying they are a B2W mom, then they tell me that they have had a job of some sort (sometimes for many years). There are two stages for B2W moms that we will be discussing: 1) re-entry and 2) full employment. Many readers of this book may be in the re-entry period and are ready to leverage their experiences for full employment. The strategy and expectation for each stage is different.

The Stacked strategy you are about to learn is effective over the lifetime of your career.

Myth 8: I can single-handedly shift the cultural perception of stay-at-home moms.

Not as a job candidate. Once you are in a position to hire your own staff, run a business, or hold an elected office, you can start making an impact on how moms are perceived in the workplace.

My expectation is that the B2W mom cultural perception will change once the eldest sector of the Millennial generation becomes the dominant percentage of executive and legislative leadership, slated between years 2030 to 2040.

Right now, a group of wealthy, aged 50+, baby boomer men are making employment and legislative decisions. The average age of congressional official is 58 years old and 81% are men. The average age of an executive in the United States is over 52 and the percentage of men is about 90%. The 2017 Senate panel on women's health issues was 100% male! I would not want my dad making my reproductive and career decisions and neither should you.

That is why this book is important. Moms need the chance to become successful leaders, but it will take time and require a strategy.

Myth 9: Employers understand that I may need to leave work at the drop of a hat.

No. Many employers are understanding up to a point. However, business needs to get done and if the staff is taking off frequently or even irregularly, it may be difficult to keep the operation afloat. There are staff equity issues as well. If the team is seeing allowances for moms, they will want perks themselves and that can create a lot of trouble for the managers.

Myth 10: Employers understand that I need many weeks or months off of work.

No. Currently in the United States, two-weeks off after a year of full-time work is still the norm. Other countries have their own norms and, if you are located outside of the United States, you will need to follow your respective country's customs.

Myth 11: I can get a job if I am angry about how our culture perceives stay-at-home moms.

No. In fact, you cannot get a job if you are angry about anything. For the purpose of interviewing and getting a job, you and your family need to be healthy, happy, and thriving.

Myth 12: Employers understand that I have to go back to work for income purposes, but I do not really want to.

No. Employers only want to hire people that want a job. The problem here is this – a job candidate tends to telegraph their unhappiness within the interview. If you are unhappy, despondent, or worried, it will come across that you are not a happy engaged job candidate. A B2W mom may need to fake happiness about her job search to be successful.

<u>Myth 13: I can put stay-at-home mom on my resume, or say it in the interview, and get a job.</u>

No. You are essentially telling employers 'I already have a full-time job and I will be moonlighting with you.' For a moment, I am asking you to think like the employer. If you were a manager, would you want to hire someone that is telling you that this new job will be a side gig. No, you would not. The duty of a manager is to make sure the team is fully staffed and that the department is meeting its metrics with engaged employees.

I find some moms get angry that their stay-at-home status is not more respected or accepted. I want to validate you here. You have one of the hardest, most-demanding, emotional, physically-exhausting, and important jobs on earth. The problem is, employers understand that too. They need to know you are ready to balance these demands. You are ready!

<u>Myth 14: I can only leave the house if the job is perfect and pays at a rate that will cover child care costs with some extra left over. Otherwise, it is not worth it.</u>

No. This thought process will kill your career transition dead in its tracks. There are many things that your first job needs to achieve, including:

1) Establishing your commitment to your career.
2) Getting you back in the swing of things.
3) Adjusting your resources to manage home and career.
4) Managing the emotional and self-worth issues of leaving the home.

That is a lot of things for one job to have to do. My goal for your re-entry job is to break-even on your child care costs. I know that is not exciting to hear, but re-entry jobs are typically a stepping stone to 'as-if-you-never-left' full employment. <u>This fact is already true</u>. I am simply formalizing it here so you can get ready for what would likely have occurred anyway. It is very rare for B2W moms to hit their dream job (and pay) straight off an employment gap. But we <u>will</u> get you there.

<u>Myth 15: My employment gap is the biggest problem with getting back to work.</u>

Yes and No. As you can tell by now, the biggest issues are the following:
• Can you make your work schedule THE priority over your children's schedule for a set period every day?
• Are you telegraphing that you actually want to work (or is it just that you have to)?
• Are you going to be a happy, stable, contributing team member or a physically and emotionally exhausted employee?

23

- Have you managed your resources so you have adequate support and you will not take time off at a 'drop of the hat?'
- Will you stay at the job at least two years?
- Lastly, has your job gap created a situation where your skills are not current?

This book focuses on an A to Z job search strategy to help you get back to work. But, we cannot do that if you are not aware of issues listed above. Now that we have uncovered the sabotaging thought patterns affecting B2W moms, we can learn and apply the correct strategy that will achieve a successful transition.

1.2 B2W Mom Core Strategy

The goal of the B2W mom strategy is to give the job market, recruiters, and hiring managers clear signals about your career commitment. I am not going to tell you how to manage your emotions or your resources. It is your job to figure that part out. My job is to give you a strategy that closes the gap on your resume to reduce the anxiety and fear the employer faces when considering a B2W mom. You are also going to learn how to create profiles that attract recruiters by keyword stacking your online resume and LinkedIn profile.

So, what can we do to create more certainty for the employers?

There are two stages to the B2W mom strategy.

Stage 1: Re-entry

This is an approximate 2-year period where the B2W mom pursues work or school experiences that will support her mid-term employment goals. This is typically a break-even financial period where the cost of resource management (i.e. child care) is equal to job earnings through non-standard work arrangements (part-time, temporary, contract) or full-time (often lesser pay and title) experiences. It can also be a period of investment in additional education.

Stage 2: As-If-You-Never-Left 'Full Employment'
This is a job move where moms leverage their re-entry experience to achieve full employment which can be defined as full-time, but also means you are making a professional income and title as-if-you-never-left the labor force. The Stacked strategy will tell you how to position your current work experience for full employment.

This next section will explore the six different strategies with specific examples of moms that I have worked with. The online class has the resume transformation which can be used as a template for your own profile.

1.3 Meet the B2W Moms

There are six go-to methods I use with my B2W moms. Most of my mom-clients use a combination of these methods for their re-entry period before moving on to full employment. I have separated them out by each mom's primary strategy.

Stage 1 of 2: The Six Effective Re-entry Strategies to Close the Gap & Change the Dialogue

1. Alternative 'reason for gap' answers (Teri)
2. Leverage a business (Sheila)
3. Leverage part-time work (Andrea)
4. Leverage a volunteer 'title-swap' (Priya)
5. Go back to school (Amy)
6. Re-enter via staffing agencies (Marie)

In the first strategy, the use of alternative answers is the focus which shifts the attention off the B2W mom status and on to other life changes.

Strategy #1. Alternative 'reason for gap' answers
If a mom has a relatively short gap of a year or two with any of the following simultaneous occurrences, it may be more advantageous to offer these options as the reason for the employment gap.

Script 1: "I left my last position before having a new job for the following reason ___."
- I decided to go back to school.
- I graduated from school.
- I moved cities.

These answers are more advantageous because they shift the dialogue away from mom work-life balance concerns. Education and relocation for work sends a 'career-commitment' message. Sometimes a number of these are true and can be added together to say 'Some major stuff went down in my life. Now things have settled and I am ready to find a job.' In the example below, I introduce a B2W mom that had graduated, moved to a different city due to her spouse's new job, and had two children. Because she moved to a new city, she needs to telegraph that her kids are situated with day care or school and that she is ready to go.

Teri (Alternative Answers Strategy #1 Example):

Teri is a B2W mom that immigrated to the United States as a graduate student. During her doctoral program, she met and married an American medical doctor-resident. They had two children and subsequently relocated across country for her husband's first job out of college. At the time of her job search, Teri had about a 2-year gap in employment.

Teri's B2W mom gap was not her only challenge. She had not worked a full-time job since 2003 and that job was outside of the United States (countries tend to devalue experience gained in different places because it feels 'unverifiable'). Although Teri had these challenges, she had a number of high-quality skill sets that we could leverage to get her back to work.

In the end, we really did not have to talk that much about being a B2W mom. She was able to tell employers, "During my graduate studies I met and married a M.D. We both finished school then moved for his job with two young children. Now that we are settled from the move and the kids are in a daycare, I am ready to get back to work."

Teri's example indicates that a mom may not always need to focus on the B2W mom status. Instead, there may have been other things that occurred that can change the conversation.

Her situation also shows the need for a comprehensive mixed approach to getting back to work.

Teri and I spent most of our time determining which of her four professional categories to focus on: 1) research, 2) copyediting, 3) teaching, or 4) statistical analysis. In other words, Teri could have had four completely different profiles. The same resume would not work for everything (*this is a key Stacked concept!).

From her skills, we determined that a part-time adjunct teaching role for two years would support a long-term goal to teach full-time. She also could achieve a part-time or full-time job as a junior editor. We decided to run both campaigns with a direct-apply strategy to teaching roles, and a 'leverage the recruiter' campaign for editing. (More on that coming up in the next chapter.)

Strategy #2: Leverage a Business

Some of my moms have their own freelance work, a business, or have grown up in a family business. A strategic use of the business can be a primary method of covering large employment gaps that facilitate back-to-work goals. It is possible to present your freelance, business endeavors and side gigs in a way that facilitates job acquisition.

With this strategy, candidates create a business name and title themselves in a way that matches the goal position. For instance, don't say you are CEO of a marketing agency when the likely job for your skill level is Marketing Coordinator. Instead, make a business, title yourself Marketing Coordinator, and present yourself as an employee working for the self-owned company.

Sheila (Leverage a Business Strategy #2 Example):

Sheila was an attorney that had 10 years of intermittent contract and volunteer assignments. With the pending relocation of her husband's work, and the maturity of her children, she decided it was time to get back to work. Due to the short-term nature of her work assignments, we wrapped up her contracts under one business entity creating a nice chunky 10-year period of work to discuss. Her goal was to get into an HR department, so she also pursued the Professional Human Resource (PHR) certificate and we focused on Employee Relations which deals with conflict resolutions and employment law. This is a great usage of her legal mediation background. With the right certifications, the creation of a business and the skill based resume, Sheila was able to get back to work.

Sheila's strategic use of both business and education investments closes the gap and changes the dialogue about her B2W mom status. She shows evidence of her career commitment.

Strategy #3: Part-Time Work

In the 'part-time work' re-entry strategy, mom does not try to go full-time immediately. This is a great way for you to:
- Practice finding a job.
- Manage your boss' expectations.
- Manage a workplace schedule.

- Arrange childcare.
- Strike the needed work-life balance.

The biggest challenge with the part-time work method is that we want it to be meaningful. The job needs to be at a level that supports one of the goal directions desired for full-time employment. Another issue is that professional level part-time work can be more difficult to find then full-time employment, but I have tips in the job search section to assist you in identifying these roles.

Andrea (Part Time Work Strategy #3 Example):

Andrea's first job was in 1987. She had not been working full-time since 2002, except for one brief interlude from 2006-2007. Andrea wanted to be near her home until her kids graduated, so she needed a flexible position. For her re-entry period, she was able to pick up a part-time job in 2014 doing office administration for a furniture retail store. About two years later, we leveraged a staffing agency to obtain a full-time temp contract which quickly resulted in a full-time offer.

Andrea's example demonstrates the use of a part-time re-entry strategy followed up by the use of a staffing agency temporary contract to achieve full-employment.

Strategy #4: Volunteer Title Swap

This strategy is recommended when someone is really stuck or absolutely committed to heading in a new career direction. Find a small business in need of assistance related to what you want to do. Ask the business owner to exchange work, paid or not, for the ability to gain experience, a title, and a reference. This is similar to an internship, but for the older job candidate it is better to call it a short-term contract. This is typically part-time work and it will probably not be an advertised job, as you will be 'making the opportunity' yourself.

This strategy works better in some professions than in others. For instance, social media marketing has a large growth trajectory right now and there is a low supply of experienced workers. Someone interested in this work could use this method to implement digital campaigns in exchange for a title and reference on their resume. If you have no experience in a certain field, this is sometimes the only way to make a move in a new direction because it provides proof of your ability to handle the new job duties.

Priya (Swap Strategy #4 Example):

Priya had been off of work for 10-years and she had no college degree. Her previous work had been selling advertising space for a radio station. A local entrepreneur needed assistance, but was short on cash. The two worked out a deal where she would be titled as the 'Social Media Coordinator' managing the website's advertising content and placement along with the business' social media marketing posts. Priya also concurrently took digital marketing classes which she added to her resume. As a result, Priya was able to obtain a full-time Social Media Coordinator role in just six months of having this unpaid experience. Two years later, she moved into a digital marketing 'full-employment' role.

Priya demonstrates that with the right unpaid opportunity, and some brushing up on skills, can be all it that is needed to move towards full employment.

Strategy #5: Go Back to School

Two years prior to your desire to return to full-time work is a great time to complete a new degree. There are so many class schedule options now. I do recommend attending an in-person community college or university if possible. Networking and socializing with local people can be important for moms.

Education is a strong positive signal to employers. It also shifts the conversation from—I took off to watch my children to— 'after my children were settled I had the opportunity to finish my degree which I had been wanting to do. Now I am ready to get back to work full-time.' Your investment in yourself and your ability to juggle the demands of school and family sends the right message to the employer.

Amy (Back to School Strategy #5 Example):

Amy had been out of work for five years and she did not want to go back to her previous role as an Elementary School teacher, a position she had held for 10 years before leaving the workforce. When we spoke, she was already taking some Master's level classes and like many 'stay-at-home' moms, she was working on the side.

Amy indicated that she really wanted to go back into a corporate administrative role, something she did very early in her career prior to teaching. I explained to her that e-Learning was hot in the corporate environment and had a better trajectory. If she would switch her Master's degree to corporate learning, we could build a nice cohesive curriculum development or instructional design profile.

What was great about Amy's story is that we made the change to her resume while she was still in school. A few weeks after the resume changes, she landed an instructional design internship before she ever took a single class in the new Master's program! The intent of your educational program is sometimes enough to acquire a new job.

Strategy #6: Staffing Agencies

One of the primary benefits of using a staffing agency is that the interview process can be very short or nonexistent. Because the job may not be a 'marriage for life,' there is less interest in the long-term motivations of the candidate. Instead, the focus is on skills and baseline ability to do the job. Also, a staffing agency is more likely to consider a functional style resume and may use assessments to verify candidate requirements.

A staffing agency usually places for positions in office administration, accounting and manufacturing opportunities. Not only can these opportunities be beneficial in making a career change, but these staffing agencies are often used by employers for other opportunities that come up because they already have a recruiting agreement with the organization.

Adecco and Kelly Services are well-known national staffing firms, but there are hundreds of local agencies.

Positions with staffing agencies often have lower expectations of their placements, which allows candidates with large gaps in their resume to obtain work and get 'their feet wet.' These contract opportunities allow for job changes that would not otherwise be possible. If you knew a $15 to $30 per hour temporary position could change the trajectory of your career and line you up for $65,000 to $100,000 per year career would you take it? Of course you would. Suspend any disbelief and concerns you may have about temp positions.

Marie (Staffing Agencies Strategy #6 Example):

Marie was the 50-year mom that I highlighted at the beginning of the book. She had a 17-year gap on her resume. Before she left the labor force, she had been a Clinical Research Assistant (CRA). This was my first B2W mom coaching experience and it was a doozy. How was I going to transition her into meaningful work?

I told her we would have to leverage the family construction business to fill her gap even though she only intermittently worked there. I ran two campaigns at the same time: The first campaign focused on her previous work as a Clinical Research Associate (CRA). The second campaign focused on construction company office management.

Marie obtained a temp position as a CRA on a grant-funded medical research project with one of the top research

Universities in the country. The initial research period was successful and a multi-year grant was funded resulting in a full-time job for Marie. Within one year of accepting a $17 per hour temp contract, Marie was back to work in a $50,000 per year CRA job with full benefits and the equivalent income as if she had never left the workforce.

Marie's example demonstrates the power of staffing agencies and temp gigs in creating powerful job moves. It also shows us how a family business can help smooth the concerns of a large gap.

Stage 2 of 2: Full Employment

If you are a mom that is currently working, but have not yet achieved full employment, it is time to really formalize what you have been doing to reach 'as-if-you-never-left' income and title.

The goal of the six re-entry methods is to start getting experience again. If you have already completed this period, then it is time to perform a Stacked campaign to achieve full employment.

It *may* take three job moves depending on the level of skills gained during re-entry. I have included 'step-2' full employment resume examples as additional templates for your use to demonstrate how moms leveraged their re-entry experience to pursue full-time work (find the templates via the class www.karengurney.com/mom).

1.4 The B2W Mom Strategy Summary

You can help recruiters and employers to see you as a non-scary, viable candidate by demonstrating a 'career-commitment' through evidence of recent work or school experience. The first two years may be nothing more than a break-even period, depending on how long you have been absent from the labor force. If you are already in your re-entry period, then it is time to leverage what you have for full-time income. There is also a percentage of B2W moms that will deploy strategies in this book and achieve as-if-you-never-left income and full-time hours immediately. Use the online class to see a discussion of before and after resume transformations.

Author Disclaimer: I think it is important to tell you that I am not, in fact, a mom. I am a career coach and Director of Corporate Outplacement that has successfully served the B2W mom segment of the labor force. I do not pretend to understand everything you are going through and encourage you to use multiple resources in managing the emotional and resource challenges that you are facing. For many years, I did not write this book due to my non-mom status. However, my B2W mom clients encouraged the book due to the successful implementation of the Stacked strategy in their career goals.

There is so much I need to teach you about finding your dream job, writing a resume, preparing for interviews and understanding salary negotiations. The fact is, you have to learn what every candidate needs to know *in addition* to your unique 'close the gap' B2W mom strategy.

The next thing we need to cover is the different types of recruiters and what motivates them so that we can prepare the resumes, online profiles, and interview answers that recruiters love to see and hear.

> Homework

Get downloads of each example and review the video lesson at www.karengurney.com/mom. The use of these six strategies is a critical concept to understanding what you must do to transition into full-employment as a B2W mom.

Now we will learn how target the right jobs to apply for using the Core-3© strategy. We will use what we learn at this stage to build resume content and online profiles.

Quiz 1: B2W Mom Strategy (T/F)
1. ___ I can put stay-at-home mom on a resume and get hired.
2. ___ The employer needs to offer work-life balance to moms.
3. ___ I can single-handedly shift the cultural perception of stay-at-home moms.
4. ___ Employers understand that I may need to leave work at the drop of a hat.
5. ___ Employers understand I need many weeks or months off of work.
6. ___ I can get a job if I am angry about how our culture perceives stay-at-home moms.
7. ___ If I cannot get the perfect job, it is better to stay at home.
8. ___ If I cannot make more than the cost of daycare I should stay home.
9. ___ There are six-strategies to pave the way to a great job and income.
10. ___ A temp job will go nowhere.

Chapter 1: Answer Key (T/F)

1) False: Recruiters fear back-to-work moms and if you focus on your B2W status, you will limit your employability.
2) False: Moms need to say that the job is their #1 focus and that they have child care support.
3) False: Not yet. Get the job, become a leader, start changing minds.
4) False: Moms need to manage their resource to focus on work for a set schedule.
5) False: In the U.S., two weeks off is considered the norm.
6) False: Anger of any kind does not get jobs.
7) False: The first job paves the way to the perfect job and shows employers proof that you are ready.
8) False: The first re-entry job may only pay for the cost of care but it paves the way for a full employment 'as-if-you-never-left-the-labor-force' goal.
9) True: There are six go-to strategies for the B2W mom.
10) False: Temp jobs often result in full-time income with that contract or the next opportunity.

Chapter 2: Get Recruiters to Work for You with LinkedIn

Recruiters are using online and company databases to seek out qualified candidates for open positions every single day. A typical job candidate is not getting calls on their resume because of one simple reason: recruiters cannot find them. This is true for internal HR recruiters and for third party external recruiters. For the B2W mom, you will encounter many different types of recruiters and understanding what motivates each type is important to getting that next position.

The first step in any job search, regardless of any other issues with your candidacy, is the ability to be found.

You are about to learn the fastest and easiest methods to get calls for the jobs you want. Yes! You can bring recruiters to you and double your interviews by using cutting edge recruiter search training via LinkedIn. Before we discuss how recruiters use the LinkedIn Recruiter Application, let's debunk the nine most common job search myths.

This chapter includes the following lessons:
2.1 – Nine Most Common Job Search Myths
2.2 – The 3-Step Recruiter Process
2.3 – Types of Recruiters and Why This Matters
2.4 – 'Leverage the Recruiter' Strategy Recap

2.1 Nine Most Common Job Search Myths

Here are some of the common concerns that people have before jumping in:

Myth 1: I have to know what job I want to succeed.

No. In fact, what I am about to teach you is the most effective method of identifying job opportunities and career changes that are actually available to you right now (and, how to build a resume and online profile to get them).

Myth 2: I have to 'network' to make this work

No! This answer may be shocking; networking is actually the *last* tactic you should be using in your job search. It takes a very long time to build a network robust enough to help you find the job you want. Note: I am not saying don't pursue networking over the life of your career. I am simply saying that when you are ready to get interviews, there is a much faster and effective way to get job interviews (and offers).

Myth 3: I have to go 'door-to-door' to get a job.

No! I know there are books that say this is the best way to get a job, but that is not the way hiring is done for professional level roles and you risk upsetting employers and ruining your reputation. Besides, if you really *want* to do that, I can already tell you that you should be in outside sales. For the rest of the non-selling population, there is a better, easier and more professional way to get job interviews.

Myth 4: Hiring is 'all-who-you-know.'

Absolutely not! The concept that hiring is based entirely on who you know is not only ineffective common wisdom, it is 100% wrong. You can double your job interviews overnight and bring recruiters straight to you for the jobs that you want, without knowing a single person at your future employer.

Myth 5: I have to spend hours and hours blasting hundreds of the same resume.

That is not an effective technique. However, I am going to teach you how to leverage some easy online methods that yield results overnight once you know what to do.

Myth 6: I have to go to Career Fairs and do some bizarre 'Guerrilla Marketing.'

Career fairs are typically soul-sapping experiences that should also be one of the last steps in your career search (not the first). Nothing I teach you in this book will put you in weird uncomfortable situations. The biggest irony in hiring is that the simplest and most comfortable methods yield the best results.

Myth 7: I need a paid LinkedIn Premium Account.

Not at all. At the time I am writing this, there are very few advantages to a paid 'Premium' membership. However, LinkedIn plays a very important part of what I am going to teach you to do to double your interviews.

Myth 8: I need to have a college degree.

The techniques taught in this book are valuable for anyone who uses a resume to apply for a job.

Myth 9: I need to take an online class.

No, but you will want to. As a bonus for purchasing this book, I am offering my award-winning class for **free**. You will want the downloadable templates I offer to make implementation of these concepts much quicker. www.karengurney.com/mom.

Now we know what does not work, let's find out what does.

2.2 The 3-Step Recruiter Process

When recruiters look for candidates via the online databases or through their employer-based Applicant Tracking System (ATS), also called the Talent Management System (TMS), most resumes do not surface even for the most qualified candidates, creating what is referred to as the "resume black hole." When you know how recruiters search, you can keyword-stack and optimize your profile so that you are produced as a qualified candidate in the recruiter search. My mom clients assume they are not getting calls because of their employment gap. That is only partially true. All candidates are facing the bottomless black hole where your resume is sucked up into cyberspace never to be heard from again. Once we know how recruiters work, we can change that.

To understand how recruiters search for candidates, we will use LinkedIn.com - the most popular website for careers, as our vehicle. Most users of LinkedIn understand that this is a free social media website for our professional lives. However, most job applicants have not been exposed to the "recruiter" app. This search application is used by Human Resource professionals to seek out profiles for their "ready-to-fill" open jobs. In this chapter, I will show you the instructions that LinkedIn offers recruiters for this application, which also reveal the popular current job candidate search methods. The recruiter search process is the same whether it is via LinkedIn, online job boards or an employer's internal Applicant Tracking Systems (ATS).

The #1 Way to Learn How Recruiters Work
LinkedIn Recruiter Search Application

First, we will examine the core techniques that recruiters use and then we will discuss each one in greater detail.

Recruiter 3-Step Search Process
Recruiters do a three-step process within the recruiter application.
> Step 1: Keywords
> Step 2: Location
> Step 3: Narrowing Terms

Step 1: Keyword Search

When LinkedIn teaches recruiters how to use their recruiter application, their training tells recruiters to use keywords, not titles, as the first search method to identify the right candidate. This may come as a surprise to job search candidates that have been taught do to a reverse-chronology resume that focuses on title, industry, and professional category.

This disconnect between resumes and recruiter searches leaves highly qualified professionals drowning in the deep dark end of the candidate pool. The last time your resume came up for air was probably only for a direct match to your most recent title, and for good reason: that is focus of most resumes. Title will indeed become important later on in the process. However, at the beginning, keywords are the primary way candidates are found. Therefore, you need to understand the in-demand keywords for your background so that you are being produced as a candidate during the recruiter search.

In the example LinkedIn gives, a recruiter is searching for the keywords "SaaS sales" (SaaS means Software as a Service). When a recruiter searches LinkedIn for this keyword combination, there are over 400,000 results! This result is similar for many other keyword searches. It is not possible or efficient for the recruiter to review 400,000 candidates so they must reduce their options. It would seem that this is where title would come in but, not yet.

Step 2: Location search

After keywords, recruiters use location to narrow down their list. Location goes beyond the direct search and affects overall hiring. There is a large and reliable statistical link between attrition (the rate at which employees quit their jobs) and a distance beyond a 30-minute commute to work. In other words, employers find that employees who have to drive farther quit their job sooner. This statistic is even higher when the job candidate has moved to a completely different metropolitan area. The quit rate of relocation employees is reported to be as high as 80% in under two years. Employers obviously do not want to hire job candidates who are going to quit. (*There is a special lesson later in the book about geographic relocation strategies*). For now, we will assume that you are seeking a job close to your home.

Step 3: Narrowing terms

The Keyword-Location search combination will still produce too many results, requiring the recruiter to narrow the field even more. The following fields are the next most popular options.

Narrowing Terms:
- Title
- Industry
- Rank
- And years of experience.

The following search terms start defining the level of experience the candidate would be expected to have for the targeted positions.

Title
The fastest job move a person can make is often based on their most recent title. One would think that this would be the first search term, not the third. However, an experienced professional may have a variety of titles that are closely related and which are often the same across many different types of

positions. Therefore, as noted earlier, keywords and location are a more reliable source of quality results for the recruiter. A caveat about titles: Once a candidate surfaces in the search and their profile is scrutinized in depth, a candidate's title progression as it relates to the position will actually be the most important factor in the hire. But first, a professional must be found using the other criteria.

Industry
The industry in which the person has worked in can be very important to some positions, while to others it may be of limited importance. Therefore, the use of industry as a search method will vary greatly.

Rank
Rank has to do with whether a person has a lower hierarchical title, mid-manager, Director-level, Vice President or Executive. It is important to have your profile match the level of rank that is reasonable to attain based on your background so that you can surface for the most likely job opportunities.

Let me give you an example. A single entrepreneur who owns a marketing firm may title themselves as Director of Digital Marketing, even if they have no team. However, in a company with 2,000 or more employees, a Director of Marketing will likely have a team with multiple direct reports. A recruiter may find this single entrepreneur and eliminate them from the pool of candidates due to company size. On the other hand, this person may have excellent experience for roles like Social Media Strategist or Digital Account Manager. Due to their

Director of Marketing title, they may not surface for the jobs that match their actual level of qualifications.

Years of Experience
In a search, a substitute for rank is often the number of years of experience. Employers may prefer depth of experience, versus title and rank achievement, especially in technical roles. It may seem like more years are always better but you are seeking a direct-hit match to recruiter expectations.

This LinkedIn training on the recruiter application has given you a good idea of what is important for online profiles and resumes. Recruiters rely on a 'direct-hit' match to their keyword search terms. As a mom, you can leverage the same 'direct-hit' keyword-stacking tactics to beat the black hole and surface as a candidate.

However, there are different types of recruiters which will impact your success. Since your career progression is depending on these professionals, it is important to understand what motivates each type of recruiter.

2.3 Types of Recruiters and Why It Matters

You may encounter multiple types of recruiters in your career. When you apply the strategies taught in this book, these various types will be calling you unexpectedly for jobs you have not even applied for, as well as from your direct applications. You want them working for *you*. So how do you do that? There is one generality that holds true for all recruiters.

Recruiters seek people for jobs, and not jobs for people.

Perhaps that seems obvious, but recruiters constantly complain that people ask them to find a job or ask the recruiter to "make them a fit." No matter what type of recruiter, they are not paid to make you or any candidate 'a fit' into their open jobs. Once you know that jobs are available and that they need to find a direct-hit match, it is much easier to understand how to effectively make recruiters work for you. Now, let's explore the differences in recruiter types.

Five Types of Recruiters
1. Third party recruiters: retained or contingent
2. Internal company human resource (HR) recruiters
3. Staffing agency recruiters
4. Executive career managers
5. Head hunters

These five recruiter types can make or break your success, but there is one group that is insanely effective for my re-entry B2W moms (Hint: It is type #3).

Type 1. Third Party Recruiters: Retained & Contingent

Third party recruiters are major players for leadership and technical roles. In the case of accounting, finance, information technology or any position that is management level or above, you are more likely to get a call from one of these recruiters than from an internal company recruiter who received your direct application. If a job pays over $65,000 per year a recruiter is probably seeking a professional that will best fit. These recruiters like to pick up the phone and call prospects. There are examples where a job candidate applied for a job but, instead of getting a call from the company's HR department, a third party recruiter found them online for the very same job. This means these recruiters cannot be ignored if you are in certain fields or level of employment.

Keep in mind that no matter what level you have attained, you absolutely should want to get these calls. Many candidates tell me they only want calls from internal recruiters, however it is much faster and easier to leverage a third party recruiter than any other type.

Popular national names in third party recruiting industry are Robert Half for Accounting and TEKSystems for I.T., but there are hundreds of thousands smaller players in different locations. Do not expect a niche firm like Robert Half to place a customer service professional. Some recruiters seek out all sorts of jobs but many agencies have niches. These professionals tend to focus on identifying talent for jobs that pay over $65,000 per year, but I have seen calls on some entry-roles as well.

When you get a call unexpectedly, meaning you do not remember applying for the job or company, it is usually from a third party recruiter. These professionals mine online databases for "passive candidates." LinkedIn is a perfect place to do this because many professionals create profiles even if they are not currently seeking a new position. Making your resume and online profile attractive to these recruiters is an important strategy to make the fastest and most profitable career change.

If a third party recruiter is calling on your resume or LinkedIn profile, it is an indication your profile is properly optimized and that your skills are in hot demand; it may also indicate a short supply of talent in the market. In other words, you are doing your career, resume, profile and job search correctly.

What are the differences between the third party recruiter types?

Employers pay an outside agency to help locate talent. There are two primary types:
1. Retained
2. Contingent

With retained recruiting agreements, the company regularly pays to have a recruiter source for particular positions and they only hire through that agreement. Contingent recruiters have no agreement with the company. This group can sometimes create a painful experience for candidates because they call on jobs that they do not formally represent. The only reliable way to spot a contingent recruiter is if they ask you to sign a contract to work with them. There are fewer and fewer of these types of recruiters. It is best to keep working the job search and not focus on the type of recruiter you may encounter.

In both cases, the recruiters are paid about 20% of the job candidate's annual salary. For someone making $100,000 that is a $20,000 commission. The employer pays the fee, which excites job candidates. They feel like they have an "agent" working for them at no cost.

Why would a company pay so much for a candidate they can find on their own?

There are a variety of reasons that the third party recruiting industry exists:
1. The employer's clunky Applicant Tracking System (ATS)
2. Applicant overwhelm
3. Genuinely hard-to-fill jobs

Let's review these reasons in greater depth.

1. The clunky ATS

The ATS, which is commonly referred to as the "resume black hole," negatively affects an employer's ability to find applicants in their own database. Believe it or not, employers have a hard time mining their own ATS which creates a false impression that there are no qualified applicants. The ATS is technologically inferior to online job boards because it does not receive as much constant investment into programming compared to LinkedIn and other online databases. If you think of how Google search has evolved over the years and the artificial intelligence required to figure out what you are searching for, it will make sense. The ATS programs are, in a word, clunky.

2. Applicant overwhelm

In addition to the ATS problem, the ease of applying for jobs online has created an overwhelming amount of applicants for open positions. Many employers, especially the top tier ones that everyone wants to work for, complain that they get over 1,000 applications per advertised job. Sometimes, it is just easier and more cost-effective to hire an outside recruiter.

3. Hard-to-fill jobs
The third party recruiting industry originally began for professional niche hard-to-fill positions. Some positions really are difficult to fill with a limited number of qualified candidates, and it requires an extensive and lengthy internet search to find the right person. Some recruiting agencies have professional category specializations allowing them to identify qualified candidates more quickly. Their finger is on the pulse, so to speak.

Some businesses are either too big or too small to be able to source the right candidates. Some companies have more money than time and it makes sense to pay agency fees. As in all things with business, sometimes it is cheaper or more effective to outsource for a specialized activity, and recruiting is one of those activities.

<u>Shouldn't a depressed economy increase the supply of qualified applicants and reduce the need to hire a third party recruiter to source talent?</u>

This is an interesting question and a completely logical assumption. However, something very different has happened. Because we have been in a depressed economy since about 2000, the employers believe they can get whatever they want. This is referred to as "seeking the unicorn or purple squirrel."

This situation can get really absurd. A recent conversation with a third party recruiter uncovered that one of their candidates, with an Ivy-league MBA and over 10 years of work experience, was a finalist for a position. The candidate was not extended an offer because they did not have a 4.0 GPA in the Bachelor's degree program. This is the type of ridiculous hiring behavior that drives third party recruiters and job candidates crazy. However, the "seeking the unicorn" strategy opens the door to two things: 1) third party recruiters who use much more effective talent sourcing methods and 2) the strategies in this book which help you win at their game.

<u>Why are third party recruiters so much more effective at recruiting?</u>
• They are the sales people of the HR industry and they are driven by a juicy commission.
• Job candidates are their product and they want to talk to as many as possible.
• They do not use technologically inferior ATS programs like the internal recruiters.
• They often list their personal email and telephone number in a job advertisement to increase how many people they talk to.
• Because there is no ATS, a <u>human being</u> will review your resume submission.
• As sales people, they jump on the phone to talk to a candidate with no hesitation, sometimes within hours of submitting the resume.
• They read newspapers to see which companies are laying off, thus creating a new stream of qualified candidates that they can sell to hiring companies.
• They will call everyone on their list to source new candidates because a qualified person is likely to know another qualified person.

- They have started taking qualified people out to lunch even if they are not actively seeking work, for the sole purpose of finding new candidates through networking.

In conclusion, third party recruiters are successful because they do recruiting the way it used to be done, **live human interaction.**

How does this affect me as a B2W Mom candidate?

A B2W mom will not likely see the best benefits of the third party recruiting industry until she performs the re-entry period. Recruiters are being paid huge commissions to find unbelievably good candidates. Unless you are in a field that is red hot and has a short supply of candidates, like programmers and data scientists, I do not expect this type of recruiter to come into play until your gap is closed.

Once you successfully close your gap, you may feel a bit victimized by third party recruiters. They are the salespeople of the hiring world. They tend to make a lot of calls with quick determinations and they quickly move on to make the 'kill' and close the sale. Some job candidates have even described these individuals as "evil" and expressed a high-degree of disgust with the field. We can offset this by actively understanding and managing these relationships.

Dealing with third party recruiters can be both exhilarating and depressing. Nothing is worse than getting a call from a pumped up recruiter telling you how great you are for a job and then never hearing back from them. However, you do want these calls! They are one of the best indicators of a perfectly optimized job search and there are some professions almost exclusively hiring this way. These recruiters cannot be ignored by the job seeker.

Type 2. Internal Company HR Recruiters

Many job candidates only want calls from companies and positions they have applied to directly. This significantly extends the amount of time it takes to get a great job. You already know that the ATS, the tool an internal recruiter uses, is technologically inferior. But in addition, internal HR recruiters are not sales people; they are motivated by screening out as many candidates as possible and typically seek to only bring in about three people for the time-consuming in-person interviews. It is very resource-intensive to hire and recruiters often have competing interests for their time. To complicate the issue, most companies hire by committee to protect from biased decisions. It is difficult to put busy employees in the room for something that is not a priority in their work. This is a sharp contrast to the third party recruiter whose one and only job is to <u>screen in</u> candidates.

An internal HR professional may be very reluctant to present a B2W mom professional with a large gap to a hiring committee. Do not lose hope though. We are already learning ways to close the gap and help the recruiter assist you.

Type 3. Staffing Agency Recruiters

A staffing agency is a type of business that employers use to fill their short-term assignments. I like to use staffing agencies to help candidates who have experienced a long period of unemployment or are returning to a profession they were in a long time ago. A staffing firm is one of the critical re-entry methods for B2W moms.

The Advantages of a Staffing Agency to B2W Moms
- There are agencies geared towards professional level work.
- The interview process for these roles is less rigorous (sometimes non-existent) which can help a job candidate get back to work.
- The agency is more focused on skills and ability to do the job than they are on gaps, length of tenure, or long-term career goals.
- Many agencies are now working in the third party recruiter space for professional-level roles which has a strong possibility for full employment.
- Some employers like to "try before they buy." Moving from temp to full-time is EXTREMELY common. Even if that employer does not work out, a good relationship with the staffing agency will mean quick placement in a new project.
- The short-term nature of the project is beneficial to moms that are trying to figure out their resources for unpredictable events like the kids getting the flu as well as predictable child care issues.
- If it turns out that a mom could not balance her competing priorities, this short-term relationship will not hurt a more positive long-term prospect.

The Disadvantages of a Staffing Agency for B2W Moms

- Many moms do not want to arrange child care for something that is not 'permanent.'
- Some moms tell me that they do not want to go back to work if the role is not 'perfect' due to the guilt, preference, or logistical challenges related to being a working mom.
- Sometimes agency roles will offer a compensation that barely covers child care costs.

I think I have adequately expressed that a break-even re-entry period is a likely scenario for most moms. You have to close that gap and show evidence of career commitment.

There is one final disadvantage to staffing agencies. Recruiters that work on the 'staffing' side of the business, versus third party recruiters, typically only call candidates who apply directly into their system. These recruiters are not out mining the online job boards for passive candidates. A job applicant has to apply directly into their systems to be found. Luckily, these tend to be quick and easy submissions. If you have not already performed your re-entry period, it is likely that you will need to leverage an agency to get back to work.

Type 4. Executive Career Managers

You know now that recruiters and staffing agencies seek people for jobs, not jobs for people. A company pays a recruiter $10,000 to $20,000 or more to get a qualified hire. Would you pay that to someone to find you a job? Perhaps, but read on.

This is where we meet an unusual type of business called the "executive career management" firm. The career management firm appears to be a staffing agency or third party recruiting firm that will act as an "agent" and call on businesses to negotiate a new job for the candidate. They work for, and are paid by, the candidate.

These companies are exactly like me, your author; they are career coaches and consultants. That is not a bad thing, except they create an impression that they are more than career coaches. You might pay $10,000 to have someone find you a job, but you may not be willing to pay even $1,500 to hire a career coach. Some people receive the coaching they need from these firms and it results in a job. However, many times job candidates that pay these firms later feel like they were scammed. My issue is the impression they create of being an agency.

These are the ways to identify if a company is an "executive career management" firm.

• They typically advertise online as if they have executive positions. (This is their primary lead generation system or sales marketing method.)
• Upon clicking on these job advertisements, there will be a general description but no employer name.
• A visit to their office will result in a highly satisfying career analysis where the candidate feels like a million bucks. (This is one of their primary sales-closing tactics.)
• The person working at this firm will discuss the "hidden" job market and how they can help tap their network to uncover opportunities.

- The person working at this firm will tell you that they have lists of recruiters in their database (this is probably true but the problem is that the recruiters may not place for your background.)
- The job candidate may receive a rigorous accomplishment inventory for homework and then must come back in a week.
- There is a sales pitch between $1,500 to $10,000 to help the candidate find a job.
- The job candidate may have the feeling that the firm will act as an "agent." (This is the other primary sales tactic.)
- The candidate may or may not get a job from the work product done by the firm.
- There is a "no refund" policy.

There is no candidate on earth that would not be excited about the potential to have someone go out and sell them for opportunities. However, these firms are not recruiters, staffing agencies or agents – they are career coaches, strategists and search consultants.

Unfortunately, there is no agency in the hiring industry that represents the candidate.

Career management firms are not "bad" because they do perform a service to help the candidate package and present themselves for new opportunities. However, the way they sell their service leads candidates to believe one of two things: 1) that their background is more in-demand than it really is and 2) that the firm will act as a recruiter and seek out (or even create) job opportunities for the candidate. Just know that you are paying for career coaching and not for job placement.

Type 5. Head Hunter

As a final discussion of recruiter types, we will talk about head hunters. Most job candidates believe that recruiters find jobs for people. It is a general belief that a 'head hunter' helps people get jobs.

There is no such thing as a head hunter!

They are a mythic beast made up by hopeful job candidates who misunderstand how hiring is done. Someone could technically call any type of recruiter a head hunter. The reason I do not like the term is because, in most cases, that person completely misunderstands what a recruiter does for a living.

The only agents for hiring are in sports and entertainment. Unless you have won the Heisman Trophy for football, or an Emmy award for acting, there is no agent out there that is going to call to find you a high-paying opportunity. Let me say it again: agencies do not exist on the candidate side of hiring. If that is what you, like many others, think about head hunters, then you will have bought into the mythic beast concept of this field.

2.4 "Leverage the Recruiters" Strategy Recap

Recruiters are seeking qualified people for their open job requisitions.

If the recruiters are of the "third party recruiter" variety, they are going to receive a juicy commission by sending a 100%

super-qualified direct-hit match, square-peg, square-hole candidate to the employer paying their contract. They intend to talk to a lot of people to find their golden egg but, ultimately, will only send a few people that they know the employer will pay them for. A B2W mom in a red hot field or that has performed her re-entry period can take advantage of this type of recruiter.

If the recruiter is an internal company professional, they are seeking to look at and contact <u>as few of people as possible</u>. Why? Because they are busy and no one is going to pay them a big fat commission check for doing more work. The less people they need to talk to the better because they do not want to create a mob of angry, depressed and rejected job candidates who think they are perfect for the stated job. The Human Resources department recruiter wants to talk to at most ten 100% super qualified direct-hit match square-peg, square-hole candidates. For the B2W mom, we need to close the gap so that they call you.

The staffing agency sits somewhere in between the company and third party recruiter, with a focus on temporary or temp-to-hire jobs. They increasingly play the role of third party recruiters because companies already use them for other types of recruiting. The staffing agency can be helpful in moving a candidate who has been out of work for a while. This is a critical player for B2W moms that need re-entry work.

With all recruiters, your job is to present yourself as a 100% super-qualified direct-hit match, square-peg, square-hole candidate for open positions using the job advertisements as a clue as to what they are seeking. You can then surface at the top of their search, so that they can get the best results, while talking to the least amount of people in the shortest amount of time.

> **Homework**

For clarity on this chapter, review the video lessons on LinkedIn Recruiter Search. This is a critical concept to understanding what you must do to be found by recruiters.
www.karengurney.com/mom.

Quiz 2: Recruiters (T/F)
1. ___ Recruiters only call on actively applying professionals.
2. ___ The best way to be found by recruiters is keyword-stacking.
3. ___ In Recruiter search, title is more important than keywords.
4. ___ Where you live is not important to recruiter search.
5. ___ Recruiters search LinkedIn differently than internal company databases.
6. ___ There is only one type of recruiter.
7. ___ Head hunters find jobs for people.
8. ___ Calls from direct applications are better than 'out of the blue' calls.
9. ___ There are agents that seek jobs for people.
10. ___ It is possible to tap the hidden job market and get calls for unadvertised jobs.

Chapter 2: Answer Key (T/F)
1) False: Recruiters call on "passive" candidates every day.
2) True: Keywords are critical to being found.
3) False: Titles are important in hiring but less important in the search process.
4) False: Location is a primary method to search for candidates.
5) False: LinkedIn searches and database searches are basically the same.
6) False: There are four real and one mythical types.
7) False: Head hunters are mythical. Recruiters find people for jobs (not jobs for people).

8) False: Both are important and 'out of the blue' calls will double your interviews.

9) False: Candidate-driven Agents only exist in sports or entertainment.

10) True: Yes, this book's strategy taps the hidden job market and doubles interviews.

Chapter 3: Your Core-3© Career Assessment

Like any job candidate, a B2W mom needs to identify jobs that leverage their existing skills. You also now know that recruiters seek people for jobs, so to get them to work for you, you need to be a direct-hit square-peg square-hole match "on paper" based on their keyword search. How do you find these keywords? The job market!

The method I use to help determine the right keywords to bring recruiters to my clients is the same strategy I use to help candidates who tell me they are hungry for a more rewarding role, want a change, or need to do something different.

There is a significant lack of information in the job market. Most people go about their career bumping into figurative walls because no one ever told them exactly how to effectively search for a job. Some find a mentor or obtain a great job straight out of college and their career grows at a steady rate. For others, their career does not match their lifestyle or work interests. In other cases, professionals may find themselves stagnating or even falling apart.

For a mom, this can be even more complex because the economy, job titles and your own wants, needs, and desires may have changed during the stay-at-home period. When a candidate does not know what to do or how to solve a career problem, where do they turn for information?

It is very common for professionals to use personality assessments like the Myers-Briggs Type Indicator (MBTI©), Gallup's Strengthsfinder©, or some other popular personality-career analysis tool. I will be the first to tell you that I love personality assessments. In fact, when I take them, I am usually listed in the category of people that love them! (Yes, there is a category for that. There is also a category for those that despise them.)

The problem is, no matter how you feel about personality assessments, they will not tell you how to get from <u>where you are to where you want to go</u>. However, each candidate has a Core-3© set of job changes based on their skills. Let's first explore some myths about career and job changing as they relate to personality assessments before investigating your Core-3©.

This chapter includes the following lessons:
3.1 – Career, Jobs, and Personality Test Myths
3.2 – The Core-3© Career Assessment
3.3 – Finding Your Dream Job
3.4 – Targeted Job Alerts
3.5 – Identifying Part-Time & Staffing Agencies

3.1 Career, Jobs, and Personality Test Myths

If you think one of the popular personality or skill assessments is going to help you identify what you should be doing, studying, applying for, or working towards, think again.

<u>Myth 1: Personality tests will help me identify rewarding work.</u>

This is just not true. When I first graduated from my Bachelor's program, I had a degree in Political Science and Spanish. I did not realize it at the time, but the job market for those skills was extremely limited. Silly me, I incorrectly thought that if a University offered a program, there was a good job potential for that degree. Following graduation, I held a job collecting on credit cards (bummer). I quit that job after two years and then sold insurance for two years (major bummer), and then I worked on a software Help Desk for three years (better but still a bummer).

From my perspective, my career was in shambles. I felt like I was stuck in dead-end jobs with no hope of leadership roles, and I really disliked my life. I had no idea where to turn - and that is when I decided to take two different personality assessments. The MBTI® told me I was an ENFP and Strengthsfinder© determined I was an Ideator that liked to relate to people and woo them. Please tell me, how could I move from dead end call center jobs into a great new position with this information????

Personality assessments do not help you change careers, jobs, or lives ... but what I am about to show you will.

Myth 2: Personality/skill assessments will tell me which fields need my abilities.

Personality and skill assessments help you become aware of your inherent *and* learned abilities. Reputable experts in psychology know that an assessment will essentially tell you what you already know. The assessments definitely will not match you to positions that are open in the market right now for your greatest skills. They also will not help you identify the skills and abilities that are in demand right now or where demand exceeds supply of workers. Only the job market can tell you that - and I am going to teach you how to tap that information.

Myth 3: Personality tests will help me identify the education or training I need to get a job.

Personality tests are woefully inadequate for identifying education programs that will result in a job. For instance, one of my clients was a Biomedical Engineer. This should be an excellent career, right? She studied for over 24 years, and worked for 10 years with another researcher. She reached the point in her career where she had to create her own funded research or she literally would be out of a job. No one told her about that when she studied for her degree. Biomedical research and STEM programs were supposed to be in-demand. Was a personality test going to help her identify new career paths for her background? No! To put her on a different career path, I used the Core-3© Career Assessment.

Myth 4: Employers do not reveal what they are looking for.

It is true that there are information shortcomings in the job market that limit great career planning. However, employers do reveal what they want, and I will teach you how to crack the code. As a coach, I get calls every day from candidates working in professional categories which I have not been exposed to in my own professional life or with previous clients. I developed my own process to assist them in understanding what their core strengths are by tapping the job market. What is great about this process is that it not only helps me understand the strengths of the candidate, it also helps my clients understand where the demand is for what they know. There is a third important benefit to using the job market as a "personality assessment": it also identifies potential jobs. This method is the most holistic way to make a career change. You have something that employers want and it can result in a complete shift.

There is one more thing to remember. After you build this list and start looking for a job, the job ads will also give you additional keywords for your job search and resume profile.

Myth 5: There is only one career change available to me.

Not true. At any given time, a person typically has at least three core moves they can make that, from an employer standpoint, are considered lateral. But for the candidate, a lateral move can mean big shifts in money, title, career trajectory, or lifestyle. The "lateral" part does not necessarily mean doing the same work; it means that the person matches at least 75% of what the employer is seeking. This should come as a relief to job candidates who think they are pigeon-holed in their career, a "jack-of-all-trades and master-of-none," those who feel they have no skills, or candidates who feel their challenges are insurmountable. Of course each person's career is linked to personal and financial interests, which adds to the complexity of the situation. My goal is to help you identify the jobs available that want what you know, and to help you position yourself for them.

3.2 The Core-3© Career Assessment

Before you jump into your assessment, let's spend some time defining the Core-3©.

Core-3© Definition

Your Core-3© are the <u>three primary career changes</u> available to you based on the following attributes:
- You will be able to read the job description and say, 'Yes, I have done that" to at least 75% of the line items in a job advertisement.
- You will have close to 100% of the mandatory requirements.
- Even if you are missing many line items, you will have a combination of one to three very hard-to-find skills, like a second language or technical skill.

Your Core-3© are not:
- Your three primary skill sets, or
- Your last three job titles.

Your Core-3© will change over time based on the following attributes:
- The skills you have gained, and
- The changes in job market demand.

Your Core-3© Assessment is the job market demand for your keyword skills.

The Core-3© can also be used to identify streams of jobs that support specific lifestyle interests. For example, a millennial seeking to climb the ladder into executive positions, a professional mom who has worked for 10+ years and wants a part-time job, or a 55-year old professional who wants to semi-retire. In this case, it can also help a mom with her re-entry and full employment goals.

Once you have identified the stream of jobs for your background, the goal is to then use this information to create a Market-Based Resume© and an online profile that capture your matching skills, thus creating the look and feel of a "lateral" career move. "Lateral" does not mean the same job, title, pay, and industry. These job moves can result in promotions or pay increases, achieve some life or work goal, or be radically different from your most recent position, while still appearing to the employer as if it was the exact work you have been doing in the recent or even distant past.

Exercise 3.2 Core-3© Career Assessment

To perform the Core-3© Career Assessment, grab a piece of paper or open a document online and write the following down with spaces in between to fill in your answers. The class has a downloadable form of the exercise.

- Professional/industry acronyms or phrases
- Certifications

- Software
- Industry "players"
- Titles
- Languages
- Target geographic market
- Titles and employers of promoted or job changing colleagues
- Jobs you have already had calls on

Job Market Search Parameters

To identify the right positions for you, you need to start with the search terms you just listed. The job market itself will reveal additional parameters. Begin the search, add more, and try different combinations to identify your Core-3© stream of jobs.

The key to building a great list is to start with a few items, try some combinations, and then use the job advertisements to continue building out your list. This is not a perfect science. Trial and error will be required by combining different items on your list to find great jobs.

Professional/Industry Acronyms or Phrases

There are certain industry phrases or acronyms that may be popular in your profession or industry. These do not have to be complex to reward you with great hits on your job search.

For instance, in the online class, I demonstrate the job search process of an Accountant. She really enjoyed forecasting. When we searched for that word, the majority of the positions were actually titled in the Finance profession, not Accounting. This was a complete game changer for that candidate. In your list, if you cannot think of any specific acronyms or phrases, move on to the next category.

Certifications

In certain professions a certification is mandatory, which makes identifying jobs very easy (for example, Project Management Professional (PMP)). If you have certifications, list and search by them. If not, move on to the next category.

Software

The software you use can create opportunities for many new types of jobs. This is the #1 method I use to facilitate a career change for my clients. It is especially helpful when the person has used or interacted with ubiquitous software pieces which are popular across an industry. Below is a list of common programs:

- SAP (Manufacturing),
- EMR (Hospital Software),
- SQL (Database Software),
- Oracle (Database & Reporting Software),
- Crystal (Reporting Software),
- Peoplesoft (Human Resources),
- and, Intermediate MS Excel (Database).

The more broadly used the software, the better for the career, but even niche software can offer some interesting streams of jobs. For those in entry or even lower-level positions, software skills can assist in making moves into analyst, sales, or account management roles, which become gateways into new professional paths which may not have been open to the individual had they not had the software experience. List the software you have touched and use the job ads to continue expanding your list.

Industry "Players"

Professionals who work with vendors or customers may be able to open doors to new career pathways based on their deep knowledge of those businesses. In addition, competitors or other businesses in the same or a similar industry may be interested in your background. For example, a marketing professional worked in paint (chemicals), and discovered that another chemical company selling through a similar distribution and store network was interested in her work. As a result she achieved a promotion in title and salary.

Titles

As you now know, this is not the first search term recruiters use to find talent. However, if you can define nothing else about your career, you do know your previous titles. Also, it can be helpful for a B2W mom to re-enter the workforce in the same or similar role she had before leaving because it limits the concerns about the ability to do the job. Remember, the re-entry job is not always our ideal. It is something to be used to achieve full-employment in a job you do want later. Getting a job that you know how to do can also limit the stress of returning to work. You may not be ready to be challenged by the job right away since going back to work is difficult enough. Another benefit of pursuing the same title and role is that it is one of the fastest ways to get a job. Eventually, this can actually result in more money, sometimes $10,000 or more, because employers pay a premium for experienced workers.

Another strategy to consider is a "'return to an old profession." Do not forget about previous titles as well. Perhaps you were on a better path in your previous position than you are now and can return to it.

A title communicates a few things to an employer. It lets them know what you have been doing recently, whether you have had an upward logical progression, your "apparent" goals based on the choices you have made, the industries you have worked in, the level of responsibility you have had, your skill level, and an approximation of your current pay rate. In other words, there is a lot of information loaded into a job title that you can leverage (or overcome) to move if you want to go in a different direction or get a promotion.

If a fast job change is the ultimate goal, look for jobs with the same title in the same industry. If the goal is a much larger change, the title is just a "jumping off" point in your search.

Add to your list the following:
• Most recent title
• Previous titles
• The title representing the most likely promotion from most recent title

- Level of responsibility: coordinator, manager, director, etc.
- Profession: accounting, finance, engineering, sales, marketing, etc.
- Industry: banking, manufacturing, healthcare, software, etc.
- Years of experience: entry (0-2 years), mid (2-5 years), experienced (5+ years)

Languages

The ability to speak a second language can often open up opportunities you might not otherwise have been qualified for, especially when combined with one or two other skills. Native or intermediate language skills are not something a person can pick up on the job. These skills can spur career changes that overcome other skill gaps. Search for languages first in your target geography, and then add different skills to narrow down the list.

Target Geographic Market

The most likely location to get a job is within 30 miles of your current home location. As discussed in the previous chapter on LinkedIn Recruiter searches, location is one of the primary ways recruiters narrow down their list. There is a negative statistical relationship between distance to work and the likelihood of a person quitting their job soon after starting. However, the United States has the most mobile labor force in the world. Around 1% of the population (or over 300,000 people) move to new areas every year for a job.

First, write down the general large city area you are interested in. Then think about secondary areas, especially the next closest cities or large locations where you have a support system. The strategy to make these moves is dramatically easier if a person is within driving distance to interview. Geography, and the impact of a move, is less of an issue as a professional attains a "Director-level" or above position.

Titles, Industries, and Employers of Promoted or Job Changing Colleagues

When job candidates think about making a career change, they often think about a total shift of profession and industry, sometimes ignoring the next logical step in their career progression. A career change that leverages what you know can move you into training, quality assurance, management, implementation, doing the same job you are doing but remotely from home, doing the same job but with travel, or seeking out that next-step senior-level promotion. These types of step-up or step-over roles in the same profession and industry look like lateral moves. But, these roles often feel dramatically different than the current role you have held in an organization.

If you are frustrated with your current role do not ignore the next step up or over as a method to change your life. The best way to identify these roles is to examine the positions, titles, and industries of your previous colleagues. If you are lost, this is a good place to start to identify the market demand for your skills which can result in a much different position and which also matches your lifestyle goals.

Jobs You Have Had Calls on Without Applying

If you are already getting calls for jobs "out of the blue," this is an indication of where the demand is for your skills in the market. It also indicates how your profiles are optimized. If these jobs do not match your goals, then it is time to change your profiles to reflect where you are going versus where you have been. However, you may want to consider one of these potential jobs. The market is telling you how your current profile is being perceived; do not ignore these signals. If this is what you want, promote it more. If it is not what you want, change your resumes and profiles.

Education

Your degree or education is also a good additional search term. In some industries, the right degree is absolutely mandatory; however, for many roles the type of degree is less important. For instance, in my searches for a client, if a job candidate has a second language I will combine the language with the word "Bachelor" to identify professional level jobs in a certain location which require the second language.

3.3 Finding Your Dream Job

Now it is time to search for the items on your list to find the streams of jobs available to you based on your background. For this task, I recommend Indeed.com. This job board has silently overtaken major competitors like Monster.com and LinkedIn.com to become the most robust job board, online resume posting, and recruiter talent search website in the United States. Because it is an aggregator, pulling jobs from multiple databases, it offers the most global view of the job market.

In 2015, the majority of my candidates who received calls from recruiter searchers came from either Monster.com or LinkedIn.com. In 2016, I saw an almost total shift away from Monster.com as Indeed.com gained in popularity. I still recommend posting to at least three general job boards and to any applicable third party sites.

However you are not at that point yet in this process. The first thing you need to do is survey the job marketing to identify your Core 3©. The job market survey will uncover additional skill sets to add to your list. This will require many searches.

The job search can be as broad as the entire country or for a select city. Once several searches are made and the stream of jobs presents itself, the next stage is to set up job alerts.

Exercise 3.3 Survey the Job Market

Begin the survey by going to www.Indeed.com and then follow these steps:

- Enter one skill word at a time to get a broad overview
- Select a geographic market
- Start with single-word specialized certification or software words first
- Assess the results and determine additional words to add

- Try search-term combinations from your list
- Keep narrowing the list until you identify a stream of job titles that have 100% of your mandatory qualifications, 75% of the line items, or a rare set of combined skills.
- Start pasting links into a Word document and track the associated keyword combo so you do not lose your work.
- Build a list of promising job angles.

Once a promising single or combined group of skills is identified, create a job alert to stay abreast of new postings.

3.4 Targeted Job Alerts

Most job boards have an automatic function to send you alerts based on previous job searches. However, they are usually very title driven. This can result in some pretty bizarre job suggestions. One example is for the title Account Manager, who can work across a variety of industries from advertising agencies to manufacturers. Although there is a tendency for these roles to be involved in expanding sales for existing customers, that is where the commonality ends. The algorithms in the job boards are not going to be able to easily differentiate the right jobs as efficiently as a professional who knows their own skills and experience. Use Indeed.com and the other job boards to set your own job alerts. There are multiple delivery options and they can be cancelled when you choose.

Job alerts can be set on proprietary systems or for specific employers. This can be very helpful for positions in government or universities that tend to have limited job advertising budgets.

It is a good idea to set up accounts and alerts for special organizations of interest.

Job alerts can also be used for ongoing research or a long-term career planning goal. For instance, some professionals are interested in understanding what is happening in their profession or industry and do not want to miss great jobs that may pop up, now or in the future. Job alerts are also helpful if a busy professional only has one day a week to review and apply for positions. Use job alerts to your benefit and do not miss anything happening in your field.

Exercise 3.4 Job Alerts

Once you test different search terms, a certain word or skill combination should produce good results. It is easiest to manage job alerts when you have an account with Indeed.com (which you will need anyway for online profile posting). After you identify a promising search, enter your email in the job alert bar on the top right hand section of the Indeed.com search page.

3.5 Identifying Part-Time & Staffing Agencies

This section is for the B2W moms approaching their re-entry period with a part-time, contract, or staffing agency strategy. The only robust website that has a helpful method of identifying part-time or temporary positions is indeed.com. When you search by your keywords, it will produce every type of job out there. However, on the left-hand margin there is an option to narrow down by the following categories: Full-time, part-time, contract, commission, temporary, and internship.

This method is something I use to identify staffing agencies and recruiters in a specific city. Not all part-time job ads will derive from staffing firms which means this method can assist in identifying companies that want part-time employees as well.

Here is an example I took from the Chicago market on indeed.com. I searched for all jobs and then narrowed it down by selecting 'Temporary.'

The national agencies popped up:
- Kelly Services
- Adecco
- Ranstaad

And then several smaller niche firms:
- Advantage Resourcing
- Brilliant Management Resources
- Veterans Sourcing Group
- Marco & Associate

Use the left-hand margin to identify your own city's unique staffing agencies.

Exercise 3.5 Identifying Part-time & Staffing Agency Roles

Begin the survey by going to www.Indeed.com and then follow these steps:

- Enter one skill word at a time to get a broad overview
- Select a geographic market

On the left-hand margin select
- Part-time
- Contract
- Temporary

- Follow the staffing agencies you find to stay abreast of new job opportunities.

>Homework
Create your list, perform the survey, and set up the job alerts. If you need further inspiration, visit the free video class to watch me perform a Core 3© assessment.
www.karengurney.com/mom.

Once a stream of jobs has been identified, it is time to build a "composite" profile that pulls the keywords from multiple job ads targeting that one position. Our next step is breaking down the job ad to create a keyword-stacked market-based resume.

Quiz 3: Career Assessment (T/F)

1.___ Personality tests help you change careers.
2.___ Personality tests help identify educational programs that result in a great career.
3.___ There are at least three different career changes available to you.
4.___ You can career change based on skills even without a matching job title.
5.___ Software skills can present completely new career avenues.
6.___ Just one search term is all you need to find great jobs.
7.___ A second language can overcome missing skills.
8.___ Indeed.com is the best job board to start your search.
9.___ The online job boards are effective at sending you new job leads.
10.___ Indeed.com is the only job board you will need during your job search.

Chapter 3: Answer Key (T/F)

1) False: No, personality tests help you understand inherent or learned abilities.
2) False: No, personality tests do not help in picking degrees for in-demand professions.
3) True: There are at least three career changes available to you.
4) True: Skills are the #1 way of changing directions.
5) True: Software knowledge can really open new doors.
6) False: Many single and combination search terms will be needed.

7) True: Language can be a strong competitive advantage that overcomes skill gaps.

8) True: Indeed.com is a job search aggregator and offers the best job market overview.

9) False: Set up your own job alerts because the job board's automatic leads are ineffective.

10) False: Indeed.com is the best place to start to identify your Core 3© career changes; other job boards will be needed to perform your entire search.

Chapter 4: Market-Based Resume© Template

So far, you have uncovered how recruiters search for candidates and you have used the job market to identify your Core-3© power job moves. Now you need to learn how to use job ads to keyword-stack your resumes and online profiles to attract recruiters for the jobs that you want. This works for both the re-entry and full employment periods.

One of the challenges of writing a career book is to offer a resume strategy that can work for every single person at all professional levels and across different industries without having hundreds of resume examples. This method does just that by letting the job advertisement and market drive your resume creation. I will be offering an example of one candidate with three different resume changes. My online video class showcases different examples for variety.

How can one resume strategy work for everyone? This may sound a little bit controversial but ... the first part of the resume has NOTHING to do with your personal experience!!

I know that sounds crazy but if you had to write a paper about Shakespeare's *Romeo and Juliet,* would you start the essay discussing your own love-life? No, of course not. And the same is true with a great resume. Your resume (and your online profile) is based on the typical job requirements of your goal position. Once you have done the Core-3© Career Assessment and have identified your power career changes, you will have already matched your background to job market need.

To start a great resume, you literally set aside your work experience for a moment and focus on the top of the resume, which is a re-write of the related job advertisements that you have found. Once that is done, then you add your *matching* background. Going back to the *Romeo and Juliet* example, would you write about *Macbeth* if the paper was supposed to be about a different play? Use the job advertisements to drive the resume, not the other way around.

The #1 Resume Hack: Write the Resume to the Job Advertisement.

This resume style takes all the hard work you did identifying different career paths for your skills, and makes a resume out of the resulting job advertisements. At this stage you optimize the resume based on the keywords necessary to allow recruiters to find you based on their search parameters. By specifically creating a resume based on the job advertisement's required and desired skills, years of experience, job title, education, and accomplishments, your resume surfaces to the top. This document is also used as a template to build your online profiles on LinkedIn, Indeed.com, Monster.com, staffing agencies, and niche professional job boards. An aligned profile helps the recruiter to assist you because it is easier for them to sell a direct-hit match candidate to the hiring manager.

With the Market-Based Resume©, <u>what matters is what matches</u>; all other material is minimized or removed. By the time you are done with this section you may ask yourself the following question: *"Why don't I just copy and paste the job advertisement into my resume?"* My dear readers, it is almost that simple!

Before you learn this powerful resume style, let's review and debunk some myths about modern resume writing.

This chapter includes the following lessons:
4.1 – Modern Resume Myths
4.2 – The 4-Easy Steps to a Resume that Gets Calls
4.3 – Cover Letters

4.1 Modern Resume Myths

A resume format that works for online profiles and internal Applicant Tracking Systems (ATS) is not the same as the old resume style. This lesson discusses or debunks many myths and common beliefs about resumes.

Myth 1: The look of the resume is as important as the content.

This is not true. There are some amazing and quite beautiful templates out there for resumes that do absolutely nothing to tell the recruiter that you are qualified for the job. In addition, some of the graphic rich, grid-like resume formats can really be hurting your chances of being found because the ATS cannot read them.

To do a quick check on how your resume is being read, log in to Indeed.com and upload your resume. Also, open your Notepad on any PC, and copy and paste the resume into Notepad, which will strip the formatting. That stripped-down version is the actual output of many ATS programs. It is not pretty, and some systems are designed to boot out resumes that cannot be read properly.

The look of the resume is less important than ...
- Matching content.
- Matching keywords.
- Matching accomplishments.

Myth 2: Modern resumes should be submitted as a PDF not a Word Document

The industry standard in resume creation and submission is a Microsoft Word Document (.doc or .docx). Even the most cursory review of the job market will indicate immediately that MS Word is the mandatory resume submission format. This is true because although Adobe PDF is popular and better at retaining its format shape, the Applicant Tracking Systems cannot read a PDF document. Instead, create and submit using MS Word. (I do like to review a PDF version of a resume to catch any strange formatting issues - a great way to proofread.)

Myth 3: Resumes should be pretty to stand out.

MS Word offers some really attractive looking resume templates. Even I think they look great. BUT, these resumes do not help you stand out with online submission. In fact, they may be hurting your chances of being found by recruiters due to issues that the ATS has with grids and images. Consider keeping a "pretty" version for your in-person networking and for online use. The goal is a resume style that focuses on matching information and keywords that the systems can read.

Myth 4: Modern resumes do not need whitespace - more information is better.

The human brain needs "white space" to discern words and images. For this reason, it is critical to maintain at least a half inch margin; .75 inch is also good. If your resume is too crammed with words, the recruiter will not be able to read it. A recruiter will read the resume from left to right with the top half of the page being the most important visual space. Create a resume that presents the most important matching information first.

Myth 5: Solid lines that go from one side of the page to another are useful.

The use of lines to create visual separations is generally discouraged because the old type of ATS, which many companies still use, cannot read them. It is better to use center justifications, ALL CAPS, **bold**, and different font styles to create visual separation.

Myth 6: Dates of employment have to be month and year.

Because many candidates have dates of employment spanning less than two years, it is recommended to tab the dates over the right and use a year-to-year date format. You will, however, be required to use the month/year (xx/xxxx) format on your job applications. I recommend year-to-year on the resume and a separate document that has month/year for employment applications. Eventually, you will need it.

Myth 7: Fancy bullets are fun!

Fancy bullets are generally unnecessary for the resume. Use the standard "•". Use tabs to move copy horizontally on the page. Note that to get dates and other information justified properly on the right, the use of tabs and spaces will also be needed to get the correct alignment.

Myth 8: I can copy lines from the internet into my MS Word document with no problem.

When material is copied and pasted from the Internet, paste it into "Notepad" first to strip any background formatting and graphics, and then copy and paste into the Word document. If the formatting within an MS Word document gets difficult, select the entire document and change your paragraph spacing to "no spacing" (in the 2010 version of the program) to remove all paragraph spacing. Sometimes it is best to start over instead of fussing.

Myth 9: Tables and graphics are great!

They may be great but the ATS cannot read them. Do not put them on your resume. Use tabs instead to create columns and spacing on resumes.

Myth 10: Times New Roman Font Size 12 is the best ever!

I love the Times New Roman font but it is no longer acceptable, because "sans serif" fonts are considered the most readable modern fonts for this computer age. The recommended fonts and sizes are Arial-11, Calibri-12, Tahoma-11, and Verdana-10. The template on the video class is Verdana-10. Sometimes if I want to be fancy, I will use Garamond-14, but for headers only.

Myth 11: The header and footer are a great place to put my contact information!

The ATS cannot read information in the headers or footers so do not use these.

Myth 12: I need my contact information on both pages.

Usually, this means putting the contact information in the header, which as I said can't be read by the ATS. It is not necessary to have your contact information on all pages of your resume.

Myth 13: It's OK to have a resume over two pages long.

The answer is no, unless it is a C.V. for an academic or scientific position that includes publications and consortium events. Studies have shown that the recruiter tends to look at the top of the resume and scan for education at the bottom on the first page. If they do not find it on the first page, they will look for it on the bottom of the second page. If they have to search, your resume goes in the trash bin. The recruiter is not going to review multiple pages of experience. The goal is to quickly show them you are a match and to get the call for an interview, not to review your entire history.

Myth 14: I need to list all 20 years of work history.

Generally speaking, you should only be listing the last ten years of work history. This can be pushed to 15 years but it is not advisable. More history tends to age the candidate and the older worker tends to have a lot of redundant or irrelevant history as well. Only keep older information if it is critical for the next job.

Here is a recap of general formatting recommendations.
• Document program: MS Word (.doc or .docx), not Adobe PDF
• Margins: One-inch standard, .75 inch, or .5 inch. Do not go too narrow.
• Lines that span the page: Do not use
• Fonts and sizes: Arial-11, Calibri-12, Tahoma-11, or Verdana-10
• Spacing: Single or 1.15
• Highlights: **Bold**, CAPS, *italics*, different fonts
• Justification: Left or center
• Listing: Standard round bullets
• Indentation: Tabs and return
• Tables and pictures: Do not use
• Colors: Do not use
• Page Numbers: Do not use
• Header and Footer: Do not use

The online class has a downloadable resume example that has the correct formatting. This can be used to create your own resume.

Myth 15. Reverse Chronology is the only way to build a resume.

This one is partially true. In the classic reverse chronology resume, the recruiter focuses on the following items: Employer/Industry, Job Title, Dates of Employment. This is an issue for professionals who want or need to move out of their industry or job title, or that have gaps, too much job jumping, or even too long a tenure at a specific job. A candidate who needs to change careers often turn to the classic functional resume that focused on the skills and accomplishments. These resumes minimize mismatching industry, titles, and dates of employment.

Recruiters tend to dislike or (I will say it more strongly) *hate* functional resumes. The recruiter wants to see immediately if the candidate's most recent work experience matches the job for which the recruiter is hiring. Unfortunately, the recruiter believes that the most recent work experience is more important than the job candidate's related skills and accomplishments. Because of this, hiring practices typically reinforce square-peg, square-hole lateral moves.

The ATS-friendly Market-Based Resume Profile© combines the reverse-chronology resume with the qualities of a functional resume in a way that does not appear to hide anything.

Below is the format difference between a classic reverse-chronology resume compared to the Market-Based Resume© style. There are four differences: 1) the use of a Title Bar, 2) a Summary of Skills, 3) Skill Highlights, and 4) matching line items and accomplishments.

CLASSIC RESUME
- Contact information
- Objective
- Reverse-chronology work experience: highlighting job duties
- Education

MARKET-BASED RESUME©
- Contact information
- Title bar
- Summary of skills
- Skill highlights
- Reverse-chronology work experience: line item accomplishments
- Education

Myth 16: I need to list every possible contact method to reach me.

The contact information includes your name, mailing address, one telephone number, and one email address. More than one of anything just clutters and does not help.

Myth 17: My email address from when I was 20 years old will work great.

Old email addresses pose a few problems. The account "handle-name" and email provider you chose 15 years ago may appear very unprofessional and outdated now. I recommend that you create an email specifically for your job hunt. Most of us are inundated with spam or even solicitations that you have signed up for, but because many employers use email now to set up a phone interview or to send you a written pre-screen, it is very easy to miss an email from an employer or the Applicant Tracking System. Make sure the email address you use is neutral sounding and is something you reliably check every day. Gmail is recommended.

Myth 18: I have to list my LinkedIn account on the resume.

This is still optional. If a LinkedIn account is listed, the profile must be optimized to support the desired position.

Myth 19: Objective or no objective?

The Title Bar, Summary of Skills, and Skill Highlights section taught in this program replace the objective and are a primary tool to beat the ATS system.

Myth 20: One resume style will make everyone happy.

One resume style and strategy gets you past the ATS to get a call for an interview, but do not expect to get great feedback about it. Resumes are extremely personal, like a work of art. Ten people can look at one piece of artwork and have different feelings about it. Do not be surprised if a recruiter calls you on your resume and provides negative feedback about length and formatting.

The truth is if the resume got you a call, it was successful!

Welcome the feedback respectfully; potentially even make changes if the recruiter suggests it will help with continued candidacy. But in many cases the feedback is the personal taste of the recruiter. If the resume got the call, it did its #1 primary job! Its second job is to make the interview conversation easier. If the format is hampering the interview conversation, or not presenting all the relevant information in an easy-to-follow format, then it may be a signal to alter the profile.

Now it is time to start looking at resumes to see how market-based profiling works. I recommend visiting the online class to not only watch the modules but grab the example and use it as a template. Free Class Link.

4.2 The 4-Easy Steps to a Resume that Gets Calls

This resume format optimizes for keywords and *skyrockets* your chances of being found in employers' systems and online by recruiters searching for you right now.

Market-Based Resume©
1. Title Bars
2. Summary of Skills
3. Skill Highlights
4. Line Item Accomplishments

4.2.1 Title Bars

This lesson could also be called **"how to include title and industry on your resume regardless of your most recent position."**

In the classic version of a resume, the "objective" section is an area right under the contact information that gives a job candidate an opportunity to state their goal in applying for a certain job. These objectives were typically weak statements that usually had nothing to do with the job advertisement. This section is completely replaced by the Title Bar, Summary of Skills, and Skill Highlights.

Title Bar Definition
A three- to six-word re-write of the goal job title typically written in bold and ALL CAPS that creates a framework for the resume profile.

The Title Bar serves the following functions:
• It uses the target job title in the resume for keyword optimization whether or not the candidate has held that title.
• It allows the resume to surface in the Recruiter's search because it is entirely based on the keywords used to find the targeted candidate.
• Once the resume surfaces, it also instantly sends a signal to the recruiter's brain that the candidate is qualified for the job.
• It allows the job applicant a method of stating the job title from the advertisement even if they have not specifically held that title.

Your most recent job title and industry is one of the primary methods that employers use to qualify a candidate for positions. Many candidates do not have a job title that is an exact fit for the position. The simple but powerful step of using a Title Bar creates a profile theme and uses the keywords that are critical to get through to the recruiter. Title bars also remind the candidate to focus on writing a matching profile for the particular job.

In the following section, I will present a recently graduated job candidate that is applying for three different positions. Based on this candidate's Core-3©, there were three great options. The item listed before the colon is the job title of the ad, and the item after the colon is the Title Bar used for the respective resume.

This candidate was a 40-year old new graduate seeking to either leverage many years of retail management for a promotion or to move in a completely new direction into Human Resources. Technically, the candidate had only one relevant title in their previous work history - Retail Manager. One of the job advertisements was seeking a Multi-Store Regional Loss Prevention Manager. The candidate had never held a position with that exact title but had done the loss prevention work. The candidate had also not held a Human Resource title but had done a lot of related work and was trying out internships as a way to break into a new field following graduation.

The process of restating the job title tells the recruiter what the resume is about and that the candidate has done this type of work. It also keyword-stacks the resume with the targeting job title so it can be found.

1. Regional Loss Prevention Manager: MULTI-STORE LOSS PREVENTION PROGRAMS
2. Human Resources Internship: HUMAN RESOURCE INTERNSHIP PROFILE
3. Retail Store Manager: RETAIL MANAGEMENT ACCOMPLISHMENTS

Exercise 4.2.1: Title Bars

In the following exercise, apply the concept of Title Bar to jobs you identified in the Core-3© Assessment.

Write the Title Bars for the start of three different resumes.
Title Bar 1 for Resume 1:
_____

Title Bar 2 for Resume 2:
_____

Title Bar 3 for Resume 3:
_____

4.2.2 Summary of Skills

The Title Bar is the first of four steps in an ATS-friendly Market-Based Resume© Template customization. The second is the Summary of Skills section, which is the area directly under the title bar. When applying for jobs, the applicant should meet the following minimum thresholds to be considered qualified for the position: 1) match close to 100% of the mandated qualifications and 2) have at least 75% of the line items in the job advertisement.

This second step offers an opportunity to repeat the important mandatory qualifications of the position including years of experience, the level of responsibility, and skills.

Summary of Skills Definition:

Summary of Skills is a rewrite of the <u>REQUIRED QUALIFICATIONS</u> section of the job advertisement which should include:
• Position title
• Education level
• Requested years of experience (each request)
• Level of responsibility
• Matching industry and profession focus

This serves as a direct-hit match to the required qualifications at the top of the resume where it will be read immediately.

Sometimes a job advertisement will say "3 years of 'x'" or "5 years of 'x'." You should literally write that out. This works - I have had recruiters read the Summary of Skills right back to the job candidate. Remember that these recruiters are going through hundreds of resumes a day so make it easy on them. The next exercises provide examples of appropriate Summary of Skills writing and scripts based on the three Title Bars from the previous lesson.

Exercise 4.2.2 A Summary of Skills Example Review

Use the following examples to help guide the creation of your summary of skills sections. Select the script that fits your situation the best for the three Market-Based Resumes© that you have started.

MULTI-STORE LOSS PREVENTION PROGRAMS
Degreed regional manager with 5+ years in drug-store loss prevention programs and 3+ years of experience specializing in employee-oriented theft, the design of sting programs, store audits, and court representation at offender prosecutions.

HUMAN RESOURCE INTERNSHIP PROFILE
New graduate with a Bachelor's degree in Business and concentration on Human Resources with 2+ years of curriculum development and 3+ years of additional recruiting, hiring and employee relations experience as a retail assistant manager, which would allow me to support the HR team immediately while also learning.

RETAIL MANAGEMENT ACCOMPLISHMENTS
Experienced retail manager with 10+ years of profit and loss responsibilities has recently graduated with a Bachelor's in Business Administration. My stores have consistently made a profit with effective merchandising, staffing, and training. In addition, I have saved money for the store through the implementation of loss prevention programs.

Exercise 4.2.2b Scripts for Creating Summary of Skills

Use the following scripts to help guide the creation of your Summary of Skills sections. Select the script that fits your situation the best for the three Market-Based Resumes© that you have started. This is a re-write of the mandatory requirements section of the job advertisement.

Script 1:
Degreed_____ (*position title written as a skill*) experience in _____ (*industry*) with _____ (*amount of years in the job ad*) of targeted experience in _____ (*skill 1*), _____ (*skill 2*), _____ (*skill 3*). My experience includes the _____ (*list of other skills*).

Script 2:
New Graduate_____(*level of responsibility*) with a _____ (*mandated degree*) with ____ (*years*) of _____ (*skill 1*) and also_____ (*years*) of _____ (*skill 2*).

Script 3:
Experienced _____ (*level of responsibility*) _____ (*job title*) with experience in _____ (*skill 1*). I am seeking to obtain a _____ (*job title objective*). In my work, I have _____ (*state an accomplishment that matches desired qualifications*).
*Note: this is the only place on a resume where using the first-person 'I' may be considered acceptable.

4.2.3 Skill Highlights

The skill highlights section is the third method that tells the recruiter a candidate is a direct-hit match to the job advertisement. This method helps preserve the classic reverse-chronology version that they prefer while still directing their attention to matching qualifications.

Skill Highlights Definition
Condensing the line items and mandatory qualifications down to two- to four-word statements focused on "hard-skills," in a 2-column format under the Summary of Skills.

This serves to repeat the "hard-skill" line items and tells the recruiter the applicant is qualified for the job immediately.

One of the more challenging things for a candidate to do is to create and differentiate these "hard-skill" power statements when job advertisements are chock full of "soft-skill" statements. Soft-skills are important but they will not get you a call for an interview. To get found and get a job offer you need to simplify your matching technical dominance. Below is a list of soft-skills and a corresponding hard-skill list to demonstrate the difference.

Soft-Skill versus Hard-Skill Comparison

Soft-Skills List
Leadership
Problem Solving
Technical Expertise
Analytical
Dependable

Corresponding Hard-Skill List
Multi-Unit District Manager Support
Store Audit Compliance & Reporting
Payroll Calculations & Accurate Submissions

Inventory Management & Analysis
Store Revenue Growth

The soft-skills are very important qualities but they must be demonstrated throughout the resume with hard-skill accomplishments, length of time at various jobs, job titles, and software or technical expertise. The soft-skills words are rather meaningless compared to the matching hard-skill list.

To examine this process, the program will refer back to the three resume examples. The skill highlights used for each resume are reduced to powerful keyword-stacked statements.

Exercise 4.2.3 Skill Highlights:
Examples with Title Bar and Summary of Skills

MULTI-STORE LOSS PREVENTION PROGRAMS
Degreed regional manager with 5+ years in drug-store loss prevention programs and 3+ years of experience specializing in employee-oriented theft, the design of sting programs, store audits, and court representation at offender prosecutions.

Skill Highlight
Shrinkage Sting Operations
Loss Prevention Court Representation
Store Audits & Compliance
Store Revenue Growth
Inventory Management & Analysis
Staff Management & Scheduling
Hiring, Training & Development
Payroll Calculations & Accurate Submissions

Multi-Unit District Manager Support

HUMAN RESOURCE INTERNSHIP PROFILE
New graduate with a Bachelor's degree in Business and concentration in Human Resources with 2+ years of curriculum development and 3+ years of additional recruiting, hiring and employee relations experience as a retail assistant manager, allowing me to support the HR team immediately while also learning.

Skill Highlight
President of Society of Human Resources (SHRM)
Human Resource Classwork
Curriculum Development
Recruiting & Staffing

RETAIL MANAGEMENT ACCOMPLISHMENTS
Experienced retail manager with 10+ years of profit and loss responsibilities, recently graduated with a Bachelor's in Business Administration. My stores have consistently made a profit with effective merchandising, staffing, and training. In addition, I have saved money for the store through the implementation of loss prevention programs.

Skill Highlight
Store Revenue Growth
Store Audits & Compliance
Staff Management & Scheduling
Hiring, Training & Development
Payroll Calculations & Accurate Submission
Inventory Management & Analysis

Exercise 4.2.3 Creating Skill Highlights: Step Three in Market-Based Resume Profile©

To create Skill Highlights follow the following steps.

1. Copy and paste the job advertisement into Notepad to strip any formatting issues.
2. Take each line item of the advertisement and look for "hard-skills."
3. Discard any "soft-skills."
4. Create a 3-word to 4-word phrase that describes each "hard-skill."
5. Use tabs to create a 2-column list of a block of skills. (Do not use the split-page or column feature in word. Use the tab key.)
6. Keep a single line for online job posting on Indeed.com and other sites that cannot preserve this formatting.
7. Use the video class to watch me break down an ad. Use the example resume as an already-formatted template for your use.

4.2.4 Line-Item Accomplishments

It is common for job candidates to create a list of job duties for their resume and leave it the same for each resume – this is not a good practice.

Line-Item Accomplishments Definition:
A rewrite of the line-item accomplishments in the job advertisement, ideally with quantified accomplishments.

This serves the following functions:

- The Line-Item Accomplishments are, at a minimum, a list of matching duties stripped right from the job advertisement.
- In the best scenario, the Line-Item Accomplishments are quantified statements that match the job advertisement.

In some cases, re-writing the line items from the job ad is all that is needed to get a call on the resume. It is certainly better than a list of duties that have nothing to do with the job. As a career coach, I consistently work with professionals for positions I have never worked with before. To assist those clients, I created a work-around hack to help develop their resume content.

Tip 1: Use another job advertisement in another city to build your resume.
Tip 2: Search for other resumes and follow their content direction.

Some job ads have very few line items listed. To help create your resume, search for the same title in another city. Find a job that that has a robust set of line items. Copy, paste, and re-write the list of duties. This helps to avoid plagiarism for the position you are applying for yet offers the most content to work from. You can also search for your competitor's resume on indeed.com and use it to brainstorm your own content.

Sooner or later, you will need to learn how to quantify your accomplishments. For readers who bristle and say "my work is not quantifiable" then, at a minimum, make sure your job duties match the line items of the advertisement. Matching accomplishments will later be needed for both the interview and salary negotiation process. Therefore, it is beneficial to develop a list of accomplishments for the resume. This skill is also critical for garnering higher incomes throughout your career.

For the Retail Manager and Loss Prevention resume examples, the job candidate will review the requested line items and then capture and communicate their value for the positions based on their past roles. Below is an example of quantified accomplishments:

- Improved C-Store revenue from an average of $65,000 to $90,000 revenue per month.
- Reduced shrinkage by 15%, controlling $90,000 of C-store Inventory.
- Supervised and scheduled nine customer service hourly employees for a 24-hour business over 5 shifts: 1st, 2nd, 3rd, and two middle or carry-over shifts.
- Increased safety and health inspection passing grades by 15%.
- Prepared payroll based on a total of 365 allowed hours with a formula that is calculated to be no more than 13% of typical monthly income for a high volume store and 9 to 10% for slower stores.
- Assisted district supervisors in managing operations of 37 district stores ranging from $30,000- $90,000 per month per store in revenue.

Line-item Accomplishment statements tend to have a few things in common:

1. They have numbers that quantify the related work.

2. They focus on the end result, not the duties done, to demonstrate success.

3. They tend to be "big picture" and relate to how the accomplishment drew more revenue or saved on expenses for the organization.

4. They create a comparison of some kind to help the reader understand why this was an accomplishment.

Providing evidence, or proof of success, can translate to more calls on the resume, more offers in the interview, and more money in salary negotiations.

Exercise 4.2.4 Creating Accomplishment Statements

Follow the steps below to begin writing accomplishment statements. At a very minimum, re-write the job advertisement line items to describe your work background.

1. Copy and paste the job advertisements into Notepad.
2. Create a line under each job requirement.
3. Underneath each line write the question: "tell me about a time when you did (fill in whatever the line item on the job advertisement is about)."
4. Accomplishment Script: Use the following script to create accomplishment phrases.

"I performed _____, which made or saved _____ (*money, time, or some other performance unit*). This was done better than _____ (*coworker, other teams, industry standard*) and impacted my employer positively by resulting in _____ (*achieving the employer's goal*).

5. Use growth rate percentages instead of whole numbers when the amount of units is not impressive. For instance, an increase of 10 units to 15 does not sound as impressive as a 50% increase.

The growth rate equation is as follows:
Growth Rate (%) = ((New-Old)/Old) * 100 or ((Present-Past)/Past))*100

In our example of moving from 10 units to 15, the equation would look like the following:
((15-10)/10)*100 = 50%

6. Reduce the scripts down to simple statements.
"Improved _____ revenue from an average of $_____ to $_____ revenue per month."
"Reduced _____ by ___% controlling for $_____."
"Increased _____ by ___%."

Many candidates believe the resume and cover letter are inseparable in the job application process. A large percentage of job applicants spend more time on the cover letter than the resume. Cover Letters should not be your focus! Lesson 3.3 discusses the topic of cover letters and its relationship to the resume and job search.

4.3 Cover Letters

Cover letters have been greatly impacted by the use of online job boards and Applicant Tracking Systems. For instance, when recruiters search for a candidate, whether internally or online, a cover letter is never scanned for keywords and it is rarely read by the recruiter. The following section discusses and debunks myths related to their use in modern career changing.

4.3.1 Cover Letter Myths

Myth 1: Cover letters are mandatory.

Career advisors will tell you that a cover letter is necessary with every job application 100% of the time. This is not true. Research has found that 80% of candidates customize their cover letter and not their resume, yet experts estimate that less than 20% of recruiters actually read cover letters.

The rise of the ATS is reducing the importance of cover letters every single day.

The majority of job candidates who have used the methods covered in this book obtain positions without ever submitting a cover letter. Even if there is a field in the ATS to upload, that cover letter will not be scanned during a candidate search or read later by the recruiter.

Myth 2: I need to add the cover letter to the resume document if there is no space for it.

Sometimes candidates will put the cover letter in the same document as the resume. This is not a good practice unless specifically requested by the employer. The ATS may parse data to prefill fields in the application, which will not work with the cover letter potentially damaging your submission.

Myth 3: The employer adds space for an optional cover letter so they must want one.

No, when it is noted as optional it is just a reflection of employee expectations. If the employer wants one, they will tell you.

Myth 4: The cover letter is a second opportunity to "keyword-stack."

No – because the cover letter is not scanned, use the Summary of Skills and Skill Highlights section as a great substitute for a cover letter. It is more important to make changes to the Summary of Skills section to match the job advertisement than it is to submit a cover letter, because the software will always scan the resume. Even if a cover letter is mandated, the Summary of Skills section along with the most relevant bullet points and keywords can be slightly reworded to form the cover letter.

Myth 5: If the job advertisement requires a cover letter and I do not send one, I will still be considered as a viable candidate.

Some employers do still use mandatory cover letters as an extra exercise to help weed out candidates. When a job advertisement specifically requires a cover letter, you must submit one to be considered as a candidate.

Also, if the job is something you are very interested in, a carefully customized cover letter may indicate a higher level of interest. The great news is that a good Market-Based Resume Profile© can help quickly create the cover letter.

Because cover letters extend the time it to apply for a position, they are considered part of a "quality" strategy in this program. In the job search process, a candidate should be submitting both high quality customized materials and a large quantity of general market-based profiles. As noted above, you should submit one only if it is mandated for the position.

I will be completely transparent here. A cover letter is one of the single greatest wastes of time when it comes to applying for jobs in today's hiring climate. Any information you feel is important for the cover letter should be in the resume. It is far more important to tailor your resume to the job than to tailor a cover letter that no one will ever read.

The exercise on the next page presents a cover letter template. Change the bulleted items in the resume to read more like a composed paper instead of resume statements. The cover letter template is also available on the video class

4.3.2 Cover Letter Template

NAME
Address
Phone • Email

Date

Employer
Employer Address

RE: (Job Title and Job ID Number if Listed)

Dear Hiring Manager,

Please accept this cover letter and resume as my application for _____ (*Job Title*) position. With over ___ years (*use the years from the job ad*) of _____ (*state the primary skill listed in the job title*) experience and _____ (*list the second more important skill or industry qualification*) I am uniquely qualified for this position.

Insert the Resume Skill Highlights and Accomplishments.

I believe that my _____ (*state the primary skill listed in the job title*) experience combined with _____ (*list the second more important skill or industry qualification*) can make an impact on your initiatives. I look forward to speaking with you over the phone at _____ (*telephone*) or by email _____ (*a neutral sounding Gmail address used only for your job hunt*).

Sincerely,
(*Your Name*)

> Homework

Download the cover letter and resume template in this lesson from the online class.

• Take one job ad and write the Title Bar, Summary of Skills, and Skill Highlights to create the top of your resume.

• Add your work history only after you have created the framework for the resume from the job advertisement.

• Create a simple pre-formatted cover letter for use <u>only</u> when required by the employer. If there is just a field for a cover letter, it is not mandatory. I am serious. Do not waste your time on this unless absolutely 100% required.

Quiz 4: Resume & Cover Letter (T/F)
1.___ The first part of the resume is about your work or education.
2.___ The best way to submit a resume is in the Adobe PDF format.
3.___ The resume's job is to get calls, not satisfy the recruiter's stylistic resume ideals.
4.___ The Title Bar, Summary of Skills, and Skill Highlights replace the "Objective" line.
5.___ Your work history should cover the line items in the job ad.
6.___ You can find yourself on indeed.com and improve the results
7.___ Quantified accomplishments need to be on the resume.
8.___ A single resume will work to get you hired.
9.___ A customized cover letter and template resume is best.
10.___ A cover letter is needed for most submissions.

Chapter 4: Answer Key (T/F)
1) False: The first part of the resume is a re-write of the job advertisement. Yes, it needs to be true to you, but it should be about the job advertisement, not you.
2) False: No, no, no, no - stop submitting PDF resumes.
3) True: If the resume got you the call it did its job no matter how the recruiter feels about the style.
4) True: The objective line is dead and even joked about among HR and resume writers.
5) True: Copy, paste, re-word, and add accomplishments matching the line items.
6) True: Scan the competitors use of keywords and add more to your resume.

7) True: Numbers typically play well on the resume. Eventually you will have to quantify.

8) False: Ideally you customize the top of each one and have three core resumes.

9) False: Customize the resume as often as feasible and have a templated cover letter (only when requested). The resume is always scanned or read; the cover letter is never scanned and rarely read.

10) False: If a cover letter is not mandatory, do not submit one.

Chapter 5: LinkedIn and Online Profiles That Tap the Hidden Job Market

LinkedIn and the online job boards are the engine that drive a job search capable of doubling your interviews and leveraging recruiters. Once you have created the resume profiles based on the Core 3$^©$, then the LinkedIn profile can be created.

Recruiters are searching these databases every day to fill their open positions. In addition, most offer "quick apply" options using your profile which can ramp up your job search immediately.

LinkedIn and the online job boards allow a job candidate to tap the hidden job market in a way that has never existed before in history. When jobs were primarily advertised through the newspaper, there was no way for employers to access a database of talent for their positions. As well, before the turn of this century, to access the hidden job market of unadvertised jobs the candidate was forced to develop and maintain a network of contacts. Now employers and candidates alike can succeed by searching these databases.

Before we discuss the strategy, let's review some myths.

This chapter includes the following lessons:
5.1 – LinkedIn and online job board myths
5.2 – LinkedIn profile optimization

5.3 – Monster profile optimization
5.4 – Indeed profile optimization
5.5 – Other job boards & niche sites
5.6 – Check the competition, boost rankings, get more content

5.1 LinkedIn and Online Job Board Myths

Myth 1: The ATS, LinkedIn, and Online Job Boards are programmed differently.

No. The software programming of all the hiring software systems and the way recruiters search for candidates are essentially the same. However, the online job boards receive more consistent investment to help improve search results. In addition, because third party recruiters cannot tap internal company databases the amount of searching done with the online job boards is more extensive.

Myth 2: The resumes for direct application and the online profiles are different.

No. The resume you create will be used for both direct application and the online job board profiles. There are some unique aspects of LinkedIn, Indeed.com, and Monster.com (how attention is drawn to keywords, and some pre-populated box formatting issues with the resume upload) but, in essence, they are the same.

Myth 3: LinkedIn is the primary online database that recruiters use to find talent.

No, not yet. LinkedIn began as social media tool for professionals before it became heavily used for recruiting. As more and more professionals used the job board, LinkedIn started leveraging the website for revenue-generation by selling the recruiter app and employer job posting. It is the #1 job board for I.T. positions if for no other reason than because it is easy to search for certifications that are used throughout the I.T. profession. But professionals will need to leverage more than one job board to double their interviews.

Myth 4: Online job boards are better than networking for tapping the hidden job market of unadvertised jobs.

This one is actually true! Recruiters are searching these job boards every day for un-advertised jobs. A highly optimized profile on the job boards, including LinkedIn, is the most effective method an active or passive job search candidate can use to be targeted for the hidden job market. It is much easier, faster, and efficient than networking to tap this market.

Myth 5: LinkedIn is not used in a background check.

LinkedIn is used to screen, but not after an offer is made. It is more common for the recruiter to scan the LinkedIn page before even calling for an interview, so it is very important to control your professional image before you apply. LinkedIn is very important in this process, but it should not be your last stop in creating your campaign.

Each of these systems is unique in how it harnesses the power of keyword-optimization. I will discuss my three current favorites: Monster.com, LinkedIn.com, and Indeed.com. I also recommend creating profiles for niche websites in your profession or location.

5.2 Monster.com and Professional Categories

Monster.com is the original online job search database that fine-tuned the concept of professional category assignments. Before there was keyword-search, recruiters would use professional categorization offered by Monster. But what if the candidate does not understand all the categories they belong to in the job market? What is great about Monster.com is it offers a glimpse into how the recruiter perceives the candidate. As an effective job board for your resume, Monster.com has declined in the United States but it is still hot in Canada and offers some important lessons.

Let's review some concepts that you have covered thus far. You know now that you have to help recruiters find you by optimizing your resumes and profiles for keywords and popular recruiting search terms. As a professional, you cannot be defined with just one term. Most of us do multiple duties using various skills within a single position. Most professionals are well-qualified for at least three power moves which are often in different job categories, the Core-3©. In addition, a candidate may be qualified for a step-up, step-down, or a step-over into a different industry which is another Core-3©. Let's use Monster.com to demonstrate how this operates, because it is the most robust job search database in regards to professional categorization.

When creating a profile in Monster, one of the first selections to make is that of professional categories and sub-categories. Here is the first Category and Subcategory you will find on Monster.com.

Category 1: Accounting/Finance/Insurance

Subcategories:

1. Accounts Payable/Receivable
2. Actuarial Analysis
3. Audit
4. Bookkeeping
5. Claims Review and Adjusting
6. Collections
7. Corporate Accounting
8. Corporate Finance
9. Credit review/Analysis
10. Financial Analysis/Research/Reporting
11. Financial Control
12. Financial Planning/Advising
13. Financial Products Sales/Brokerage
14. Fund Accounting
15. General/Other: Accounting/Finance
16. Investment Management
17. Policy Underwriting
18. Real Estate Appraisal
19. Real Estate Leasing/Acquisition

20. Risk Management/Compliance
21. Securities Analysis/Research
22. Tax Accounting
23. Tax Assessment and Collections

As you can see, in the **Accounting/Finance/Insurance** category there are 23 subcategories that are specialized skill sets for the candidate. An applicant will likely fit into at least three of these sub-categories. Each subcategory can be Core-3©. In addition to subcategories, a job candidate may have worked across more than one primary category.

On Monster.com there are 25 categories. Listed in parentheses is the number of subcategories for each primary category.

1. Accounting /Finance/Insurance (23)
2. Administrative/Clerical (11)
3. Banking/Real Estate/Mortgage Professionals (11)
4. Biotech/R&D/Science (8)
5. Building Construction/Skilled Trades (14)
6. Business/Strategic Management (15)
7. Creative/Design (10)
8. Customer Support/Client Care (10)
9. Editorial/Writing (6)
10. Education/Training (13)
11. Engineering (14)
12. Food Services/Hospitality (9)
13. Human Resources (8)
14. Installation/Maintenance/Repair (16)
15. IT/Software Development (13)
16. Legal (9)

17. Logistics/Transportation (17)
18. Manufacturing/Production/Operations (16)
19. Marketing/Product (13)
20. Medical/Health (15)
21. Other (3)
22. Project/Program Management (5)
23. Quality Assurance/Safety(11)
24. Sales/Retail/Business Development (19)
25. Security/Protective Services (9)

A professional in Category 1: Accounting/Finance/Insurance may work on the Category 15: IT/Software, Category 16: Legal, or Category 22: Project/Program Management. The Monster database really demonstrates how many categories and sub-categories one professional can belong to. If you have been feeling pigeon-holed in your career, this should give you hope that a job or career change is possible across a span of your skills and abilities by understanding how to re-orient your profile to different categories.

Let's stop for a moment and think about this. If the recruiter is looking for an Accountant that has worked in Audit but the job candidate's current resume is focused more on their financial analysis and reporting work, the recruiter cannot find that candidate in the database even though they may want that job and are qualified. You can help the recruiter find you by making their job easier, versus hoping an employer will come across your resume and spend time figuring out if you are qualified. The easier you make it for them, the easier it will be for you.

You can double your interviews by picking the right categories, aligning the resume, and matching the profile, sometimes in less than 24 hours. The online class presents a candidate named Lisa, and we will discuss her example here. To see how I optimized her Monster.com, LinkedIn.com, and Indeed.com profiles, use your free video course link (www.karengurney.com/mom).

Monster.com Professional Categorization: Lisa's Example

Lisa is an accountant who worked in many accounting roles. In her last role she was a Controller, one of the highest accounting titles, but the organization was small with only $4M in revenue. Lisa was willing to consider several accounting titles. In this case, we will focus on the ways I optimized her Monster.com profile based on the different aspects of her background.

On Monster.com, for Lisa's resume there are a number of selections under Accounting that I could pick but, like your Core-3©, Monster.com only allows you to select three at a time.

The recruiter is going to use these to narrow down their list of candidates, so it is important to try three and then rotate among your different Core-3© resume profiles (assuming that you want to do three different campaigns). For Lisa, she has done all of these subcategory options:
- Audit
- Corporate Accounting
- Corporate Finance
- Financial Analysis/Research/Reporting
- General/Other: Accounting/Finance

- Tax Accounting

For her first campaign, I focused on financial analysis and audit. So I selected Audit, Financial Analysis/Research/Reporting, and to be sure I caught all possible inquiries, also General/Other: Accounting/Finance. Lisa has worked in different categories that are unique to an industry, like product licensing. If the market was good for those skills, I would try a later campaign focused on subcategories of her other qualifications. Monster.com has the most developed method of all the job boards of narrowing down a job candidate's skills for professional categorization. Even though Indeed.com is more popular than Monster.com in the United States, this particular job board really emphasizes the importance of "categorizing" your resume so that the recruiter can find you and say "this person is qualified."

I do need to add one last caveat: Monster.com, and increasingly Indeed.com, tends to generate a lot of spam emails. No matter the profile, a professional will get calls for sales positions. Ignore any emails or calls that do not specify a title related to your resume.

5.3 LinkedIn.com Profile Optimization

LinkedIn is best known as a social network representing your professional life. However, as we know now, recruiters are using it to source passive and active job candidates. To increase the likelihood of being found, and to also properly represent your career, LinkedIn offers many sections you can add to your profile. Some of these qualifications are important for recruiters to find you and, after they find you, pre-qualify you as a candidate. This is a listing of sections that require your attention.

1. Profile picture
2. Headline
3. Geographic setting (i.e. City)
4. Industry
5. Connections
6. Summary of skills
7. Work history
8. Education
9. Certifications
10. Skills (recommendations)
11. Endorsements
12. LinkedIn job alert preferences
13. Recruiter push

In the following section, I will review each of these, and will offer a strategy and compare it to what I did for Lisa. You may not want your current employer or network to be notified of what changes you have made to your profile; you can turn the "Notifications" off. The changes will still be public but an alert will not be sent to your network.

Profile Picture

Needless to say, your profile picture is the first impression that a recruiter uses to understand who you are across a broad dimension of demographics. In the United States, we do not put pictures on our resumes as happens in other countries. Because of this, LinkedIn is often cross-referenced by recruiters even when a candidate has directly applied to the employer.

Technically this increases the type of demographic bias that U.S. employers are supposed to avoid. However, the option is to either have no profile at all or to control your online image using LinkedIn.

My recommendation is to find a local photographer that specializes in talent headshots to take your picture. This means no JCPenney and Sears photography, or friends taking your picture at the local park. When Googling to find the right photographer, search for the word "headshots" or "talent photography" in your city. An appointment with a true headshot or talent professional will include a makeup artist/hair stylist and numerous outfit changes. Do not leave the face of your professional career to a selfie on your phone. Get professional hair, makeup, and photography.

I also use a free profiling tool, Carol Tuttle's *Dressing Your Truth*, to identify my client's power-colors and style. Google her program. This image coach has built an impressive free analysis tool that will help you identify your power color and style. You do not need to join her program to identify your type, but you may want to for additional information. For my clients who do not want to join this program, I Google their "type" with the word "Pinterest." There are other people who share your type and who have created boards for different styling. There are Pinterest boards for both men and women, and Tuttle's program applies to both. Once you take new photos, post them on photofeeler.com to get feedback on how the image is perceived from a LinkedIn professional standard.

This extra step in boosting your physical image can be valuable to a B2W mom. Your last professional photo was probably before your children were born. Getting ready for a photo shoot will force you to do needed updates to your wardrobe, hair style, and make-up. Most moms are not happy with the changes to their post-baby bodies. You will be shocked what a real talent photographer can do for you. (I feel I am the least photogenic person on earth yet a real photog was able to unlock something inside of me.) Allow a true artist to unlock your beauty in a way you never thought possible leaving you feeling great about yourself and your job search.

Headline

Your headline should be very similar to the Title Bar on your resume. LinkedIn will generate a headline from your most current position, but that is not what you want to use. Unless it is "Product Manager" at General Electric or some other well-respected business, it is best to create this on your own.

After you perform the Core-3© assessment, identify a stream of jobs, and write the resume to the job, you will have the right headline for LinkedIn sitting right at the top of your resume. This can be typed in CAPS or first word capitalization. Play around until it displays the way you want. Note: LinkedIn will override what you put in with your most recent position unless you uncheck the box. This can be annoying, so you may want to wait until you input your work experience to do the final tweak on the LinkedIn profile.

Lisa Headline Example on the Online Class:

In the class, Lisa's headline is "Financial Analyst at Audio Stream." This is good because that matches the direction she wants to go in, however if she decided to focus on Controller jobs, she might use Controller, Financial Planning and Analysis (FP&A) and/or Audit headlines. You always want to focus on a headline that matches your primary goal position for your campaign. This can always be changed and rotated for different campaigns.

Geographic Setting

At the top of your profile, under your headline, there is an option to set your city. As you know, where you live is an important search keyword for the recruiter. If you want to get calls choose the city where you want to work, not where you live. You may feel this is dishonest and I know this is not ideal, but on a base strategic level, to double your interviews where you want to work you have to match the selections made by the recruiter. I am expecting, as a B2W mom, that your profile will be where you are living and that this will not be an issue.

Industry

The industry selection is the one I dislike the most on LinkedIn for many of the same reasons as the geographic selection. If you recall from the Monster.com training, Monster offers hundreds of professional subcategories as well as industry settings. I ignore the industry settings in most cases. What *you* actually do is your professional category. What your *company* does is your industry. These are totally different aspects of your qualifications, but LinkedIn only offers one selection, which makes recruiter search by category difficult, if not impossible.

My recommendation is to choose the closest selection to what you want to be doing professionally (professional category) not the type of industry you want to be working in. For instance, I selected Human Resources because that is how the market perceives my work. Technically, from my perspective, my work falls more under Professional Training and Coaching. This is a balancing act - you must think about the most likely selection by the recruiter. In the case of LinkedIn, most recruiters bypass industry and focus on keywords and the other selections anyway.

Connections

LinkedIn is about being social, which means connecting with the people you know. There is a baseline of connections of 500+. My recommendation is to get to 500+ as quickly as possible. This means loading your email lists and then, as people connect with you, using the LinkedIn "recommended connection" opportunity to connect with many more cross-connections. When performing a connection campaign, you may get an interview if the headline is set correctly, especially for digital marketing and sales people. However, my goal here is primarily to make you appear "highly-connected" or popular. You may not in general be interested in "being popular," but for your job search, this indicates a networked person that is dedicated to developing professionally. That is the message you want to send.

Summary of Skills

LinkedIn offers a Summary of Skills section. Copy and paste the top part of your carefully crafted resume to attract a certain type of job. The goal of this section is to keep the recruiter focused on your matching skills when their search produces you as a candidate. In our online class example, Lisa wants to focus on financial analyst and forecasting roles versus "Controller" positions. Therefore, she pasted the top of her resume right into the Summary of Skills along with the headline for the resume. You will need to do some formatting to make sure it looks correct.

Lisa's Summary of Skills Example from the Online Class

FINANCIAL FORECASTING ANALYST PROFILE
From working in managerial accounting, financial accounting, and financial analyst roles, I have developed a strong acumen for analyzing, forecasting, and budgeting organizational finances specifically for system implementation, process improvement, new product development, lending, cash flow, and expenses. In every position I have held, I presented the most detailed forecasted comparisons for evidence-based managerial decision-making that generates revenue and saves money.

Forecasting: Sales & Cost of Goods Sold
Internal Control Systems
Internal Reporting: P&L and Balance Sheet
Daily & Annual Cash Flow Analysis
Cost Analysis
Bank Financing

Internal Audit
Variance Identification
Systems Evaluation & Implementation
International Billing Policy
Month End Close

You can use this top portion of your resume and the Summary on LinkedIn to laser-focus the recruiter's attention.

Work History

There are two aspects of the work history that are important: The LinkedIn "generated title" selections and "years of experience."

Title Selection

The LinkedIn system generates title options that will be slightly different from the title you have. Use the closest-match LinkedIn *pre-formulated* titles to improve your ability to be found. Consider selecting titles that reflect your goal position versus your actual title (within reason). Your LinkedIn profile is not a legally binding application; the goal is to be found, and using the system the way it is designed improves those chances.

Years of Experience

The next area of concern is "years of experience." If the job advertisements are requesting five or ten years of experience, it may make sense to consolidate all of your experience with one company under the most recent title. To improve honesty in representation, create a "title transition history," a list of your title progression with dates, under the one title. In some cases, it is better to have one single employer with all years of experience in one post and list the title transition under that post, rather than to separate them out. In other cases, it is actually better to break out your own experience into multiple titles from your Core-3© so that your profile will surface in a variety of search terms.

Whichever strategy is selected, remember to present what matches your goal position. Any random or unrelated positions, short term temporary positions, or even work detail that does not support your goal position should be left off the profile. Overall strategy: Think of LinkedIn as a brochure for the job you want. What would you put on that brochure?

Education

Do not include your high school education. Once you have your Bachelor's degree, it is no longer important to display an Associate's, unless that program is directly related to the goal position. Education is not a primary search term, but a baseline degree is a pre-requisite for most professional positions. For the most part, it is not necessary or even desirable to list anything below a Bachelor's degree.

Certifications

Certifications are critically important to hiring and also serve as a keyword search item. Make sure your certifications are listed on your LinkedIn profile and your resume. When seeking jobs, use certifications as a primary search term to uncover new streams of opportunities. You may also consider adding an important certification to your last name space on LinkedIn so that it displays immediately. You can do the same with the resume. This is ideal for a Certified Public Accountant (CPA) or any role that requires mandated licensing to perform the work.

Skills & Endorsements

LinkedIn offers an opportunity to list skills that people can easily endorse. Endorsements are not recommendations, which are a more detailed write-up; these are "hard" skills that are likely to be searched as a keyword. The system allows you to input them and periodically will ask connections to endorse those skills. The best way to get more endorsements on a skill is to endorse someone else's skill. This prompts a system email to request the person that you endorsed to in turn endorse you. Do not let LinkedIn generate these and leave it to chance! Create "hard skill" endorsements that match the job you want and then start endorsing your friends so they will be prompted to endorse your skills.

Recommendations

After the profile is created, invite people to write recommendations. As a consultant, these have been extremely valuable to me and are basically mandatory for any professional. Although recommendations will not necessarily help the recruiter find you, they do help recruiters evaluate you as a candidate during the selection process.

Set Your Job Alert Preferences

Indeed.com is the most important website to set up customized job alerts because it aggregates job postings from multiple websites offering the most robust job market information but, it does not pull from LinkedIn. Therefore, a separate set of job alerts will need to be set up on LinkedIn and Indeed. In LinkedIn, click on Jobs and then Preferences to set up job alerts for positions posted by companies.

Set the locations of interest, the range of your level of professional ability, and in the section that asks for industry, select your professional ability as well as industry. If LinkedIn does not have an item as a category, you will not be able to add it. This section is limited and honestly, not my favorite. LinkedIn's industry list is not as robust as it should be but you can still select as many professions and industries that make sense.

Set Up Recruiter Push "Let Your Next Job Find You"

Buried underneath the job alert preferences is a handy little hidden section that allows you to notify recruiters of your job interests for 90 days.

Go to the Jobs and then Preferences on LinkedIn and then under the job alerts is a section that says "Let Your Next Job Find You."

• *Share career interests with recruiters?* Switch this to "On."

- *What field are you interested in?* Choose the best option from the list that matches your professional background. Choices are limited - do your best.
- *What roles would you like to be considered for?* Pick at least three titles that surfaced from your Core 3©. (LinkedIn has to have the title in its database for this to work. Start typing and select from the auto-generated titles.)
- *What job types are you interested in (Check all that apply)?* Full-time, Part-time, Contract, Internship, Remote, Freelance
- *When can you start?* Anytime
- *Share your job preferences?* On

There are more advanced features for LinkedIn that are explored in later chapters but they take much longer. The goal in this chapter is to get a highly optimized job search campaign up and running as fast as possible that will draw recruiters to you and, when you apply for jobs, will provide a profile that matches the resume.

5.4 Indeed.com and the Top of Your Resume

It is no secret by now that Indeed.com is a career coach's best friend. Because the database aggregates from other websites along with employers posting into the system directly, Indeed.com is the database of choice for job research. There are many reasons that a job applicant needs to be on this site:
- Job research,
- Job alerts,
- Salary survey,
- Posting a searchable resume that recruiters can find,

- Indeed "quick-apply" job submissions, and
- Quality Check: Search for your own profile to see where you stand (and grab more content).

Job Research

In chapters one and two, we discussed the importance of aligning resumes and profiles with core skill sets sought by recruiters. The goal is to get calls for jobs without applying, double your interviews, make easier career transitions, experience reduced periods of unemployment, obtain pay increases, and find more rewarding work by matching background to market need. Indeed.com can help with this and more.

Job Alerts

There is an email bar on the upper right hand side of the page where you can enter your email and it will send alerts for new jobs fitting the criteria you set. Your own self-generated job alerts (using the right search terms for the stream of jobs in your Core-3$^{©}$) are much more reliable than the system-generated ones.

Salary Survey

In Chapter 7 on salary negotiation, I will cover how to use Indeed.com to perform a salary survey, a critical skill in salary quoting and negotiations.

Resume Posting

In addition to seeking jobs and market information, you can also post resumes which are searchable by employers. My candidates are increasingly getting job interviews from recruiters that are identified through a search of the Indeed.com database. In 2016, it appears that recruiters are leaving Monster.com and moving quickly to Indeed.com. The more job applicants using a database, the more attractive it is to recruiters.

Whether you are in an active or passive job search, your resume needs to be on Indeed.com. One of the great things about Indeed.com is that an applicant can really see how an Applicant Tracking System parses data. When a system user uploads a resume, the ATS pre-populates fields just as employer's tracking software does. This is one great method to identify resume formats that may not work well in the system.

There is one more drawback to the Indeed.com resume upload system. The top of the resume as taught in this book gets removed or pushed to a bottom section, and the skills or certifications are not broken out by the system. Therefore, extra work will be needed to make sure all of the correct information is present. Copy and paste your Summary of Skills and put it into the detail of the most current Job so that when the recruiter prints the detail it will print out as if you built the resume that way. It will be necessary to break out each skill and add how many years you have done it.

All of this work is definitely worth it. Once the resume is uploaded correctly and the skills and certifications are broken

141

out, a recruiter can find you more easily in the system based on keyword-search.

Indeed.com "Quick-Apply"

The Quick Apply option is one of the most effective ways to get calls quickly. Many employers allow the user to rapidly apply using their Indeed.com profile or by doing a simple upload of a resume. The higher level the position, the less likely for this option to be available, but for most positions under $80,000 per year this is often an option. There is no faster way to get the calls rolling in right away.

5.5 Other Job Boards & Niche Staffing Websites

Other job boards tend to have fewer options to ensure a recruiter can identify a candidate. My clients never get calls from CareerBuilder, Ziprecruiter, and other random job sites. I have stopped using anything but indeed.com, LinkedIn.com, monster.com, unique industry job boards, and for readers outside the U.S., there will be country-specific boards as well.

Niche Staffing Firms and Professional Organization Websites

There are certain fields that have entire staffing firms dedicated to professional placement or that have professional organizations with a career section. For instance, when I have an applicant in Accounting and Finance, I use the Core-3[©], determine which stream of jobs we want to go for, write the resume to that profile, adjust LinkedIn, Monster, Indeed and then I post their resume on www.roberthalf.com.

Another example of a niche site is the "New England Journal of Medicine" for physicians, or the American Society of Training and Development for the corporate Organizational Development (O.D.) fields. As you search for jobs, the various staffing firms that represent different jobs will pop up. Do not overlook these powerful sources of jobs.

Government and Universities

Most local, state, and federal government positions are not advertised on the popular job boards. Since most universities are public institutions within the government retirement system, they are included in this list. My public institution colleagues indicate the reason that these jobs do not appear on Indeed.com, LinkedIn.com, or other popular websites is because there are limited funds for posting jobs, and sometimes there are even regulations prohibiting paid advertising. Whatever the reason, if you want a public job you will need to create a profile and job alert on www.usajobs.gov, www.governmentjobs.com, and straight to your local municipal, community colleges, and university websites. These organizations have a lengthy hiring cycle, sometimes up to nine months before they even review applicants. A personal reference is often needed for these roles. If you need a job fast, run a simultaneous campaign for corporations and government. These jobs are a 'long game' that require a significant wait time.

5.6 Check the Competition, Boost Rankings, Get More Content

Now that your resume is online, you can check your work using indeed.com. My goal is to get your resume profile into the top 10 results for your keywords. If you are #1 on indeed.com for your keywords you will theoretically be #1 in the employer's ATS and on the other job boards. Using indeed.com as a quality check is a final method to ensure complete dominance in your keywords.

The #2 Resume Hack: Boost ranking and content with keyword counting using Indeed.com resume search.

This concept is a 'reverse engineering' of your resume and online profile. The quality check helps in the following ways:
• Get a numerical count of the keywords needed to surface as a top candidate.
• Get more matching content by using your competitors' resumes.
• Understand how others are positioning themselves.
• Get a deeper understanding of the issues Recruiter's face in identifying talent.
• Optimize for indeed and roll the changes to all profiles to improve rankings online and in the employer's ATS.

I use the quality check to make sure my clients are ranking in the top 10 for the selected campaign, keywords, and positions that surfaced during the Core-3© assessment.

Exercise 5.6 Indeed Resume Profile Quality Check

Log in to your indeed.com account and proceed with the following steps:

- At the top of the main screen, click on the 'find resumes' option.
- Enter in your target city.
- Enter in your target title or keyword combinations.
- Survey the top-ranking resume results.
- Take a count of how many times the keyword shows in the resume.
- Observe the competitions title, employer, and other data to understand the competition.
- Go to your profile and keyword stack optimize the resume and title section.
- Have a count as high or higher than the top three competitors.
- Wait a few hours for indeed.com to adjust to the new information.
- Refresh your screen with the search terms and see how you improved.
- Keep adding and adjusting until you show in the top 10 results.

>Homework

- Review the video class for LinkedIn and Job Board optimization.
- Identify your job boards and open accounts with same login.
- Create the LinkedIn.com profile.
- Post your resume on the job boards.
- Perform a quality check via indeed.com 'find resumes.'

- Keyword-stack optimize the accounts.

Quiz 5: LinkedIn and Online Job Portals (T/F)
1.___ Recruiters only call on actively applying professionals.
2.___ Professional Category and Industry are the same thing.
3.___ The online job boards are the "engine" of the double your interview strategy.
4.___ The advantage to Monster.com is superior professional categorization options.
5.___ Monster's disadvantage is spammy emails.
6.___ LinkedIn is the most popular site for recruiters.
7.___ Indeed.com is becoming more popular because more job applicants are using it.
8.___ Indeed.com does not need to be tweaked, just upload the resume and apply.
9.___ System-generated job alerts are as good as manually-created ones.
10.___ "Quick Applies" in Indeed.com kick off the campaign.

Chapter 5: Answer Key (T/F)
1) False: Recruiters call on "passive" candidates every day.
2) False: What you do is profession. What your company does is industry.
3) True: The online job boards, when optimized, get you more calls.
4) True: Monster.com has the best professional categorization for recruiter search.
5) True: Unfortunately, a job candidate will need to manage some spam.
6) False: LinkedIn is the most popular source for I.T. recruiting. Indeed is very popular for other professions but an applicant needs to leverage multiple job boards.

7) True: Recruiters naturally gravitate towards the most populated active job boards.

8) False: Indeed.com needs two tweaks: 1) Add the Title Bar, Summary of Skills, and Skill Highlights to the job detail of the most recent position so that the output will reflect your actual resume and 2) Add Skills. Use the quality check to identify changes.

9) False: Always create your own alerts based on your Core-3© strategy.

10) True: Yes, use the "Quick-Applies" to get things going.

Chapter 6: B2W Mom Campaign Kickoff

The goal of this chapter is to set up the exercises in order of completion, to create an effective campaign within a few hours. This is also a recap and complete B2W mom strategy.

For the purpose of this section, we will skip the myths and get right to the strategy.

This chapter includes the following lessons: The 12-Steps to the B2W mom Campaign Kickoff
6.1 – Core B2W Mom Strategy Selection
6.2 – Core-3© Assessment
6.3 – Setup Job Alerts
6.4 – Breakdown Job Ads
6.5 – Line Item Accomplishments
6.6 – LinkedIn Profile
6.7 – Post Resume to Job Boards
6.8 – Perform an Indeed.com Quality Check & Optimization
6.9 – User Indeed.com and LinkedIn 'Quick-Apply'
6.10 – Apply to at least 10 Jobs
6.11 – Ongoing Applications
6.12 – Manage Phone & Email Screens

Exercise 6.1 B2W Mom Strategy Selection

Determine which of the six strategies, or combination of options, you are going to use to close the gap, perform the re-entry period, or leverage existing re-entry work that you have been doing to achieve full-employment. The six ways presented in the B2W mom strategy are as follows: 1) alternative 'reason for gap' answers, 2) leverage a business, 3) leverage a volunteer 'title-swap,' 4) leverage part-time work, 5) go back to school and, 6) re-enter via staffing agencies.

Exercise 6.2 Core-3© Assessment

Select a few search terms from your background on Indeed.com. Common terms relate to software, certifications, industry phrases, and titles. Use the job ads to identify more search terms that were not on your original list. Search by the new terms and expand the list of possible power career changes. Once you identify the search terms that produce the best stream of jobs, create your own job alerts.

Exercise 6.3 Set Up Job Alerts

Set up your own job alerts to stay current on new job postings.
1. Perform a search of your terms and verify that the results support your goals.
2. Enter your email to set up job alerts.
3. You will be sent a confirmation email.
4. The alert can be cancelled at any time.
5. Use these alerts to stay on top of new potential jobs within your parameters versus the unreliable system-generated alerts.

Exercise 6.4 Breakdown Job Ads and Create Top of Resume

From similar jobs, create a composite Market-Based Resume© to one stream or multiple streams of jobs.

1. Break down the job ads into core keywords, phrases, and qualifications.
2. Write a Resume Title Bar/Headline.
3. Write a one- to three-line Summary of Skills straight from the mandatory qualifications.
4. Create a list of matching "Skill Highlights" that are two- to four-word breakdowns of the line items and mandatory qualifications.
5. Do this for each resume matching the Core-3© strategy.

Exercise 6.5 Line Item Accomplishment Work History & Education

Complete the resume by inserting your work history and education for each profile.
1. Rewrite each line item in the job and when possible add a quantified accomplishment related to each line item.
2. Write about the relevant work experience over about 10 years.
3. Leave out unrelated work unless this creates a gap.
4. Add your education towards the bottom of the resume.
5. What matters is what matches the requirements. Avoid unrelated details.

Exercise 6.6 LinkedIn Profile

Now use the resume to create the LinkedIn profile.
1. Use the resume's Title Bar to make the LinkedIn profile headline.
2. Select the goal city.

3. Select your profession (not industry) from the industry setting.
4. Copy and paste the resume's Summary of Skills into the LinkedIn Summary of Skills (correct any alignment issues).
5. Create work history, but consider consolidating positions within one company into one posting.
6. Let the system present the closest matching title to your goal title. (LinkedIn is more like a brochure than legally-binding application.)
7. Enter your Bachelor's degree and higher (or your Associate's degree if you have no Bachelor's degree). Do not add high school.
8. Enter Certifications.
9. Create individual skills that other people can endorse.
10. Connect with over 500 people using your email and suggested connections.
11. Endorse other people's skills so that they will be prompted to endorse yours.
12. Seek out detailed recommendations.
13. Set up custom job alerts.
14. Set up recruiter push.

Exercise 6.7 Post Resume to Job Boards and Tweak

In the following exercise, follow the steps to post your resume to multiple job boards.
1. Identify the job boards that are popular to your area or industry field. As stated earlier, the most popular national websites are:
• www.Indeed.com
• www.Monster.com

2. Tweak the resume to make sure it looks good and keyword-stack the Indeed.com profile by breaking out skills.
3. Identify niche job boards, professional organizations, and staffing agencies.

Exercise 6.8 Use Indeed.com to Perform a Quality Check

Once you have posted your resume, use the indeed.com 'search resume' feature to examine the competition, to get a keyword count for optimization, and to identify new content that might be missing from your resume. Keyword stack optimize the resume with the correct keyword numerical count. Check your ranking a few hours later, keep optimizing, flow the changes through to your other profiles.

Exercise 6.9 Use Indeed.com or LinkedIn 'Quick-Apply'

1. Once the LinkedIn and Indeed.com profiles are created, search for jobs and apply for all of the "Apply through LinkedIn" or "Easily Apply with Indeed" to get as many applications out there quickly as possible.
2. Customize the top of your resume when a job is of particular interest.

Exercise 6.10 Apply to at least 10 Jobs Immediately

1. The auto-apply function allows a job candidate to get the ball rolling immediately.
2. There will be a number of great jobs that do not have a "quick-apply" option. The goal for the kick-off should be at least ten matching jobs for the campaign kick-off.

Exercise 6.11 Ongoing Applications

1. The manually created job alerts will continue to send new jobs as they become available.
2. Your online profiles will be available for recruiters to locate when they are searching for jobs related to the keywords in the position.
3. Perform "quick-apply" and manual applications every two weeks.
4. Applying for jobs takes both quality and quantity. Plan on applying for many, but with a matching profile.

Exercise 6.12 Manage Phone & Email Screens

1. The campaign kick-off will generate emails and calls from your direct application and also from recruiters searching your type of profile. You need to control these calls - never do on-the-spot phone screens.
2. Prepare for every phone screen as if it were an in-person interview.
3. The following chapter will cover phone screen preparation and the rest of the job acquisition process.

>Homework
Complete the steps in the Campaign Kickoff.

Quiz 6: B2W Mom Kickoff Campaign (T/F)

1.___ The first steps to kickoff is choosing you B2W strategy and doing the Core-3©.
2.___ System-generated job alerts are as good as the ones you manually create.
3.___ The top of the Market-Based Resume© leverages the job advertisement.
4.___ Your work experience should be a re-write of the line items of the targeted job.
5.___ The resume you create is used to build the LinkedIn profile.
6.___ You can post the resume to the job boards with no tweaks.
7.___ The "quick-applies" on Indeed.com and LinkedIn.com do not work well.
8.___ Quality is more important than quantity of applications.
9.___ You can rely solely on recruiter search and not worry about direct-applications.
10.___ You will only get calls for the jobs you apply for.

Chapter 6: Answer Key (T/F)

1) True: Your success begins with finding the right job ads for your needs and background.

2) False: A human is still more intuitive than a computer. Create your own alerts.

3) True: The top of the Market-Based Resume© is a rewrite of the job advertisement and it is CRITICAL to doubling your interviews.

4) True: Forget "job duties" and focus on re-writing and capturing accomplishments that directly match the line items of various related jobs.

5) True: The Market-based Resume© is used to build the LinkedIn profile.

6) False: Most job boards, especially Indeed.com, will require some tweaking.

7) False: Quick-applies spur the job search.

8) False: You need both a quantity and quality strategy.

9) False: You will need to perform on-going applications to keep your campaign alive.

10) False: You will get calls for all sort of jobs and it is very important to control these telephone calls and emails using the information in this book.

Chapter 7: Phone Screens & Interview Preparation

The methods taught in this book will stimulate calls that require cutting edge interview and salary negotiation strategies. This section explores the common myths and beliefs about the interview process.

*Note: This section works in conjunction with Salary Negotiations chapter. Both chapters should be reviewed prior to taking a phone screen or even before applying for jobs.

This module includes the following lessons:
7.1 – Interview Myths
7.2 – Phone Screen Interview
7.3 – Common Phone Screen & Interview Questions
7.4 – Reason for Each Question & Strategy
7.5 – Interview Worksheet Scripts
7.6 – Explaining Terminations and Dismissals
7.7 – Behavioral Interview Questions
7.8 – Questions for Them
7.9 – What Not to Say
7.10 – Building an Interview Portfolio or Project
7.11 – "Thank You" Letter

7.1 Interview Myths

Myth 1: The ability to do the job is the primary focus of phone screen interview questions.

No - the resume has already pre-qualified the candidate. Although these skills will be verified, there are two other primary questions on the mind of the recruiter.

1. Will this candidate be a <u>happy</u>, productive, and non-disruptive employee?
2. Is this candidate <u>stable</u> and willing to remain in the position for at least two years?

To get these answers, the recruiter will ask a list of common interview questions that seem innocent but are the source of most candidate rejection. The phone screen has little to do with your ability to do the job.

<u>Myth 2: The most capable employee is the one that gets the job offers.</u>

The reality is that the person who wins the job is not always the most capable job candidate. The winner is the candidate who performs the best in the interview, and the majority of that performance is based on the content of their answers.

<u>Myth 3: You can get a job that you are not sure you want.</u>

Job candidates tend to talk themselves out of applying or interviewing for jobs because they are unsure about the position. If they are unprepared to interview, they will naturally want to know more about the job before saying they want the position. Uncertainty kills great career moves because employers only want to hire people who want the job.

Tip: My recommendation is to treat every job as if it were your dream job until you have enough information to determine otherwise.

The hiring process may be easier to understand for those readers who have done sales. Hiring is similar to sales in that the candidate needs a pipeline of opportunities. The rule of thumb in sales is closing 4% of opportunities. Although the pipeline for hiring does not need to be as wide and deep, it is more advantageous if the job candidate is talking to more recruiters/hiring manager/employers versus focusing on one single lead (company and position).

Once you get the job offer, then you can decide to decline or accept based on the offer and interview experience. Go for it, be excited, and be flexible, and then when the job offer rolls in, negotiate, accept, or walk away.

Myth 4. Interviewers ask you what they want to know.

No. There are few times when the recruiter asks straightforward questions about a person's background and tells the applicant their concerns about their candidacy.

The majority of the time, the interviewer will ask other common questions to uncover the true goals and attitude of the job candidate. That is why so many interview questions are strange and seem like they have nothing to do with your work experience. The more conscious, aware, and prepared you are for these questions, the more likely you are to get a job offer from the interview.

Myth 5. The phone screen is a "nothing" interview

The phone screen is actually the most challenging of all interviews because the employer is actively using the call to remove candidates. You as the candidate have to perform well and be excited about a job that you know little or nothing about, and you typically are forced to perform these interviews in a distracted state - while driving, working, during childcare, or even when resting. An unprepared, distracted, or uncertain job candidate does not move forward.

Myth 6. The recruiter has been trained how to interview.

Even though there are books and consultancies dedicated to helping hiring managers to overcome making decisions based on their unconscious emotional reactions to candidates, in most cases, the interviewer will have had little formal training. This module teaches you how to control the interviewer's unconscious reactions to give them what they need to choose you!

Myth 7. If I am applying for the job, then it is obvious that I will stay in it.

No, your application does not mean you will stay. Your job transitions tell the employer how likely it is that you will stay on the job. No matter what you actually say, they will use your transition history as the "truth."

Early in your career it is acceptable to have two up to even five two-year positions. However, by the time you are in your thirties, you are expected to have "found" yourself. The employer will rely on your job transition history to predict the length of time you will stay in the job unless you make an exceptional effort to explain why this job will be different. That is why job transitions are silent job killers, and why we see questions about your reason for leaving during the applications, phone screens, and interviews. It is a never-ending process to explain yourself.

The resume already presents a story to the recruiter. If a candidate switches jobs frequently, or even at regular intervals, this indicates to the recruiter that the candidate will leave in a similar timeframe. If this is a step down, meaning the candidate appears overqualified for the job, the recruiter is almost always worried about the candidate leaving when they find a job of greater responsibility or pay. If the career change is completely different, the recruiter may feel they have no evidence at all that the candidate will remain in the position. The more work you do to create a storyline that explains your job transitions in a way that supports the position you are interviewing for, the better the job hunt will be.

Myth 8. Work happiness and joyful happiness are the same thing.

This is definitely not true. The recruiter is concerned about whether the candidate will be happy on the job. Being happy does not mean being joyful. In this case, it means being a consistent producer that does not make trouble for the managers or team members. If the job candidate states that their most difficult person or challenge is similar to the current team environment, this may indicate that the employee will not be happy. If the candidate is accustomed to working for a large organization and is applying at a small one, this may cause the employee unhappiness. Any answer or previous background that does not match the new job can be a signal to the employer that the candidate will be unhappy, unproductive, and disruptive. To diffuse this issue, your answers should indicate how you solved problems and worked with a wide range of people. In addition, it is important to not become rattled or upset during the interview.

Myth 9: The in-person interview will focus on technical questions related to the job.

Yes, but technical questions tend to come after the common interview questions. There is a portion of the interview that will focus on all the reasons not to hire you. These are the three silent job killers: job transitions, goals, and salary. All of the common interview questions are designed to determine what is "wrong" with the candidate. The other portion will examine your technical abilities (which can include a review of work history) and increasingly also behavioral questions.

Behavioral questions are a psychological blend of interview methodologies to uncover if you are capable but also indicate if you will stay and be a happy employee. Instead of asking, "Tell me about a time you did (technical ability)", the interviewer will ask you something like, "Tell me about a time you had to solve a problem related to (technical ability)."

These questions tend to put the candidate in a defensive position and often leave a great, qualified candidate stumped. This should not be the goal of an employer who is seeking top talent, but this trend is not going to change any time soon. The key to successful behavioral interviews is to take the line items of the job ad and plug them right into the behavioral questions to come up with great work samples. These robust and targeted work examples win jobs. Even if behavioral interview questions are not asked, this preparation will give you the type of content employers love.

Myth 10. I only need to prepare and practice my answers.

There are two aspects of interview preparation: 1) content for answers and 2) performance related to appearance, speech, and physical mannerisms. Every case is highly individualized, but the best advice is to "look" like the job you are going for," even if that means sitting outside the offices before your interview to see what people wear to work. A good program to search and sign up for is Carol Tuttle's free "Dressing Your Truth" which teaches you your power colors, clothes, and more.

Myth 11: I can wear the same clothes to an interview that I typically wear to work.

This is often not true. Once we have been at an employer for a long time our image tends to decline. It is the same thing as when we go to sell a house - it often looks cleaner and better decorated the day we put it on the market than any day that we lived in it.

Wear a suit that is reflective of the professional environment. Dress better, but not too much better, than the people coming out of the office. If the organization is casual, wear a casual suit anyway, just to be safe.

Tip: Buy new clothes to interview in, visit the salon or barber, and make sure you look almost as good as you would on your wedding day.

The interview is like dating for a work marriage. Make sure you look better than you normally would for a day at the office. If you are not feeling good about yourself, then you will need to "fake it 'til you make it."

Myth 12. I can be honest about the negative things that happened at my previous job. The
interviewer asked me, so I need to be honest.

Candidates want to be able to reveal all the bad things that have happened to them and still get hired. Companies want to eliminate candidates with "bad things" in their background. What is ironic about the "honesty" issue is that employers are afraid of being lied to, and in most cases, candidates tend to be ultra-honest and discuss things that have no place in the interview.

The interview is a not a "tell-all" session; it is a performance. Know that you cannot be angry or say negative things in an interview and get an offer for a job.

Even though you will be asked about having a difficult time with a coworker, supervisor, or with work performance, it is important to create and practice specific answers that are true but may not be the first ones you would like to talk about with the prospective employer. Focus on great work examples that show problem solving based on the recommendations in the following lessons.

Myth 13. Practicing and memorizing interview answers sounds robotic.

Conventional wisdom might say that practicing interview answers sounds robotic, however Human Resource and hiring managers often share that if candidates take time to prepare for their interviews it translates to being interested in the position. Just as you would prepare for a presentation at school or work, so must you prepare for this important one-time performance. Record yourself on a webcam and practice with a friend or college career office. Practice, practice, practice!

Myth 15. I can prepare for every single possible interview question.

Unfortunately, this is impossible. This interview preparation course is not designed to include a comprehensive listing of every interview situation. If you pick up an interview book, you will find hundreds of questions listed. The goal of preparation is to have a strategy for the biggest problem areas candidates experience and the most challenging questions, in order to be prepared for surprise questions with grace and ease.

Myth 16. The interview is a 2-way evaluation where the candidate also assesses the company, the position, the salary, and the benefits package.

No, the interview is not a 2-way evaluation. It is a sales pitch by the candidate about how they match what the company wants so they can get the offer. Only when the candidate achieves the offer does this turn into a 2-way discussion.

Myth 17. I am my own worst enemy in my interview.

Yes, this one is unfortunately true. It is not just in the interview - job candidates sabotage their own job search progress every day in the following ways:
1. Pre-deciding whether a role is good or bad before applying.
2. Pitting one job offer against another to appear more attractive.
3. Taking the stance that "you are interviewing the employer as much as they are interviewing you."
4. Not preparing for job interviews using the strategies I will teach you.

Think about your job search as if it were online dating.
• Will you meet someone if you sit in your home and not reach out to anyone?
• Can you tell if someone is great just by looking at their picture or reading a brief profile?
• Once you do reach out, would you tell a prospective date that you are playing the field?
• Would you tell a good prospect that you might have a better option waiting in the wings if they make you a better offer?

- Would you tell your current spouse (i.e. your current employer) that someone is more interesting to you and they need to come up with reasons for you to stay?

These tactics do not result in a great relationship and they will not get you hired. Apply, be open, tell each employer they are your "preferred option," and remain enthusiastic until they propose (make an offer). Then, and only then, can you evaluate the option based on everything you have seen and heard.

7.2 Phone Screen Interview

So far we have covered how recruiters use electronic systems, both their internal software and also the online job boards, to source candidates. You also know that you can use these systems to your advantage to double your job interviews with the campaign kickoff process.

All of this work leads to one thing: phone screens (and increasingly email, written, and video screens).

Have you ever had a phone interview that seemed to go so well you were a shoe-in for the position, and then you never got a call back? We are about to explore the human psychology around interviewing and how to turn a lackluster performance into an interview performance that lights up the recruiter's mind so that they are silently saying "yes, yes, yes."

If you knew how many unprepared, nonresponsive candidates a recruiter talks to every day, it would be easy to see that it is very exciting to talk to a professional that ticks all their boxes, that is enthusiastic, that absolutely wants the experience. Before we get into what works, we need to look at the contributing factor in phone screen failures on both the candidate and the recruiter side.

Candidate Side of Phone Screen Failures:

Job candidates fail at phone screens all of the time because:
1) They are not able to create winning answers for a job they knew nothing about 5 seconds ago.
2) They are not sure what to quote for pay, what the job actually does pays, what they are willing to accept, or how the job could be leveraged for long-term salary growth.
3) They are not sure they even want the job or will stay with it since they just got the call.

Most candidates either think these phone screens are not important, or they start to hate them because they are not moving forward for jobs they are qualified for and, upon reflection, that they would want to consider if given more time to evaluate the option.

Recruiter Side of Phone Screen Failures:

Recruiters fail to find the best candidates for their jobs because:
1) They expect busy job candidates to do well on these interviews, even though they did not know a single thing about the job 5 seconds before the call came in.
2) They assume the candidate has one salary figure they will work for and if it fits, great; if not they boot the candidate.

3) They assume the candidate can determine, in a very short span of time, if they will be happy and stay.

Recruiters love phone screens because they can really boil the pool of applicants down quickly but they dislike them because they inherently know there are great candidates that they are rejecting quickly. They just don't have time to think about that.

To be successful a recruiter must call many candidates in a short period of time, and they tend to be sourcing for many positions at one time, not just the one job. To maximize their time, they want to talk to you right then and not schedule into the future.

Phone screens tend to be a scheduled part of an internal recruiter's day, while this is literally the job of third party recruiters. If a recruiter has to schedule a call, especially an internal recruiter, they will often miss the call because they get sidetracked by other priorities. This upsets candidates and creates a feeling that the recruiter is unprofessional. This is an unfortunate part of the process but keep in mind that one missed phone screen does not necessarily reflect poorly on the company. Two or three misses and you may want to move on.

Remember that the goal of the recruiter is to find a qualified match for their position who will also be happy with the job, the pay, the location, and the work. The recruiter needs to hear one word – "yes." When they hear a lot of "yes" and "I have that experience" responses from the candidate, it creates a "yes" reaction in their mind. When a candidate says "no" or "I do not have that experience," or "I am not sure I want to do that," or "I can learn it" it creates a "rejection" reaction in their mind.

A job candidate that is able to relate how their work matches the needs of the job is displaying the type of emotional intelligence that employers love. This is not lying or deceiving. This is thoughtfully thinking about your past and relaying the pertinent information to create more confidence in your candidacy.

A candidate needs to say "yes" as much as possible and use a deflection technique for a "no" response.

Winning Phone Screen Responses

There are three ways to improve your phone screen and interview performance:
1. Say "Yes!" to all non-skill based questions,
2. Take a message, ask for the job ad, schedule for a later date, and prepare,
3. And learn how to deflect, substitute, and re-direct a "no" or "I do not have it" for skill-based questions.

Remember, you can always cancel an in-person interview later if it really is not something you want, assuming you, like many candidates, want to keep your choices open and allow yourself time to consider the option.

Create the Yes Reaction to Non-Skill Based Questions

<u>**Non-skill based conditional response examples that kill jobs**</u>

- Recruiter Question: I have a job that is a lower title than your current position - would you be interested?
>Job Candidate Response: I am not sure but I would like to hear more.

- Recruiter Question: I have a "road warrior" job that requires 90% travel - would you be able to do that?
>Job Candidate Response: Hmmm, I don't think all that travel fits into my lifestyle but for the right opportunity I would consider it.

- Recruiter Question: I have a job that is a 3 month contract - would you be willing to leave your full-time job to consider it?
>Job Candidate Response: Why would I ever leave a full-time job for a 3-month contract? No, but keep me in mind for full-time work.

- Recruiter Question: I have a job that would require relocation to a city that you could not even place on a map - do you want it?
>Job Candidate Response: I might consider moving but only to "x" city.

'Yes' Examples:
- Recruiter Question: I have a job that is a lower title than your current position - would you be interested?
>Job Candidate Response: Yes! (no, matter what.)

- Recruiter Question: I have a "road warrior" job that requires 90% travel - would you be able to do that?
>Job Candidate Response: Yes! (no, matter what.)

- Recruiter Question: I have a job that is a 3-month contract - would you be willing to leave your full-time job to consider it?
>Job Candidate Response: Yes! (no, matter what.)

- Recruiter Question: I have a job that would require relocation to a city that you could not even place on a map - do you want it?
>Job Candidate Response: Yes! (no, matter what.)

The goal in the phone screen is to keep the "ball in the air" so you can actually compete for the job. If you offer conditional responses, you are eliminating yourself from the pool of candidates. Your second option is to take a message and prepare your answers.

Matching-answer preparation for scheduled phone screens

The following set of lessons will explain how to build matching answers that get results. Controlling the time and place of the phone screen increases your success rate, therefore it is recommended that the first few phone screens be scheduled. Take a message, get the job advertisement, prepare the matching answers, and schedule the screen.

Managing a true "no" about a skill-based question

Sometimes you will be asked if you have a skill and it will be impossible to say yes. We now know in hiring psychology if you say "no" or "I do not have it," a disqualification response is created in the mind of the interviewer. So what is the option if you truly do not have experience with something? Deflection, substitution, and re-direction. I will use the role of an accountant to demonstrate.

• Recruiter Question: Do you have a Certified Public Accounting (CPA) license?
>Job Candidate Response: In my current and past accounting roles I have performed audits and worked with public accounting firms as required for this position. I can also study and sit for my certification over the next two years.

• Recruiter Question: We are seeking an Accountant with experience with the Big 4 Accounting firms; I do not see that on your resume.
>Job Candidate Response: I have 20 years of experience working on audits as required for this role.

• Recruiter Question: This position requires a Bachelor's degree in Accounting but I see you only have an Associate's.
>Job Candidate Response: I have an Associate's and five years of experience directly matching the requirements of this role. I can also study and complete my Bachelor's in Accounting.

• Recruiter Question: We are looking for direct experience with the SAP ERP.
>Job Candidate Response: I have 10 years of experience and have worked on the large accounting software suites.

The answers deflect, substitute, and re-direct the interviewers towards your matching qualifications. This avoids the silent disqualification process and forces the recruiter's mind into a "yes" position.

7.3 Common Phone Screen & Interview Questions

As stated earlier, phone screen questions are designed to eliminate candidates. The following questions will pop up throughout the interview process but they are very common for the phone screen. First, I will present the question and explain the reason for it, and then will provide a strategy.

Common Phone Screen Questions List

1. So tell me about yourself.
2. Why this job?
3. Why did you transition from one job to another or why do you want to leave where you are?
4. What are your greatest strengths and what makes you a good fit for this role specifically?
5. What are your weaknesses?
6. What is your greatest accomplishment?
7. What are your 1-, 2- and 5-year goals?
8. Are you thinking about pursuing additional education?
9. What would be your dream job?
10. What are your salary expectations?

If you took a message and scheduled the phone screen, you can prepare matching answers to each one of these. Use the next lesson to understand the psychology behind each question and the strategy to respond to each.

7.4 Reason for Each Question and Strategy

The goal of each answer is to trip the internal "yes" response in the recruiter's mind. We want them "firing on all cylinders." If there are obvious "no" issues like a missing skill, certification, non-matching industry, or seemingly illogical job transition, this is an opportunity to turn that "no" into a "yes." The way to do this is to reiterate over and over that you are a match for the job, that you want the job, that this job matches your goals - yes, yes, yes! Each question below has a tip that works in most scenarios.

Q#1: So tell me about yourself.

This is an open-ended question that many candidates do not know how to answer. You may ask yourself "Should I talk about my family, my personal health regimen, my last job, my current employer, my life story, or what?" The answer to this question is easier than you might think.

Tip: The Summary of Skills portion of the resume is the primary answer to this question, with a few added touches.

In one to three sentences, describe how you have the required skills and background of the job advertisement. Select additional positive personal and family information that demonstrates your stability as a candidate and as a person. End the answer with the reason you are leaving, or left, your most recent employer.

For the B2W mom candidate this means telegraphing that you are supported and that the kids are healthy. The difference between telegraphing and normal answers is that many of the concerns an employer has will remain unspoken. Therefore, a B2W mom needs to find other non-obvious ways to discuss her career readiness while answering other questions. Mention if you have family nearby, a helpful spouse, if the kids are in school, if the children are mature, or that you have reliable sources of childcare.

This open-ended question is the first great opportunity to send the message: "I am qualified, I will be happy, and I will stay in this job."

Q#2: Why this job?

The employer looks at the position they are offering as their priceless gift. Even though a job candidate is exchanging their time for that position, the employer does not quite view it that way. Like a gift giver, the employer wants to hear that this gift of a job will be appreciated, that you will use it well, and that it is the most important thing that could happen to you. Employers do not want to give their gift to anyone that does not want the present.

Tip: Say "This job is a perfect blend of skills and experience that I have and enjoy using the most."

When we tell the employer why we want this job we have to express three things: 1) that this is the next logical step in our career progression and 2) that we can do the job (matching strengths and qualifications), and 3) a unique list of items that employers like to hear about their company (listed below).

- Growth (if there is growth)
- It is an industry leader
- New developments in _____ (state new developments in the organization, industry, or field)
- The work environment
- Better hours and schedule
- It is closer to home
- Larger or growing organization that has greater long term opportunity
- Smaller organization that is more to my style
- Stability
- Better overall package (versus just more money)
- New industry that offers a new trajectory for my skills.

Be careful using the following:
- More money (they will be concerned that you will leave when you find more)
- Less stress or better work-life balance (suggests you are having psycho-emotional issues)
- Getting back into the work force (in most cases you don't want to shift the focus of the interview to current unemployment)

Q#3: Why did you transition from one job to another and why are you looking to leave where you are?

Other than title and industry, one of the primary items recruiters use to evaluate a good candidate is their "reason for leaving" answer. This can first appear on the job application, phone screen, or in-person interview. This is the #1 silent job killer. The interviewer is really attempting to predict whether you will stay and be happy based on your previous behavior.

Remember, they are afraid of you as a B2W mom because they are unsure if you will stay, be happy, or productive because your 'stay-at-home' status indicates home, and not work, is your first priority. We need to change that to get hired.

For the B2W mom candidate, how you handle this question will make or break your success.

I need you to look at your stay-at-home activity as an opportunity, like a luxury (even though we know it is hard work). Then I need you to express stability and support (even if you have none.) The next section presents scripts to deal with jobs before the gap in employment, re-entry, and the next position after re-entry.

Q#4: What are your greatest strengths?

Candidates often state qualities that are difficult to prove and sound relatively meaningless like "I am a hard worker, dedicated, and experienced." Instead, use the list of matching skills from the job advertisement that you used to build the Market-Based Resume©.

Tip: Your greatest strengths are everything in the job advertisement that you have.

Choose accomplishments that demonstrate your related skills. Reiterate that you are a match for this job.

Q#5: What are your weaknesses?

This question seems like a no-win situation for job candidates. To manage the potential negative impact of this question, job candidates will often give an answer like "I am intense, a perfectionist, or a workaholic." Those answers are better than a truly negative answer like "I am frequently late for work," but that is still not good enough. B2W moms may want to use their gap in employment as a weakness. This may be valid but it is a good idea to have some career-orientated responses.

Tip: If the industry is different for you, state "I have not worked in this industry but I have done all of the tasks and do not feel it will be an issue." If there are mandatory requirements from the job ad that you do not have, tell the employer that you have other skills that balance any missing items. Do not say you are a quick learner! Instead, give an example of how you picked up a skill or industry quickly.

Only give the recruiter more than one weakness if they ask for it. The most common weakness is a lack of industry experience. Select missing line items versus mandatory requirements for this answer unless the missing item is very obvious. It is better to manage these issues head on and turn a silent "no" into a "yes."

Q#6: What is your greatest accomplishment?

This question is critical because you want your accomplishment to match the job's need and be a powerful statement of your qualifications. Unfortunately, many people do not believe they have a greatest accomplishment.

Since being a B2W mom is not considered work, you cannot use 'raising great children' for this answer. We want this to be an accomplishment related to the job. If you have already been in your re-entry period, then you may have a current example. If not, you will need to use the past.

Tip: Find a work example (or school example if you really do not have one with work) that supports your candidacy for that particular job.

If you have done the work to build a strong accomplishment inventory and that matches the position, then this question will be easy to answer.

Q#7: What are your 1-, 2- and 5-year goals?

The correct answer to this question is surprisingly not creative. Remember, the recruiter wants to know that you want the job you are applying for, that you will be happy in the position, and that you will stay in it for a period of time, usually at least two years. However, there are some cases in which a job requires ambitious candidates that want fast movement. In other positions there is no growth and the recruiter is seeking a candidate that wants no or limited advancement. For the first one to two years, "the job you want" needs to be <u>this job</u>, not one higher, lower, or different. An employer is not going to hire you for a job if you tell them you really want a different position.

Commons reasons candidates do not get an offer is by stating a desire for growth when there is none, or stating the desire to stay at a certain level when the recruiter is looking for someone who wants to grow.

Tip: Use the formula below 99.9% of the time.

The majority of the time this is the answer:
1-year goal: Get this job.
2-year goal: Excel in this job.
5-year goal: Grow as the organization needs my skills.

The five-year answer can be a little more complicated. If this is a high growth organization, say you would like to grow and let the organization use your skills as needed. Be careful of sending the message that you want your boss's job. If the organization is small or there is no room for movement, then state that you are happy to stay in the position. Even if you do not actually want to work at that level for the rest of your career, it is important to state that you will be happy if you want the job offer. Then you will need to move on once you get experience.

Q#8: Are you thinking about pursuing additional education and certificates?

Sometimes an employer will find a candidate they are excited about that is missing important qualifications for the job. Many candidates may be tired of studying or amassing more skills and want to just "learn on the job."

Tip: Always answer "yes" to re-education.

This question is an excellent signal that the employer is interested in the candidate. If a candidate answers no, they are essentially telling the employer that they are not interested in doing what is necessary to succeed in the role.

Q#9: What would be your dream job?

In most cases, the job you are interviewing for has to be your dream job. There are some exceptions where the employer understands you will be moving on but is willing to hire you. For instance, if you just graduated and are working at a job unrelated to your degree, your employer may say, "I know you are just with us until you find a professional-level job."

Tip: Every job is your dream job to continue interviewing and get a job offer.

With few exceptions there is only one answer to this question. You need to tell the employer, "This job is my dream job because it leverages my skills and abilities and (the other benefits it offers)."

Q#10: What are your salary expectations?

There is an entire lesson in the book and online program dedicated to salary negotiations. It is important to reiterate that a candidate must match what the employer is willing to pay to get a job offer.

Tip: This salary quote is the amount needed to "keep the ball in the air." It is not necessarily your overall salary goal; it is the amount assigned to the position by the company. Learn how to guess what that is based on title and job description.

For the B2W mom this is an even more complex because there may be a discount on your re-entry position reflecting the risk they are taking on you. Determine and quote what the job pays. Shoot for a break-even with an overall goal of getting the best job with the greatest trajectory on your post re-entry full employment transition.

If you are in your re-entry period, there may or may not be a discount depending on how good your re-entry role was in terms of skill, title, and pay. Like any candidate, you will need to become quite savvy at guessing the value the that employer placed on the position which is covered in the salary negotiation section.

We all want the most money we can get but we may be happy with what the employer is offering, if we only knew what that was. The first part of the salary negotiation module teaches you how to predict what a job pays so that you can quote "desired salary." If the employer stated a salary range in the job advertisement, then that is what they are willing to pay. If they have not, then you need to perform a salary survey either through knowing someone inside of the organization or through the internet. In addition, you need to understand the value the employer has placed on the job based on the written job requirements. Common advice in salary negotiations is to have the employer name the first figure, but sometimes that is just not possible or likely. It is best to be armed with a strategy and to be prepared to negotiate.

7.5 Interview Worksheet Scripts

Fill in these scripts to prepare answers to the most disqualifying interview questions.

Common Interview Question #1: So tell me about yourself.
"I am a _____ (select the title of the job) *professional with* ___ (state the number of years they list in the position) *in the following areas:* _____ (list one to three skills from the job advertisement) *in* _____ (list the related industry).

"I also possess ___ (list an extra skill or accomplishment). *I am interested in this company because of* _____ (research the company or industry and list the reason for interest)."

Then, make an expression of personal life stability:

"I am from this area" and/or *"I have a strong support system here."*

Then state the reason for leaving the most recent position:

"I am leaving my current position and seeking to work in this role because _____ (state the reason for leaving.)"

Tip: This is similar to the Summary of Skills.

Common Interview Question #2: Why this job?

This job is exactly what I am looking for because it is a great use of my existing skills. The job is seeking the following qualifications which I have: (list of job ad items, especially required qualifications, that you have.)
My current position has shifted and is not using the core skills that I have, that you (the new employer) *are seeking. You are seeking someone to perform the types of things I enjoy doing.*

"This is the exact work I have been doing, so I know that I can be effective. I am interested in this organization because of _____"

- *Growth (if there is growth)*
- *The company is an industry leader*
- *New developments in ____ (state new developments in the organization, industry, or field), or*
- *The work environment*
- *Better hours and schedule*
- *It is closer to home*
- *Larger or growing organization that has greater long term opportunity*
- *Smaller organization that is more to my style*
- *Stability*
- *Better overall package (versus just more money)*
- *New industry that offers a new trajectory for my skills*

Be careful using the following:
- *More money* (they will be concerned that you will leave when you find more)
- *Less stress or better work-life balance* (suggests you are having psycho-emotional issues)
- *Getting back-to-work* (we don't want to shift the focus to unemployment in most cases)

Common Interview Question #3: Why did you transition from one job to another, and/or why are you looking to leave where you are?

"I moved from my employer because _____. (Select one or a combination of the following options.")
- *The next position was the next step in my career path of _____ (a skill that the next job has)*
- *I moved because I enjoy doing _____ (a skill that the next job has)*
- *A better use of _____ (a skill that the next job has)*
- *A return to an industry*
- *Closer to home*
- *Better hours*
- *Some unique aspect of the future work environment*

Tip: It is rarely good to say you are moving for money because the employer may feel you will just leave when the next better offer comes along. See the section for managing terminations and dismissals.

Q#3: Why did you transition from one job to another and why are you looking to leave where you are?

Any jobs before your gap in employment should show a logical upward progression.

For the other previous positions on your resume. Use the following advice.

Tip: The top four most acceptable answers for reason for leaving are the following words: 1) promotion, 2) relocation, 3) back-to-school, and 4) reorganization/shift in company priorities.

Why you move from one job to the next and how long you stay in a job is one of the most important and overlooked aspects of a good interview strategy. The solution is to make each transition appear like a positive cohesive career strategy that has led up to the next job interview.

Promotion does not necessarily mean more money or a higher title. This catch-all word can be used to leverage anything that meant a step in a better direction.

Relocation is a great option if a person moved to another city, but only use it once or twice as the reason for leaving or you may appear "lost."

Reorganization as a reason for leaving can work even when there was not a huge layoff; if the employer decided you were not worth retaining, they "reorganized." It is important not to reveal negative information related to a previous employer, become emotional, or to appear as if you are wandering aimlessly through your career.

Jobs Before Gap in Employment Script
"I left my 'previous' position(s) due to promotion, gaining new skills, or breaking into a new industry. In the last position before my gap in employment, I had the opportunity to take care of my children during their formative years. I am seeking to get back to work now that my children are settled."

Re-entry Script
"I left my last employer because I had the great opportunity to stay-at-home. Not everyone has this possibility and I am glad I was able to do it. However, now I am ready to get back to work and continue my career."

Also mention or telegraph the following:
"I have the following support system:
- supportive spouse,
- family in town,
- great childcare,
- kids in school,
- kids are mature, and
- everyone is healthy and happy."

Stage 2: Leverage Re-entry Script
"I am leaving my current employer because it has been an excellent position since I returned back to work after staying at home for a period of time. The position, while excellent, is only (mention the option that fits)
- part-time,

- *only using a portion of my skills, or*
- *the job is moving in a direction away from my greatest skills which this new position needs* (list the skills).

Q#4: What are your greatest strengths?

My greatest strengths for this role is that I have ____, ____, ____ (make a listing of the all the mandatory job requirement line items that you have).

Q#5: What are your weaknesses?

"My greatest weakness for this position is that I do not have _____ (make a list of requirements listed in the job ad that you do not have but only discuss one or two), *but I do have* _____ (list something in your background that is similar and demonstrates that this missing quality is not going to hinder your ability to do the job), *and with my other skills in* _____ (list other strengths), *I do not believe this will be an issue."*

Tip: One of the best options is to say "I have not worked in this industry but I have worked in other industries where I have gained relevant professional experience." However, there may be serious weaknesses or missing qualifications that should be dealt with head-on.

"I have increased _____ (revenue, time, or units of production) *by doing* _____ (list a skill related to job).*"*
or

"I reduced _____ (money, time, or units of production) by doing _____ (list a skill related to job)."

Tip: Choose an accomplishment related to the work you will be doing in this future position if you have one.

Q#7: What are your 1-, 2- and 5-year goals?

1-Year Strategy: *"Get this job, learn my job, and be effective."*
2-Year Strategy: *"Exceeding expectations in this job."*
5-Year Strategy: *"Grow according to the needs of the organization."*
"Move up (if there is a high expectation of growth or a large organization)."
"Stay happy where I am (no growth or small organization)."

Tip: You need to want the job you are interviewing for to get an offer. In most cases, you need to want it for at least two years.

Q#8: Are you thinking about more education/training?

"Yes, I want to pursue any training, certification, or additional education required by my future role."

Tip: If the employer asks about training and education, you need to say yes to be considered as a candidate.

Q#9: What would be your dream job?

"This _____ (state the position title) is my dream job." or

"Working in this field and using _____ (list of skills related to this position)."

Tip: You need to want the job you are interviewing for to get an offer.

Q#10: What are your salary expectations?

"Based on a salary survey of similar positions, my years of work experience, knowledge of the field, educational background, and that I have these skills _____ (list the relevant skills), I feel that this position's range is between $_____ to $_____." (State a ten thousand dollar range.)

Tip: See the Salary Negotiation Section.

7.6 Explaining Terminations or Dismissals

Besides the gap in employment for a stay-at-home mom situation, you may have been fired at one time. Employers do not like to hire people that have been fired.

Tip: Never say the words fired, dismissed, or terminated.

Not all situations are the same. In many cases, you can manage the situation without indicating that anything negative happened. At the very worst, the candidate will indicate reorganization or shift in business priorities. On the application use the following strategy for the "reason for leaving" boxes that are so common now.

Answers for "Reason for Leaving" Boxes on the Application
• If the employment gap is over 12 months, and there is no way to close the gap: stay-at-home mom returning to work.
• If there was no gap in time between positions: Promotion.
• If the gap in employment less than 3 months: Promotion.
• If you moved during the transition period: Relocation.
• If you went back to school during the transition: Back to school.
• If many people were let go at one time: Reorganization.

Try to use the word "reorganization" only once for transitions in the past five years. If reorganization is used too often the employer will assume you are a problem employee. During the interview, explanations will require more than a one-word answer, but keep it brief. Use the following selection to understand how to frame each response.

More Elaborate Interview Answers for "Reason for Leaving"

Promotion Option:
Employers want to hire people that are in-demand, experienced, and easy to work with. They also want to hire a person that understands how to build and maintain a career. A promotion will need to be explained in greater detail during the interview. This is not necessarily an increase in title; it can also be an increase in or focus on different skills, a better work environment, schedule, or pay.

Relocation Option: Move to a Different City Following a Termination

It is common for job candidates to move back to their hometown or away from their current location following a dismissal. You can use this move to your advantage by focusing on the move to a different city and not the termination itself as your "reason for leaving." If you moved back to your hometown, then state that you had a need or desire to be near family. If this move is because your spouse got a job in a new job market, then state that the career transition was due to spousal relocation. If you moved to another job market in order to seek new opportunities, then state that you moved because your old market had limited opportunities compared to the new market. Moving to and from markets sounds good to an employer and can help avoid more difficult discussions like terminations. Make sure to say that you have a strong support system where you moved because a lack of support can make an employer nervous.

Back-to-School Option: If You Were in School or Went Back to School
Employers respond well to an employee that went back to school to gain new education as a positive career transition explanation. If you have gone back to school following a termination, then state the following: "My long term goal was to go back to school, so I decided to take this time to pursue my education." Education almost always sounds great to the employer.

Option 4: Re-organization
The economy and companies shift their priorities every single day. If the company decided you were not worth saving, say they reorganized the department. Explaining that the

employer's changing priorities resulted in a dismissal is fairly common. This also applies when an organization has gone through a large, well-publicized re-organization.

State that the company reorganized or shifted their priorities, or your position's priorities changed and moved away from the important skill sets that this new employer needs. It is important to state that there was a business change, or change in management priorities, that resulted in the termination.

The exercise below includes scripts to aid in explaining terminations to future employers and to your network. First, a scenario is presented with a script that is better than saying "I was fired from that job." These scenarios and explanations are listed in order of preference. If the scenario is true, use the script provided. If not, move to the next option in the list. The final explanation is the least desirable but, if no other scenario fits it is better than the alternative. Feel free to combine scripts if multiple scenarios exist.

Scripts for Explaining Terminations
Select the scenario that most closely matches your situation and use the corresponding script.

Stay-at-Home Mom Re-Entry: Gap over a year long
"I had the opportunity to stay at home to raise my children and I took it. Now I am ready to get back to work."

Stay-at-Home Mom Post Re-Entry: Gap over a year long and in the past

"I had the opportunity to stay at home to raise my children and I took it. I have been working at ___ and it has been great. I am seeking new work now because (select the one that matches)

- *That position was temporary, a contract or part-time and now I want full-time hours.*
- *I am ready to use a greater percentage of my skills than the current role.*
- *I am ready to use a certain set of skills that you need that my current job does not need and they are the ones I love the most.*
- *This job is closer to home which makes more sense for me.*

*You want to avoid pay as a reason because it concerns employers that you will leave at the next higher paying opportunity.

Promotion: small gaps between jobs
(This method completely avoids discussing the loss of the job by focusing on the job that quickly followed).

"I moved from my employer because _____. (Select one or a combination of the following options.")
• *The next position was the next step in my career path of _____* (a skill that the next job has).
• *I moved because I enjoy doing ____* (a skill that the next job has).
• *A better use of ____* (a skill that the next job has).
• *A return to an industry.*
• *Closer to home.*

- *Better hours.*
- *Some unique aspect of the future work environment.*

Relocation: move to a different city following a termination
- *"I wanted to move back home to be near my family."*
- *"I moved to this location because my spouse found (or was relocated for) a job here."*
- *"I moved to this location for better opportunities and I have always wanted to live here."*

Back to School: if you were in school or went back to school
- *"I was in school and I decided to focus on completing my education."*
- *"I had wanted to go back to school and I took the opportunity when it presented itself."*

Reorganization:
- *"This employer promised me the job would use _____ (name a skill that the new job has), but that was not the reality, and because that is what I want to do I am applying for this position."*
- *"There was a large reorganization and multiple people were let go (or a whole site was shut down)."*
- *"The company reorganized or shifted or my position's priorities away from _____"* (state a job skill that the new job offers or some other business or industry change resulting in the termination). *I enjoy using my skill sets in _____ (state the skill sets the new job will use), so that is why I am applying for this new position."*
- *"The company reorganized or shifted their priorities. I realized in that position that I really enjoyed doing _____* (skill the new

job offers) *and/or I really enjoyed working in* _____ *(industry of the new job), so that is why I am applying for this new position."*

*Avoid having to explain a termination gap and a B2W mom gap in your job search. It is just too much for the employer to digest.

7.7 Behavioral Interview Scripting

There has been a rise in behavioral interview questions during interviews. Once you get past the phone screen, the employer will start asking questions that test your capability to do the job. The behavioral questions are a way of actually combining all three questions (are you capable, will you be happy, and will you stay) into one question.

Behavioral interview questions are more common for in-person interviews and less common for the telephone screens that tend to focus on the common interview questions.

Tip: For the behavioral questions, create one very specific problem-solving example for every line item in the job advertisement.

Do not leave a single question unanswered. Include even interpersonal dynamic issues because the employer will be focused on who you can and cannot deal with. For instance, take a line item and create a problem solving example in which you had a disagreement with a boss, vendor, or client. It may have been a very personal issue for you, but for the purpose of the interview, think of it more as one-time operational disagreement. Do not select answers about things related to your work hours, pay, or benefits. These questions are about problem solving related to the position.

For instance, if you are applying for a project coordinator position for tradeshows, select two tradeshow projects and answer all of these questions in the framework of that example to provide an in depth presentation of your experience. Maybe for example your boss felt that things should be done differently. Provide evidence of how you managed this issue.

Sometimes these questions may appear redundant and you may want to say, "I just answered that." This is common in a panel interview or a series of one-on-one interviews when multiple people are not listening to what other people are asking the candidate. It is important to not say, "I just answered that question," since that will trigger a strong 'No' response in the mind of the interviewer. Be ready to answer the same basic questions over and over.

The exercise below includes common behavioral questions and scripts for suggested answers.

Behavioral Interview Scripts

Create examples for every line item of the job advertisement. Be specific and choose examples that show you know how to do *this* job even if they are not from the most recent employer. Use the sample scripts to get your creative juices flowing.

With each question and answer, check in and ask yourself: "Is this answer showing them a great example of how I operated on a daily basis with this type of work? Can I show a great accomplishment related to this type of work from the perspective of problem-solving?"

1. Copy and paste the line items of the job into this preparation sheet.
2. Relate each line item with one of the behavioral questions below.
3. Create a powerful work example that shows how you solve problems related to this job.

Q1. Give an example of an occasion when you used logic to solve a problem (insert a line item in the job ad).

One day while doing _____ (state a business, client, or departmental problem that you were dealing with that pertains to a line item), I faced a problem where I lacked _____ (state a situation, process, or issue). To fix it, I did the following _____ (describe your process to solve the problem).

Q2. Give an example of a goal that you did not meet and how you handled it (insert a line item in the job ad).

One day while doing _____ (state a business, client, or departmental problem that you were dealing with that pertains to a line item), I faced a problem where I lacked _____ (state a situation, process, or issue). I was unable to fix the problem because of _____ (describe the barriers to problem resolution), so I did the following instead _____ (describe your process to work around the barriers and manage the problem).

Q3. Describe a stressful situation at work and how you handled it (insert a line item in the job ad).

One day while doing _____ (state a business, client or departmental problem that you were dealing with that pertains to a line item), I encountered a stressful situation. The problem was that the _____ (state a client or departmental problem that you were dealing with). I was stressed out due to the following _____ (state the stressors). To manage the process, I did the following _____ (Describe your process to successfully resolve your stressors. Suggestions include: I took a step back to gain perspective. I spoke with each person involved to determine a solution. I got buy-in from different people by explaining the importance of the issues.)

Q4. Have you ever made a mistake? How did you handle it?

Change this question to "When did you make a mistake (insert a line item in the job ad) and how did you handle it?" (Just because it is framed as a question, do not think it is optional to answer.)

One day while I was working on _____ (state a client or departmental problem that you were dealing with), I made a mistake doing _____ (state a mistake but make sure it is not too bad). This mistake resulted in reduced efficiency in completing the task. I corrected the problem by doing _____ (describe your process to work around the barriers and manage the problem). *I have learned from what happened and, as a result, have had many positive resolutions after that one mistake.*

Q5. Did you ever not meet your goals? Why?

Sometime a question seems optional. You may be tempted to say 'I have met all my goals.' To help facilitate the best answers, change this question to "When did you not meet a goal (insert a line item in the job ad), why, and how did you handle it?"

At one point in the project (state a client or departmental problem that you were dealing with), I did not reach the goal of _____ (state a goal, milestone, or deadline). The reason I did not reach the goal was because (state business reasons for not reaching the goal. Suggestions include: I needed information or assistance from other departments and, since I was not in control of that aspect, I had to communicate the missed deadline with the client/department/managers and attempt to find a workaround solution.) I was able to overcome this, which has resulted in _____ (state the result).

Q6. Give an example of a goal you reached and tell me how you achieved it (insert a line item in the job ad).

"I succeeded in doing _____ (an item listed in the job ad) by doing this ____ (using skills from job ad - This should be your greatest accomplishment for this position)."

Q7. When have you gone above and beyond the call of duty (insert a line item in the job ad)?

I put in more effort and hours to help a colleague/supervisor/department solve or achieve the following _____ (describe something that was outside of your professional duties).

Q8. How did you handle a difficult situation with a supervisor (insert a line item in the job ad)?

At one point during a project, my supervisor asked me to work on something else. But my performance was evaluated by the completion of the _____ (describe how you went above and beyond by working on and resolving both issues).

Q9. Have you handled a difficult situation with another department (insert a line item in the job ad)?

Change this question to "When did you handle a difficult situation with another department (insert a line item in the job ad) and how did you handle it?"

One day while working on _____ (state a departmental problem that you were dealing with). To manage the problem, I did the following _____ (describe your process to solve the problem).

Q10. How did you handle a difficult situation with a client or vendor (insert a line item in the job ad)?

One day while working on _____ (state a client problem that you were dealing with). To solve this problem I did the following

_____. (State your problem solving process. Suggestions include: *Because their expectations were vastly different than what we could accomplish, I explained what could be done in regards to the issue and was honest about resolution times as well. The explanation and honesty turned them into one of my biggest fans.*)

Q11. Describe a decision you made that was unpopular (insert a line item in the job ad) and how you handled implementing it.

At one point in the project _____ (state a business, client, or departmental problem that you were dealing with), *I had to make an unpopular decision. To implement my concept, I got buy-in by doing the following* _____ (explain your process).

Q12. Describe a time you made a risky decision (insert a line item in the job ad)?

At one point in the project _____ (state a business, client, or departmental problem that you were dealing with), *I had to make a decision that I knew I was going to take ownership of or that my boss would not fully agree with* _____ (describe the risky decision and why it was risky). *This decision or experiment was* _____ (state the ways it was a successful and unsuccessful decision). *Through this decision, the business or I grew in the following ways* _____ (state skills and experiences gained).

Q13. Did you ever postpone making a decision (insert a line item in the job ad)? Why?

Change this question to "When did you postpone a decision (insert a line item in the job ad), why, and how did you handle it?"

While working on _____ (state a business, client, or departmental problem that you were dealing with), *I had to postpone implementing* _____ (state what was postponed) *because of* _____ (state why you had to postpone it). *The result improved* _____ (state how the postponement improved the result).

Q14. Have you had to convince a team to work on a project (insert a line item in the job ad) they weren't thrilled about? How did you do it?

Change this question to "When did you convince a team to work on a project they weren't thrilled about (insert a line item in the job ad) and how did you handle it?"

While working on _____ (state a business, client, or departmental problem that you were dealing with), *I had to convince the team to do* _____ (state what had to be done). *The team was not thrilled about this because of* _____ (State the business reasons they were not happy. Suggestions include: The change would ask for a lot more from each team-member. To get the best results we worked on prioritizing and also focusing on the time frames so we could see an end to the extra demands. We also worked as a team to ensure completion of everything on our plate.)

Q15. Have you ever dealt with company policy you weren't in agreement with? How?

Change this question to "when did you deal with company policy you weren't in agreement with (insert a line item in the job ad) and how did you handle it?"

While working on _____ (state a business, client, or departmental problem that you were dealing with), *one of my employers in particular asked me to do* _____ (state something that you did not agree with from a business perspective). *To deal with the situation, I* ____ (state how you worked this out with the manager or performed it anyway even if you did not agree).

Q16. Were you ever asked to break the law? What did you do?
No, and if I was asked, I would never do it. (This is the answer in most cases and you need to seriously consider if you want the job if it is not the right answer.)

Q17. Give an example of when you did or when you didn't listen.
I did not listen to my _____ (state who you did not listen to. Suggestions include a client, coworker, vendor, boss, department, or student) *and it resulted in problems with* _____ (state an issue relevant to the job that occurred from not listening). *I realized from then on that I needed to listen when* _____ (state a business situation where improved listening resulted in performance on future projects.)

Q18. What do you do if you disagree with your boss?

Change to "When did you disagree with your boss over a change in procedure and why? What was the outcome?"

At one point while working on _____ (state a business, client or departmental problem that you were dealing with), *I did not agree with my boss on how to proceed with* _____ (state a goal, milestone, or deadline). *The reason I did not agree was because* _____ (state business reasons for not agreeing with your boss). *The result of this disagreement was* _____ (state whether you went with your boss's decision or if your boss went with your decision). *By taking the time to work through the problem together, we were able to achieve*____ (state reaching a goal).

7.8 Questions for the Employer

Candidates need to ask great questions of the employer to ensure that they are selected for the position. These questions can really excite the employer. It is not just the questions that are important; your specific responses can really set you apart from the competition.

TIP: This is one of your greatest and final chances to create a "yes" reaction in the mind of the recruiter.

Sometimes these questions can make or break your chances at the job because:

- Some interviewers are bad at their job and you will need to take over the interview anyway.
- If you create a conversation and identify the needed skills, you can offer answers that match their needs.
- Questions show your interest in the position and organization.
- Recruiters love great questions.
- They can set you apart from other applicants.

Some recruiters are not very skilled at interviewing. You may have to take over the interview to express your qualifications. These questions can allow you to uncover additional needs or address any lingering concerns. Any answer and example you have prepared should be used if the interviewer does not seem capable of asking the right questions. In the case of a bad interviewer, ask and answer your own interview questions by telling the recruiter "I want to tell you about this experience I had."

The most important aspect of these questions is that they must be in the form of a conversation, an opportunity to re-affirm your candidacy. Every time the recruiter provides an answer, you need to say, "I have done this exact work" or "I have faced this exact challenge and here is an example." If the recruiter is not asking many questions, this is the opportunity for you to say, "I have some great examples you may want to hear about." Then, proceed by telling the recruiter, "This is the exact work that I have done."

The exercise below includes the questions to ask an employer and your suggested response.

6.9.1 Exercise: Questions for Them

After every response the recruiter gives to the questions below, say one of three things:
- "I have done this exact work; here is an example…"
- "That is the exact work I am doing right now; here is an example.."
- "I have faced this exact challenge and here is what I did to solve it…"

… and explain when and where this has occurred in your work history.

Questions about the position:
- What are the three top priorities you have identified for this position?
- What does the organization feel is the most important thing I can do to be effective in the first 90 days of my employment?
- Is there an annual performance review and what are the performance metrics for this position?
- What structure does the organization foresee for this role and by when?

About the company or team:
- What are trends for this team and how does it impact the company?
- What do the team and organization value the most?
- How has this team and organization been received by customers/departments?
- How does this role fit into the team?
- In the most recent press release from the company_____; how does that affect the company's trajectory?

About the industry:
- What new trends are affecting the company?
- What does the organization value the most?
- How has this organization been received by customers?

About the recruiter:
- How did you find your way into the company?
- What about this work have you enjoyed most?

The Close (for each interview segment):
- Based on this interview do you have any lingering concerns about my candidacy that I can address?

Then respond to their concerns and select one of the following closings.

- I am very excited about this opportunity and look forward to hearing back from you. I want this position and to work for this company.
- I hope that I have demonstrated that this is the exact work that I have been doing. I would like this position and look forward to contributing to the organization (or team).
- I know that you are just as interested as I am in finding the right fit. Based on our conversations about the role, I know that this fits my background and goals and that this position and organization is the right fit for me.

Tip: Remember, whatever the recruiter says, it is important to say
"I have done this exact work"
or

"I have faced this exact problem" and explain when and where this has occurred in your work history.
This method gets job offers.

7.9 What Not to Say in an Interview

Although recruiters often express concerns about a candidate lying about their background, most people are incredibly honest (sometimes painfully honest). Some candidates treat the interview as a tell-all breaking news event. Sometimes, they accidentally reveal negative information that they may think is positive.

Remember, there are three primary questions on the mind of the recruiter:
1. Will the job candidate stay in the position for at least two years?
2. Will the job candidate be happy or least not disrupt the team dynamic?
3. Can the job candidate do the work?

Do not accidentally release any information that may tell the recruiter that your life is being disrupted or unstable. Here is a list of information that is best to keep to yourself.

Poor Health or Death of a Loved One

Any mention of poor health from either you or a family member has no place in the interview. This extends to your parents,

About the industry:
- What new trends are affecting the company?
- What does the organization value the most?
- How has this organization been received by customers?

About the recruiter:
- How did you find your way into the company?
- What about this work have you enjoyed most?

The Close (for each interview segment):
- Based on this interview do you have any lingering concerns about my candidacy that I can address?

Then respond to their concerns and select one of the following closings.

- I am very excited about this opportunity and look forward to hearing back from you. I want this position and to work for this company.
- I hope that I have demonstrated that this is the exact work that I have been doing. I would like this position and look forward to contributing to the organization (or team).
- I know that you are just as interested as I am in finding the right fit. Based on our conversations about the role, I know that this fits my background and goals and that this position and organization is the right fit for me.

Tip: Remember, whatever the recruiter says, it is important to say
"I have done this exact work"
or

> "I have faced this exact problem"
> and explain when and where this has occurred in your work history.
> This method gets job offers.

7.9 What Not to Say in an Interview

Although recruiters often express concerns about a candidate lying about their background, most people are incredibly honest (sometimes painfully honest). Some candidates treat the interview as a tell-all breaking news event. Sometimes, they accidentally reveal negative information that they may think is positive.

Remember, there are three primary questions on the mind of the recruiter:
1. Will the job candidate stay in the position for at least two years?
2. Will the job candidate be happy or least not disrupt the team dynamic?
3. Can the job candidate do the work?

Do not accidentally release any information that may tell the recruiter that your life is being disrupted or unstable. Here is a list of information that is best to keep to yourself.

Poor Health or Death of a Loved One

Any mention of poor health from either you or a family member has no place in the interview. This extends to your parents, siblings, spouse, and children. When you walk into an interview, everyone needs to be healthy at that moment. Discussions about health and death are depressing and can potentially indicate to the employer that you are not healthy or that you have problems at home that will take your focus away from the job. However, a strong fitness regime or physically active family can send a positive message to the interviewer. Focus on presenting information that states, "I am healthy and my family is healthy."

Hobbies & Affiliations
Sometimes there are unusual hobbies or affiliations that are better left out of the discussion (depending on the job and interview). Sometimes associations can be a deciding positive factor in a hire if the recruiter has similar interests. It is important to look at clues but to tread carefully about unusual hobbies. Focus on presenting information that states "I am normal and not into 'weird' activities."

Family Laundry
Your network influences your image. Like health issues, do not mention family members with criminal records, children out of wedlock, divorce, unemployed, poor health, mental issues, and congenital disorders. Also, do not mention if you have no family or friends in the area. Sometimes there is positive family information like a brother in the military or an aunt that is an elected official. This information contributes to the "pillar of society concept." Focus on presenting information that states, "I have a strong, stable healthy network of family and friends."

Children

This is probably one of the most difficult issues. Children are not a "negative" in general, but for the interview, they are problematic because childcare can distract an employee from their work. Talking about children too much tells the employer that the job is not the most important thing in the person's life. For men, this can be different because culturally there is an accepted notion that children spur the man to provide, which means the job should be his primary consideration.

When asked directly about children, of course answer honestly. However, also mention how much support you have, how healthy they are, or how you have worked while raising them with no problem. Focus on presenting information that states, "I have been a stable top performer in school and at work while I have raised my children and I have a strong support network."

Weddings

Men are not likely to talk about weddings other than to announce their status, but for women this can be a real negative. Younger women can become obsessed about their weddings, which can mean that they will be distracted at work. In addition, a wedding may mean time away from work for the event, the honeymoon, and the possibility of pending children for childbearing-aged women. Overall, men should mention an upcoming marriage, but women should avoid this issue or downplay it. Focus on presenting information that states, "I am available to work and this job (and my career) is my priority."

INTERVIEW "WHAT TO SAY AND NOT SAY" CHECKLIST
Use the following as "rules of thumb" about the personal information you reveal.

AVOID
- Death of a family member
- Illness of family member
- Personal illness
- Criminal records
- Non-mainstream hobbies
- Children out of wedlock
- Unhealthy children
- Personal or family unemployment
- Mental health issues
- Drug use
- Congenital disorders
- Childcare issues
- Issues with divorced spouse
- Divorce
- Getting married soon (women)

MENTION
- Personal fitness routines
- Family members with strong fitness routines
- A strong base of friends and family in the area
- A strong support system for childcare
- Successfully educated family members
- Successful business owners of legal enterprises
- Mainstream, interesting, or relevant hobbies
- Children, but also mention strong support system with childcare
- Children who are active in sports or school activities to underscore healthiness
- Gainful employment of spouse and family members
- Stable engagements, marriages, and relationships

7.10 Interview Portfolio

An interview portfolio is a method the job applicant can use to demonstrate evidence or proof of abilities to the recruiter. The portfolio is especially important in situations where the candidate needs to express ambition and high productivity. Most candidates do not make this extra effort, but it can make the difference between a job offer and a salary increase.
For instance, if you are a web designer, you might evaluate the company's webpage and discuss recommendations. Some employers are actually requesting projects or written case studies instead of a first interview. The following exercise is an additional way to get noticed by employers.

The employer will be very impressed if this is a growth-oriented position or one that is sales or marketing-oriented. It may be best to hold off on using this method for low growth positions because it may frighten the employer, sending the message that the candidate wants more than the position can offer, unless it is directly related. In addition, for someone with limited experience like a new graduate, it can appear boastful. However, it is good to learn this method as soon as possible because you will need it for your annual performance reviews and salary increases.

This exercise presents a checklist of items to include in a portfolio.

Interview and Performance Appraisal Portfolio Checklist

Create a binder or make a spiral bound presentation. Check off and include these items.

Checklist:
____ Emails and positive feedback from customers, vendors, coworkers, and staff.
____ Picture of awards granted and certificates.
____ A portfolio of projects and personal contributions in the process.
____ A list of publications and work-related social media and blog items, if applicable.
____ List of met or exceeded accomplishments per performance metrics.
____ Exceptional performance reviews.

7.11 Thank You Letter

Sometimes a candidate would like to submit a thank you letter following an interview. This may or may not help and there is no way to tell if one of your interviewers enjoys this special touch. A poorly written or illegible personal note can actually hurt a candidate. If the applicant was not a strong candidate for the position, a note could tip the scales for this particular boss, but in many cases this will not be a deciding factor for a candidate. Since there is no way to determine if a post-interview "thank you" can help, the following rules will at least ensure it does not hurt your chances of continued progression.

Rule 1: Get Business Cards

It will not be possible to send a note if you do not have contact information for the interviewer. In most cases, business cards are presented at the beginning of an interview or you may request it at the end. If the interviewer does not seem receptive to you, do not press them for their card.

Rule 2: History of Bad Grammar/Poor Writing

If your English papers from school were heavily marked up by your teacher, or if you received low scores for writing, do not write a letter.

Rule 3: Poor Handwriting

If your handwriting is not legible, send an email the same day as the interview to everyone you interviewed with. Follow the letter template below, and use email unless you have great hand writing.

Rule 4: Great Handwriting

If your handwriting has received comments for its beauty or readability, send a hand-written note. Buy beautiful stationary, potentially with your initials in script or something that is professional and sharp. Have your notecards with you prior to going into the interview. If this is a large organization, find a location (your car for instance) to write the cards immediately for each person. If you did not get their business card, record each interviewer's name at the top of your "questions for them" sheet or on a tablet. Write a three to five sentence note following the template below. Walk back into the building and offer the cards to the receptionist. If this is a small organization, there is no receptionist or walking back in does not make sense, have your stamps ready and drop the notes in the mailbox the same day as the interview.

Rule 5: Content

During the interview, take some notes and mark down areas of concern for the interviewer. What were they focused on? What questions did they have that were different from other interviewers? Who is the actual hiring manager you would be working under? That person is the most important one to impress but all interviewers should be addressed.

With your list of notes about the type of skill(s), needs, and concerns that each person stressed during the interview, speak directly to those issues on the "thank you" letter. You can write the same note for each person, but it will be far more effective to show a personalized approach. At the very least, the most important person to write to is your direct hiring manager. In the letter, briefly address one to three skills, needs, or concerns you discussed. Finish the note by re-affirming your interest in the position.

Use the following template to assist in writing your notes.

6.12.1 Thank You Letter Template

(Name of Contact),

Thank you for meeting with me to discuss your needs for the _____ (Title) position. Based on our meeting, I felt the strong sense of urgency in finding a dedicated team member that will take care _____ (Skill/Need/Concern 1), _____ (Skill/Need/Concern 2), and _____ (Skill/Need/Concern 3). I am very interested in this position and I am ready to contribute to the team and organization.

Sincerely,

Name

>**Homework**

Prepare for interviews and control the engagement, especially the timing of phone interviews. Getting a job offer is as much about demonstrating that you will be a happy, non-disruptive team member that will stay on the job as it is about skills. Only when these issues have been satisfied will a candidate be judged on their technical capabilities.

Quiz 7: Interviewing (T/F)
1.___ A great phone screen is about saying "yes" as much as possible.
2.___ Phone screens are focused on your ability to do the job.
3.___ You can quote the same "desired salary" for all jobs.
4.___ Your "reasons for leaving" past jobs are critical to interview success.
5.___ The phone screens are casual and are primarily for appointment-setting.
6.___ Behavioral interview questions are specific problem solving examples
7.___ "Questions for them" should focus on company history
8.___ I can get a job offer if I say I was fired "with cause."
9.___ The best candidate is the one that can do the job the best.
10.___ Salary negotiations typically begin at the time of the job offer.

Chapter 7: Answer Key (T/F)
1) True: The more you say "yes" the more likely it is to move forward with the process.
2) False: Phone screens are focused on your career goals and salary expectations.
3) False: "Desired Salary" must match the position, not your goals, to move forward.
4) True: Why you left each one, and how it relates to the position in question, is critical.
5) False: Phone screens are used to ruthlessly weed out candidates.
6) True: Behavioral questions require specific problem solving examples for each line item of the job ad.

7) False: "Questions for them" allow a candidate to re-affirm candidacy, decrease hiring uncertainty, demonstrate strong interest, and trigger a "yes" in the recruiter's mind.

8) False: Employers do not hire people who say they were fired "with cause."

9) False: The best candidate can do the job AND will stay on the job and be happy.

10) False: They usually begin in the phone screen.

Chapter 8: Salary Negotiations and Desired Salary Quoting

This book has covered the many important parts to getting a new job. All these steps set the stage for quoting salary or performing final negotiations. This area is very misunderstood by job candidates and it has a staggering impact on careers.

It is estimated that 85% of employers expect job candidates to negotiate salary. The reality is that only 37% to 44% of candidates enter into some type of negotiation. The lack of salary negotiating in your career can cost an average of $500,000 in lifetime lost earnings. In addition, women are much less likely to negotiate than men. A partial contributor to the female gender pay gap (where women make 77 cents of every dollar a man earns) is a reluctance to negotiate. Another contribution to the gender gap is that a percentage of moms stay home with their children and their income never recovers.

For the B2W mom, my goal is to get you back to full employment, making your worth, within a 2-year period post re-entry into the labor force. For those moms that consider themselves as B2W but have technically been working, it is time to get some more income.

The fact that the salary topic comes up so quickly in the job search process, sometimes on the application itself, adds to the complexity of this topic. Salary negotiation fears are not without merit. A bad negotiation can end the job offer.

Let's explore some salary myths and common beliefs so that you can get back to full employment as soon as possible.

This lesson will cover:
8.1 – Salary negotiation myths
8.2 – What to quote for desired salary
8.3 – Performing a salary survey
8.4 – New hire salary negotiations
8.5 – Salary adjustment, negotiation, or both

8.1 Salary Negotiation Myths

Myth 1. Salary negotiations begin after interviews when the offer is made.

In the past, salary negotiations were the final step in the hiring process or, for existing employees, a part of the performance review. Now salary negotiations often **begin at the point of application** to a job.

The following list presents the five points where a salary negotiation may occur:
1. At the time of application,
2. During the phone screen,
3. In the first in-person interview,
4. At the point of a job offer, or
5. During a performance review.

When "Desired Salary" is used too early in the process, the question essentially turns into the "Guess What the Job Pays" Game.

Here are the rules of the game:
- The employer uses a field in the Applicant Tracking System or asks a question on the phone screen about salary.
- If you answer wrong, you will not be called for further interviews.
- If you answer correctly, you may continue and might ultimately end with a job offer.

Negotiations don't even begin if you cannot guess what the employer has decided the job is worth.

Below are examples of three different sales positions. The same candidate will apply, and is qualified for, all three jobs.

3 positions, 3 salaries, 1 applicant

What answer should the candidate give in the desired salary field on the application or during the first interviews?

>Position 1: Outside Salesperson with one to three years of experience requiring a high school diploma.

>Position 2: Sales Territory Manager with three to five years of experience preferring, but not requiring, a Bachelor's Degree.

>Position 3: Sales Manager with three to five years of experience requiring a Bachelor's degree.

These three jobs do not pay the same amount.

If the same figure is quoted, this candidate will not likely advance or get a job offer. If this candidate needs a job, and would consider any of these three, they must figure out what each one pays.

The biggest takeaway is that salary negotiations begin with guessing the value that the employer has placed on the job. If you don't get that right, you won't get an interview or an offer.

Myth 2. Salary is not used to screen out a candidate.

When applying for a job, the employers may elect to create pre-programmed fields inside the Applicant Tracking Systems to eliminate candidates that do not meet a certain range of salary amounts. These same questions may also be asked during an initial telephone screen or first in-person interview. If salary is discussed this early, the employer is using this information as a way to screen candidates – one of the primary methods to do so.

Myth 3. Your desired salary quote is what you want to earn.

No. The desired salary, if you want to get the job offer, is how much the job pays.
The goal of this module is to educate you on determining what an advertised job is worth as indicated by:
1. The value that employer has placed on the position,
2. The prevailing wage information, and
3. How to have a salary conversation with the employer.

Myth 4. You will be told that your stated salary range is acceptable.

The recruiter may tell you that the quoted range is acceptable or they may just continue on with further interviewing. If you are moving along in the process, this is a strong indicator that the stated range is acceptable.

Myth 5. Once the employer makes the offer, the interview process is complete.

No. When the employer is ready to make an offer, the salary negotiation is used as the **final interview** in the process. It is important to know that you are still being evaluated for the job based on how you perform in the salary negotiation.

Myth 6. The candidate will lose if they throw out the first number.

As long as the candidate knows the value of the job, understands the prevailing wages in the professional category, and demonstrates the ability to state their value, a candidate should be in a better position even if they state a range early on.

Myth 7. Once you are hired, it is almost impossible to negotiate salary, so you better get it right first.

This one is partially true. Once you are hired at a job, it is often challenging to get an employer to offer a raise over three percent up to ten percent *without a promotion*. To get paid more money for the <u>same job</u> requires significant evidence, proof of skills, accomplishments, and industry wage information. The section about existing employee salary negotiations does discuss this, but it is also important to consider how to get a promotion, which is a more likely method of achieving a large increase in many cases.

No matter when the salary negotiation takes place, the formulation of a matching salary requires an understanding of how much the employer and the market values the position. In the following two sections, we will focus on understanding the signals an employer is making about the position's pay rate.

<u>Myth 8: Salary negotiations are always possible and there is always $10,000 or more wiggle room.</u>

If a person has virtually no experience in the field, salary negotiations are almost impossible. For a job candidate that has one or more years of experience, there is usually room for negotiation, but this depends on the salary range of the position according to the following parameters.

• Jobs under $40,000 typically have a $1 to $2 per hour negotiation range.
• Jobs between $40,000 and $65,000 have about a $5,000 per year negotiation range.
• Jobs between $65,000 and $90,000 have about a $10,000 to $15,000 per year negotiation range.
• Jobs above $90,000 will have a $20,000 or higher per year negotiation range.

B2W moms in their re-entry period should be more concerned with quoting the correct amount so that they get job offers than about negotiating more. In the post re-entry scenario, negotiation may be appropriate if the skills gained in the re-entry position help overcome the previous gap. Either way, quoting correctly is much more important than negotiating for more money for a re-entry B2W mom.

8.2 What to Quote for Desired Salary

Every profession has a huge range of salaries from the entry point to leadership roles. To perform a salary negotiation, the candidate must know two pieces of information:

1. The value the employer has placed on the job - low, mid, or high.
2. The prevailing wage information about salaries for the professional category.

If we assume that every profession can range from $30,000 to $150,000, we need to become masters at reading employer signals of job value.

Indications of Job Value

To state a desired salary that matches the value the employer has placed on the position, a core skill for a successful job hunt requires an analysis of the job advertisement. This value does not have to be a mystery. There is a push for legislation to force employers to state the salary range on job advertisements to eliminate the gender pay gap, however that has not happened on a national level yet.

Employers offer three primary signals in a job advertisement that indicate whether a job pays a low or high salary:
1. The level of education,
2. Job title additions, and
3. The years of experience.

Some areas of the country and some industries will pay at different rates, but these averages offer an excellent gauge of the employer's pay rate perspective on the position. There are exceptions to every rule, however I use these methods every day with accuracy.

1. Level of Education

The level of education required by the job advertisement is a great first indicator of pay levels. The national average for earnings by degree is a consistent indicator of the likely pay within about five dollars per hour, higher or lower, than the average. The following table presents the national average pay rates based on degree level.

Average U.S. Earnings by Degree Level (Source: BLS 2010 Census)
- High School: Average Hourly Wage-$15, Annual Wage-$30,000
- Bachelor's: Average Hourly Wage-$27, Annual Wage-$52,500
- Master's: Average Hourly Wage-$31, Annual Wage-$62,500

High School/Associate's Degree Level

A position that does not require a Bachelor's degree is typically going to be in a range of pay between $10 and $15 per hour unless the job is seeking specialized knowledge, is in a known well-paying industry, or requires many years of experience. If you do not have a Bachelor's degree and make over $15 per hour, then you are outperforming the national average and would be considered to be doing well for your education level. If you make an income close to or above the Bachelor's or Master's degree level of pay, you will likely need to consider additional education or targeted technical experience to obtain a salary increase, since the current pay rate significantly outpaces the national average. A person who is overpriced in the job market can face a challenging situation. It is better to be proactive if you find yourself in this position in order to maintain income or a job, or to experience continued growth.

When a client has a Bachelor's degree and is making over $40,000 per year, and sees a position that does not require a degree, I know that the employer is not willing to pay the best rate for the job. There are some exceptions in certain fields, particularly manufacturing and industrial, where an employee can make above $65,000 per year with no degree, but these positions are becoming fewer by the day.

No matter what the job pays, if the job advertisement states that it requires a High School graduate, it is a signal that the job is on the lower level of the pay scale. If you have a Bachelor's degree, this should be a flag that this job will probably not pay over $20 per hour.

Bachelor's Degree Level

A position requiring a Bachelor's degree will typically start at no lower than $15 per hour and will likely grow to $20 per hour rather quickly with one to three years of experience. To obtain $27 per hour, or $52,500 annually, a job candidate or employee will usually need to obtain specialized knowledge or have over five years of experience. To obtain $60,000 and above usually requires highly specialized knowledge in the field or having obtained a management position. If you have a Bachelor's degree and are not making $27 per hour or $52,500 annually, then additional years of experience, specialized knowledge, a different career path, or a management position is necessary to push to the higher salary. Salaries of $50,000 to $70,000 for a candidate with a Bachelor's degree between the ages of 30 and 50 are fairly common. Earning over $70,000 requires having higher technical knowledge, holding certifications, being politically savvy, hitting a high growth company, starting with a professional category that tends to pay better, or obtaining a management position.

There are industry considerations as well. For instance, social services and nonprofits tend to pay less than banking or manufacturing.

Since these are averages, there are people making less and more than this amount, however this is a beginning indicator of the value the employer is putting on the advertised job.

Master's Degree Level

A position that mandates, or even prefers, a Master's degree, is indicating a pay rate over $30 per hour and potentially much more. However, job candidates who have a Master's degree but limited related work experience face the same entry-level career path as a Bachelor-degree holder. Experience is the key to obtaining the higher salary ranges. In some industries a Master's degree or higher is the threshold education level even if the pay is low. A Licensed Social Worker is an example of a position that may require a Master's degree but is not in a high-paying field.

In general, if the position is looking for a Master's degree, the candidate should be making over $60,000 per year. In some business fields like finance, a job ad that asks for many years of experience and a Master's degree indicates a position over $90,000.

Tip: If you have a degree that is higher than the job is requesting, then the pay rate will be reflective of what the employer is asking for, not the education level you have obtained.

For instance, if you have a Master's degree and the job is asking for a Bachelor's degree, the employer has determined the pay rate for the position of a person holding a Bachelor's degree. Your higher-level degree will be considered as in a Bachelor's degree pay rate. If a job is asking for an Associate's degree and you have a Bachelor's degree, the pay rate will be closer to the Associate's degree level averages than the Bachelor's degree level.

What if you are making a different pay rate than indicated by the national averages for your degree level? Other than looking for different job advertisements that are more closely related to your experience and degree-level, consider the following long-term strategies.

If you are being paid less than your degree level, additional experience or a job change can assist in bumping you to the higher level. Take a lower-level job and treat it like a one- to two-year school program.

If you are at the average pay level for your education, additional experience, education, a job change, or a promotion is necessary to bump you to the next level.

If you are higher than the national average for your education, examine promotion possibilities, seek out management roles, and find ways to get more specialized technical experience or industry certifications to ensure continued increases.

If you make exceptionally more than the average pay rate for your education level, examine the market to gain experience in changing trends in the field, or consider moving geographical markets to maintain income stability.

The next indication of pay level is additions to the job title. Job titles often indicate what the employer is looking for in the level of responsibility and years of experience, which impact the pay rate.

2. Level of Responsibility: Additions to Job Title

The job advertisement will of course list a job title. The title typically holds two pieces of information: 1) the professional category and 2) the level of responsibility, which directly impacts the pay rate.

The following demonstrates the correlation between the job title additions to lower and higher level pay rates.

Low-Level Pay Rates
Coordinator, Specialist, Associate, "Levels" like I or 1, Representative, Clerk, Assistant, Supervisor, Entry Level

Mid to Higher Level
Consultant, Manager, Director, "Levels" II-III or 2 to 3, Analyst, Compliance, Development

The lower-level title additions may offer below $20 per hour while the mid- to higher-level can reach well beyond $20 per hour. Unlike degree level, there is no national data for pay rate averages based on job title additions. Use the title additions in combination with the desired education level and years of experience to complete the picture of the employer's pay rate perspective.

3. Desired Years of Experience

The requested years of experience will also indicate if the position is valued at a higher or lower level. The following correlates the desired years of experience to lower and higher-level pay rates.

Low-Level Salary Ranges: 0-3 years of experience expected

Mid- to Higher-Level Salary Ranges: 3+ years of experience expected

The requested years of experience, used in conjunction with the degree level and job title additions, can offer the final piece of information on what the employer is willing to pay.

Industry, the life cycle of the organization, demand for workers, supply of workers, and geographic location all play into salary levels. However, degree requirements, the additions to the job title, and the requested years of experience, are also good indicators of the potential pay level.

The next step in the process is using your personal knowledge through you or your network to conduct a salary survey.

Use the following exercise to determine the likely value the employer is placing on the advertised job.

Exercise 8.2: Value of the Job Evaluation

Look at the job ad and evaluate the position using this guide.

Evaluation 8.2a: Salary below $20 per hour on average
Assessment – check all that apply:
1.___ Not asking for a Bachelor's degree
2.___ Uses low-level job title additions.
3.___ Asking for 0-3 years of experience

If you selected any option from the above list, it may indicate that the position will offer less than $20 per hour. Certain industries and professional categories may pay more.

Evaluation 8.2b: Salary at or above $20 per hour.
Assessment – check all that apply:
1.___ Asking for a Bachelor's degree
2.___ Uses higher-level title additions
3.___ Asking for 3+ years of experience

If you selected any option from the above list, it may indicate that the position will offer at or above $20 per hour.

Evaluation 8.2c: Salary at or above $30 per hour.
Assessment – check all that apply:
1.___ Asking for a Master's degree or professional certification as mandatory or preferred
2.___ Uses higher-level title additions
3.___ Asking for 3+ years of experience

If you selected any option from the above list, it may indicate that the position will offer at or above $30 per hour.

8.3 Performing a Salary Survey Lesson

The previous section explored the value an employer may be placing on the position. This section focuses on the prevailing market wage for similar jobs in the same industry.

There are three ways to gather salary information:

- Your own personal knowledge of the field,
- The knowledge of friends/family/colleagues/professors/mentors, and
- Performing a salary survey of related professional titles or skills.
- Glassdoor.com

In some cases, when changing careers, a job candidate has limited personal knowledge of possible salaries, therefore it is important to talk with other people who may be aware of the salary range. Beyond asking other people about the likely pay ranges, learning how to perform a salary survey is the next most important skill. Although there are industry averages, it is better to actually search for similar titles and use the job advertisements that list jobs, speak with recruiting agencies to get an idea of pay rates, and use the salary survey tool built into Indeed.com.

Indeed.com has a salary survey tool built directly into the system. Within the search function there is a "more" option that contains salary survey information. A rule of thumb is to quote an income range for the targeted position. If the candidate, recruiter, and hiring manager have different concepts of a pay rate, a salary range may save the interview and continue the process.

Quoting a single salary number that is much higher than what the recruiter is going to offer can immediately shut down the process. Quoting a range that is too wide may indicate a candidate that does not know the industry or what they want. A quote that follows typical ranges maintains a conversation. If the recruiter indicates that the range is acceptable, you will likely obtain the middle number of the range. The exercise below demonstrates how to perform a salary survey.

Exercise 8.3: Performing a Salary Survey

Follow the steps to obtain the best salary range possible.

Step 1: Who do you know that might have knowledge of income ranges for the job?

Speak to people who you know can be trusted to remain discreet with your career goals and information. Some of the most knowledgeable people about prospective salaries really should not know about your pending career transition.

Step 2: Mine third party recruiters or staffing agencies for information.
Third Party Recruiters and staffing agencies place candidates in positions every single day. They are the single best source of pay rates in your locale. If you do not know someone working in this field, look for a job being staffed by a recruiting/staffing agency and apply for it. If you get a call, you can ask the recruiter what the job pays or what they are seeing in the field. In many cases, a recruiting firm will list the hourly wage right in the job advertisement.

Step 3: Perform a salary survey
Go to Indeed.com and...
• Search by title or keyword combinations.

- Leave the city blank to get a nationwide range for the salary and the best close hits.
- Add the city to get an idea of averages in your local market.
- Keep combining keywords or title until you get job matches that are as close to the same.
- Do not rely on the title alone unless it is very standard like "accountant." Even in this case there are many job levels within a title.
- Click on "More" under the job titles that look closely related.
- Under "More" below the job advertisement there is a Salary Search option. Click on the Salary Search and a window will pop up with salary information.
- One result is not enough. Try many combinations of title, keywords, and responsibility level of the roles to get different salary ranges across the country. These ranges will offer a basis for discussion.
- Visit Glassdoor.com to gather additional salary information if available.

8.4 New Hire Salary Negotiations

Salary negotiations ideally begin once a job offer has been made. Even if a dollar amount has been discussed during the screening process, a candidate can still attempt to negotiate. At this point, the candidate, recruiters, and hiring managers have invested a large amount of time and energy into locating the right job candidate. Everyone wants to close the process as quickly as possible. Although there is usually room in a company's pay scale to offer additional income, the employer does not always consider every candidate eligible to negotiate.

Take this self-evaluation to determine if salary negotiations are likely to result in a positive discussion in your next interview.

New Hire Salary Eligibility Assessment

"Am I eligible to negotiate more money in my new hire salary?" Check all that apply:

1.___ I have at least one year of practical work experience in this field.
2.___ I have held this title or a similar title.
3.___ This is not a low-level or entry-level position.
4.___ There is no pre-stated salary placed on the job.
5.___ I have not already strongly committed to a salary amount with the employer.
6.___ I have relevant accomplishments.
7.___ This is a high-demand field with few qualified applicants.
8.___ I have knowledge that the employer pays a wide range of salary amounts.

If you selected any option from the above list, you may see positive results from a salary negotiation. If you were not able to select some of the options above, you may experience difficulties in negotiating a salary.

Negotiating a salary may be difficult at the time of hire if a candidate has no relevant experience or accomplishments, the position is entry or low-level, or when the field has many qualified applicants. An employer that lists the pay in the job advertisement will often not be open to negotiation. If a candidate was forced to state a salary history or their desired salary, negotiations may be challenging.

Typically, it is easier to negotiate if the candidate has unique matching skills that are hard to find in the labor market.

New Hire Salary Negotiations: A Balance Between Three People

A salary negotiation in a larger organization balances the wants, needs, and realities of three people:
1. The candidate,
2. The recruiter, and
3. The hiring manager.

The exception is in a smaller organization where there may not be a formal Human Resource department, in which case the negotiation is between the hiring manager and the applicant.

A job candidate theoretically wants the highest salary possible. Recruiters want a salary amount that is within the industry prevailing wage to recruit and retain the right employee. The hiring manager wants to maintain equity of pay in the department and remain within their annual budget.

Sometimes the salary figures of these three people are not in agreement with each other. The recruiter does not want to lose a candidate during a salary negotiation because it would mean starting again in the process. At the same time, recruiters and hiring managers watch negotiations closely because the candidate is demonstrating how they will behave on the job. A job candidate is still interviewing during the negotiations.

A candidate who meets the basic eligibility to negotiate has an increased potential to maintain their job offer and obtain additional benefits in this final process if they do the following:
1. Express gratitude,
2. Act decisively,
3. Properly calculate value,
4. Provide proof,
5. Be flexible, and
6. Create a positive conversation.

Express Gratitude, Even With an Insulting Job Offer

In a survey of recruiters, the most appreciated job candidates were those who thanked them for the offer. Thanking the recruiter, and even respectfully declining an insultingly low job offer, can result in continued negotiations later on for higher value positions. Some candidates have negotiated and turned around job offers that were originally significantly less than the candidate's acceptable range, if they were gracious in their reply. An employer may come back to the candidate and make a new job offer when their budget allows for more money or a higher paying position opens up. On the other hand, an employer will not call a candidate back if a previous job offer was ignored or if the negotiation was unprofessional.

Act Decisively: Timeframes of Negotiations

Recruiters like decisive candidates who know what they want. When you enter into a negotiation, you need to know what your primary points of negotiation are and maintain them. The negotiation typically only goes back and forth one time, rarely two times, for additional well-defined terms.

If the candidate adds or changes their stated desires in this process, the recruiter may determine that the candidate is an indecisive person and rescind the offer.

This decisiveness also pertains to the time needed to accept an offer. Despite the lengthy amount of time candidates have to wait during a job interview process, once the final offer has been made the candidate only has 48 hours to make a decision.

Calculate Total Value

Recruiters like candidates who can calculate the full value of all parts of the offer, not just salary. If you enter into a negotiation, it is probably for a job that requires some level of education and skills. If you are stuck on one aspect of the negotiation and cannot assess everything being offered, then the recruiter may determine that you are not as intelligent as they thought and rescind the offer. This is especially true for managerial or number-driven positions.

Proof of Accomplishments

Recruiters like a candidate who can offer proof of their value in accomplishments. A hiring decision is often made by multiple people, and so a candidate who can succinctly present their competitive advantage makes it easier for the recruiter to support their salary negotiation with the other hiring decision-makers.

Be Flexible

Recruiters like flexibility. A candidate who is flexible in alternative arrangements indicates a team player. Examples of these alternatives are a sign-on bonus, a salary adjustment later in the fiscal year, a better title, the potential for growth, stock sharing, pay for performance arrangements, or additional vacation time.

Create a Positive Conversation

The most common advice you may hear on negotiating new hire salaries is that you should force the employer to tell you a salary amount first. The thought is that whoever states the amount first is the "loser." Not only is this advice unhelpful, but it also sets up a negative interaction with the employer. For instance, if the employer asks, "What are your salary expectations?" and your response is "I am willing to review any acceptable offer," then the conversation could go back and forth and create a negative situation.

A candidate who states, "I feel I should make more" is not likely to be successful. The best way to manage the new hire salary negotiation is to be proactive and have all of the necessary facts to state the position's range and to justify why you, as a candidate, qualify for the upper part of the range. If you have adequately detailed your qualifications with references or supporting documentation, there is a strong basis for your salary negotiation. Evidence-based negotiations yield better results for both parties because the conversation is based on data.

How the candidate handles salary negotiations reflects how the candidate will behave at work. The next section presents scripts for beginning a new hire salary negotiation, what to say during the process, and what to do if the answer is no.

Exercise 8.4: New Hire Salary Negotiations

The New Hire Salary Negotiation Commitment
Answer the following with a "yes" or "no."
_____ I know that by engaging in a new hire salary negotiation I am indicating to the employer that I am unhappy with the offered pay. I have used the evaluation to determine how likely it is for this discussion to be successful or at least well received. I know that basing the negotiation on facts and information is more likely to produce a data-driven unemotional discussion that should maintain positive relations whether an increase occurs or not. If, by some chance, the employer responds negatively, I will use the Exercise 8.4C script and decision process to determine my next moves.

Exercise 8.4a: The Script
"Based on my knowledge of this field, my current salary, and a salary survey of similar titles for this type of work, I have identified that the current salary range for this position is between _____ and _____." (State a $10,000 range based on your salary survey.)

Exercise 8.4b: Scripts for When They Say Yes

If they accept the range continue with the following:

"*I feel that I am qualified for the upper range of this position because I have specific accomplishments and experience in the following skills highlighted in the job ad and the interview process _____, _____, and _____.*" (State skills and past experience in saving money or generating revenue.)

Exercise 8.4c: Scripts for When They Say No

If the recruiter states a lower range, or directly says "no", then there are a few options which depend on the comfort level of the candidate to walk away from the table.

Willing to walk away:

"*Thank you for the offer. I am still very interested in this position, however, based on my current salary and a survey of the field, I cannot go below $_____* (State the "drop dead" desired salary amount). *I might consider $_____ with a performance-based bonus and combined benefits package that offers the potential to reach $_____.*"

Willing to accept a lower salary offer:

If you are willing, or need, to accept the lower offer, but feel you may be able to negotiate on different terms, use the following script:

"*Thank you for the offer. I am very interested in this position. I can understand you wanting to see evidence of my ability to perform. I would like to negotiate a salary adjustment review based on performance in a 6-month timeframe.*"
Or …

"Thank you for the offer. I am still interested in this position. I would like to negotiate _____. (State one or more of the following.)"

- A sign on bonus,
- A salary bump in the new fiscal year,
- A performance-based bonus structure,
- Additional vacation time,
- A better job title, and/or
- Pay for education and certification.

Willing to accept the lower salary offer:
If you need to take the job but have no intention on working at that rate for a long period of time, consider the following strategy:
- View this position as a way to be paid to "go to school." If you are not getting the pay that you want, then it may be that you need experience. Many positions are worth an increase of $10,000 or more with one year of experience.
- Seek a salary adjustment to the prevailing industry wage at the next performance review. (The next section covers this strategy.) It may take a full year to obtain this increase.
- If you cannot obtain an adjustment, seek a new position within one to two years.
- It may be necessary to re-evaluate the value of the position in the market. Maybe this career path is not worth as much as you thought.

Scripts for a rescinded offer in which the employer walks away:

If the employer terminates the job offer during the negotiation process, or you walk away from the job offer, use the following script:

"I very much appreciate being considered for this position and salary negotiation. Although it did not work out this time due to _____, I hope that we can keep in touch about future possibilities."

8.5 Existing Employee Salary Negotiations Lesson

Salary negotiations for existing employees are different from those for new hires. Employers generally will not exceed a ten percent increase in salary. To achieve higher salaries, you may need to seek a promotion to a higher pay rank. Promotions typically include a different title and higher level of responsibility, while salary negotiations can be for a current position. This section is dedicated to salary negotiations for the position an employee currently holds.

There are two types of salary negotiations for an existing employee: a salary adjustment or a raise. There is one universal HR tip for existing employee negotiations: if you are not meeting or exceeding expectations, do not expect an increase in salary.

Other than performance, there are additional instances where an increase in salary is not likely. Use the evaluation below to determine if your situation fits into this scenario.

Evaluation 8.5a: Existing Employee Salary Negotiation: Less Likely

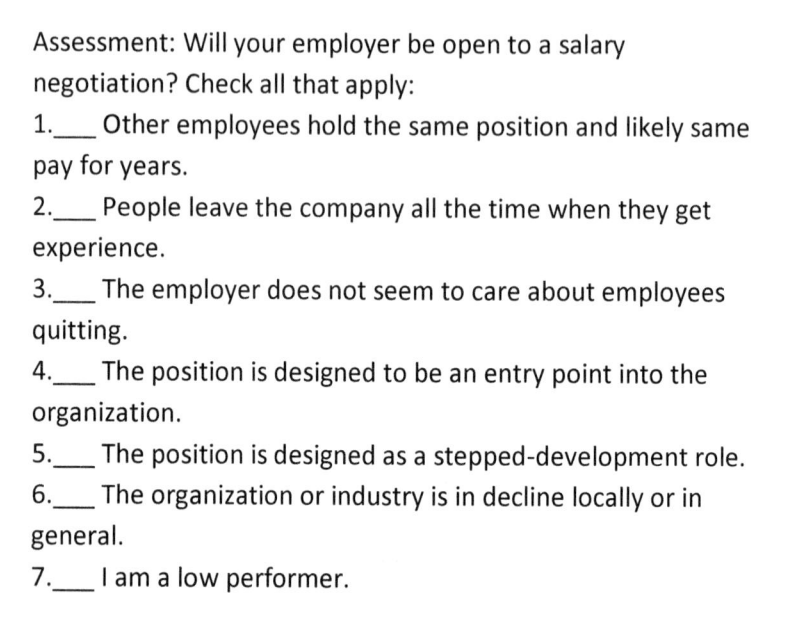

Assessment: Will your employer be open to a salary negotiation? Check all that apply:
1.___ Other employees hold the same position and likely same pay for years.
2.___ People leave the company all the time when they get experience.
3.___ The employer does not seem to care about employees quitting.
4.___ The position is designed to be an entry point into the organization.
5.___ The position is designed as a stepped-development role.
6.___ The organization or industry is in decline locally or in general.
7.___ I am a low performer.

If you selected any option from the above list, it may indicate a challenge ahead in having a salary adjustment or raise discussion. If many employees hold the same role at the same pay rate, or if an employee at a low pay-rate has been willing to remain in the position for years, the employer may believe that the job is paying well enough. If people leave the company all the time and the employer does not seem to care about them going, then it is an indicator that this is an "entry-level" organization with no plans to increase wages.

If the company is known for hiring people into "entry" positions, then the person must seek work in other departments or a promotion in the same department for a wage increase. If the position was designed as a development role from the start, then obtaining a higher wage based on the market rate is unlikely.

Some organizations or industries are shrinking in the local or greater economy, which can create salary increase issues or the proverbial "can't get blood from a turnip" situation. Even though salary adjustments are based on the prevailing wage, if an employee is a low performer they will not likely get a raise.

Although there are cases where a salary negotiation is not possible, there are equally as many instances where an employee can obtain a raise. The following sections discuss the difference between the salary adjustment and a raise discussion with corresponding assessments and scripts for a positive outcome.

Salary Adjustments

A salary adjustment typically applies to a job candidate that was hired at an entry-level and has now gained one to two years of experience. It is not uncommon for an entry-level job candidate to be worth $10,000 or more in a short period of time. The challenge is that employers do not typically like to make large jumps in salary. Salary adjustment conversations are a way to get the employer to make a bigger leap in income than they normally would consider by proving the job pays more.

Salary adjustments are an easier discussion to have than merit-based raise conversations.

Why would an employer pay less for a job than the prevailing market wage?

The reasons can include:
1. Income equity amongst workers,
2. A high tolerance for employee turnover,
3. A sign of an "entry-level employer," or
4. A lack of knowledge about prevailing wages.

The first three employer types may not be open to a salary adjustment discussion, but the fourth situation may be open to discussion if the employee can demonstrate proof of a higher prevailing wage in the market.

<u>Income Equity</u>

Some employers and professions require income equity, a standard income rate across employees performing similar duties. This is common in large call centers or any type of profession that has many people working the same job. In this case, the employer reduces the complexity of their pay structure by creating a uniform salary system. This method also reduces potential issues with employees talking to each other about pay and reduces the possibility of a salary adjustment.

<u>"Don't Let the Door Hit You on the Way Out" Employers</u>

There are employers that can be classified as the "if you do not like it, quit" type. In this case, the organization is willing to exchange the threat or reality of people quitting in exchange for low pay rates. An employer with high attrition or many people quitting is not likely to change their ways.

"Entry-level" Employers

There are employers that tend to hire at the entry level. A small business may offer a dynamic, rich experience but is not be able to pay much. For instance, a start-up or a nonprofit that is not well funded can often offer an exceptional work experience. These employers may not want to lose great employees, but there is little room in the budget to prevent employees from leaving once they have gained experience.

Other types of employers have entry-level positions that they deliberately use to develop new employees. These can be formal development positions or the general way the company hires new employees. These types of employers use the entry-level experience to separate the low-performers from the high performers for future promotion. In this case, a salary adjustment is not possible and the only way to grow is to perform well and seek a promotion.

Overall, entry-level employers are critical in the job market because they tend to have lower requirements for their new hires and allow entry-level or career changers to gain experience. However, if an employee obtains one to two years of experience, and there is no promotion pending, they will have to move on to another employer to get an increase.

Lack of Knowledge about Prevailing Wage

This is the most likely employer type to offer a salary adjustment. Some employers or managers literally have no idea what the market rate is for certain jobs. In this case, the employee needs to educate the employer. This may occur when it is a small organization or a business startup, when you would report to a boss whose professional background is different from yours, or in a business where you are the only professional in a certain category. Gathering market information and presenting it to the employer for a salary adjustment discussion may result in a positive discussion.

The following evaluation demonstrates a likely scenario for success in a salary adjustment discussion.

Evaluation 8.5b: Salary Adjustment Evaluation – More Likely

Assessment: Check all that apply:
1.___ There are no or few employees with your title or professional background.
2.___ There is a small or ineffective HR department with no wage analysis experience.
3.___ The organization is young and inexperienced in wage issues.
4.___ The last person that held the role was hired many years ago.
5.___ I have upgraded my skills justifying more money in the market.
6.___ I can provide evidence of prevailing wage information.
7.___ This organization or the industry is in a growth or mature phase.

8.___ I am a high performer that has met or exceeded expectations.

If you selected any option from the above list, it may indicate an easier salary adjustment discussion. If someone is the only person in a professional category, the employer may be unfamiliar with the prevailing wage for an experienced person. For instance, a manufacturer may have one or two I.T. employees. The employer is accustomed to wage discussions in manufacturing, not I.T. If the previous person held the role for many years, they may have been happy with a lower pay and the employer may think that is normal. It is possible to educate the employer with the facts. The same can also be said for organizations that do not have a formal or large Human Resource department.

Lastly, the organization or industry may be on the rise or at its peak, offering additional increase opportunities. In this case, educating the employer on prevailing wages may be possible.

Salary Adjustments and Performance

Even though a salary adjustment is based on the market rate for the position, an under-performing employee will not likely receive a raise. Therefore, a salary adjustment conversation must also include some level of merit-based performance evidence by the employee. The following section discusses raise discussions followed by scripts for each type of salary negotiation.

Raise Negotiations

Both raise discussions and salary adjustments require an employee who is meeting or exceeding expectations. Salary adjustments typically apply to the transition from an entry-level candidate to an experienced candidate, while raise negotiations are for the life of your career and are merit-based or pay for performance.

As with new hire salary negotiations, a salary adjustment discussion requires diplomacy and awareness. Once you enter into this discussion you are essentially saying, "I am not happy with my pay." Sometimes employers do not react well to this information which can be career-limiting. It is important to use the evaluations in this section to determine the perspective of the employer on pay rates so that a salary discussion does not threaten your ability to keep your job or limit your career movement in the company. The next assessment evaluates the likelihood of a positive discussion.

For raise negotiations, use the following evaluation to determine how like it is to obtain a merit-based increase.

Evaluation 8.5c: Raise Negotiations – More Likely

Assessment: Can I get a raise? Check all that apply:
1.___ The organization has a hard time finding qualified employees.
2.___ I consistently outperform my co-workers.
3.___ I can provide evidence that my actions generated revenue.

4.___ I can provide evidence that my actions saved the company money.
5.___ My previous performance reviews have been good or great.
6.___ My previous performance reviews properly document my accomplishments.
7.___ I have upgraded my skills in some way that justifies more money.
8.___ The company is in good financial condition.
9.___ The organization or industry is in growth or mature phase.

If you selected any option from the above list, it may indicate an easier, more successful raise negotiation. If the company cannot find qualified workers, you consistently outperform other colleagues, there is evidence of making or saving the company money, performance reviews are consistently high and all accomplishments are documented, there has been an upgrade in skills, and the company is in a financial position to offer a raise, then it should be possible to have this discussion.

There is an important point to learn as early in your career as possible: Is the organization or industry on the rise, at its peak, or in decline? The answer may influence salary increase and promotion opportunities. The organization's financial health and industry trends are governed by a growth curve.

Increases in salary or promotions are largely dependent on what stage the company or industry is in. The introductory, or startup, periods usually have lower pay scales with the possibility of performance incentives. The growth stage offers a wave of progressive promotions and increases. The maturity stage includes high wages but much fewer promotions. The decline stage often offers exceptionally high wages, called legacy expenses, but there is also little movement and a high potential for layoffs.

Observe your organization and industry to evaluate what movement is possible. It may be worthwhile to attempt to switch companies or industries to ensure continued progression. Identify a start-up company by observing if there are few employees and if the company is being funded by investors until a customer base is achieved. A growth company will be investing in new buildings for expansion. For younger employees, this is a good option to ride a wave of growth. Mature companies have typically been in the same building with limited growth or the growth is from international market penetration. The decline stage typically looks like an aging infrastructure and a reduction in workforce from its peak operating period.

The following section includes exercises for salary adjustment and raise negotiations.

Existing Employee Salary Negotiations

Exercise 8.5a: Salary Adjustment or Raise Negotiations Commitment
Answer the following with a "yes" or "no."
_____I know that by engaging in a salary adjustment or raise negotiation discussion that I am indicating to my employer that I am unhappy with my pay. The employer may not react well to this discussion creating an adverse relationship. I have used the

evaluations to determine how likely it is for this discussion to be successful, or at least well received. I know that the more information and evidence I produce, the more likely I am to have a data-driven, unemotional discussion that should maintain positive relations whether an increase occurs or not. If, by some chance, my employer responds very negatively, I am ready to leave them and move on to another position with a company that will pay my worth or the worth of the position in the market. If they say no, then I will use Lesson 8.5D to make my decision on my next moves.

Exercise 8.5b: Salary Adjustment

Fill in the salary adjustment script:
"*When I came on board, I was excited for the opportunity to contribute to the organization. I am still completely dedicated to* _____ (name of employer). *However, with* ____ (years of experience) *in the field, I have performed a salary survey and have found that the prevailing wage for this position is in the range of* _____ *to* _____ (be prepared to provide evidence). *I know that I came on with limited experience, but that has changed. I would like to discuss a salary adjustment to the prevailing market wages for someone in this position with this many years of experience. What are your initial reactions or feelings to what I am proposing? Were you aware of these differences in pay that existed in the market? What is the* _____ (employer name) *view on market-wage salary adjustments?*"

Exercise 8.5c: Salary Negotiation

Include any of the phrases that apply.

Hard to Locate Employees Script

"*I really enjoy working here and, as we know, the company has had a hard time finding qualified employees with the following skills _____, _____, _____. With ___ year(s) of experience, I have gained this technical ability. I have performed a salary survey and have found that the prevailing wage for this position is in the range of _____ to _____ (be prepared to provide evidence). What is your perception on my value to the team? Have you been aware of my increase in technical skills?*"

Outperformed Colleagues

"*I really enjoy working here and, over the past _____ year(s), I have outperformed my co-workers on a number of metrics _____, _____, _____, yet I am making the same amount of money or have only seen an increase of _____ (salary increases). Based on my contribution I believe my value is _____ to _____ (the goal should be the mid-range number). What is your perception on my value to your team? Have you been aware of these differences in performance? What is the _____ (employer name) view on pay for performance?*"

Generated Revenue

"*I really enjoy working here and over the past _____ year(s), I have generated _____ in additional revenue for the company, yet I am making the same amount of money or have only seen an increase of _____ (salary increases). Based on my contribution, I believe my value is _____ to _____ (the goal should be the mid-range number). What is your perception on my value to your team? Have you been aware of these* differences in performance? What is the _____ (employer name) view on pay for performance?"

Saved Money

"I really enjoy working here and, over the past _____ year(s), I have saved _____ (amount saved) *for the company, yet I am making the same amount of money or have only seen an increase of* _____ (salary increases). *Based on my contribution I believe my value is* _____ *to* _____ (the goal should be the mid-range number). *What is your perception on my value to your team? Have you been aware of these differences in performance? What is the* _____ (employer name) *view on pay for performance?"*

Great and Well-Documented Performance Reviews

"I really enjoy working here and, over the past _____ year(s), I have had excellent performance reviews with documented accomplishments in the following metric areas (provide a list), *and yet I have only seen an increase of* _____ (salary increases). *Based on my contribution I believe my value is* _____ *to* _____ (the goal should be the mid-range number). *What is your perception on my value to your team? Have you been aware of these differences in performance? What is the* _____ (employer name) *view on pay for performance?"*

Upgrade in Skills

"I really enjoy working here and, over the past _____ year(s), I have acquired the following _____ (new technical skills, certifications, and education), *yet I have only seen an increase of* _____ (salary increases). *Based on these additional skills I believe my value is* _____ *to* _____ (the goal should be the mid-range number). *What is your perception on my value to your team? Have you been aware of these differences in performance? What is the* _____ *(employer name) view on pay for performance?"*

Salary Adjustment & Raise Negotiation Combined
"When I came on board I was excited to get the opportunity to contribute to the organization. I am still am completely dedicated to _____ (employer name). However, with _____ (years of experience) *in the field, I have performed a salary survey and have found that the prevailing wage for this position is in the range of* _____ *to* _____ *(be prepared to provide evidence).*

Over the past year(s) I have done the following (list and provide evidence of skills, accomplishments, and accolades).

Based on these additional skills and the prevailing wage for these skills in the market, I believe my value is _____ *to* _____ (the goal should be the mid-range number).
What are your initial reactions or feelings to what I am proposing? Were you aware of these differences in pay that existed in the market? What is the _____ *(employer name) view on market-wage salary adjustments especially in light of my accomplishments?"*

Exercise 8.5d: "What to Say When They Say No" Script

"I really enjoy working here and want to continue to grow. What would I need to do in the next year to reach the income range of ____ to ____?"

- Have the feedback formalized into your review process if possible.
- Give the employer time to make the adjustment. This lets them know you are serious about staying and it buys them time to get it in the budget and speak to upper level decision-makers if necessary.

What to Expect When Implementing This Lesson

- For career changers who are taking a job at an entry-level company or breaking into a new field, remember you have to get experience first. In a very short period of time (one to two years) you may be able to increase to a much higher salary level quickly.
- For experienced new hires, gather the facts, maintain gratitude, and you can be well on your way to more money.
- For existing employees, do not get discouraged. Your manager does not know what you do all day or what you have accomplished. It is your job to protect your salary and position advancement by maintaining a portfolio of accomplishments to make it easy for your boss to see your value.
- Be sure to create a conversation with the employer to avoid a negative backlash. The goal is to keep building evidence to support your claim for more money.
- Keep it positive. Continue to thank the employer for their offers and consideration.
- If salary negotiations do not garner higher pay, seek a promotion or prepare to move to another company to earn more money.

8.6 Alternative Negotiation Item Quick Reference Sheet

In general, you only want to negotiate on three items. Most candidates focus on salary but there are alternatives. Refer to the list below for the three types of compensation that can be up for negotiation: Direct, Indirect, and Expense Allowance.

Pick the items based on:

1) likelihood of success,
2) whether you were recruited or courted for the job,
3) the items that makes sense due to the dynamics of the position, and
4) the most important items to you.

Tip: Remember to thank the employer for the job offer, express excitement, and use your scripts before negotiating!

Direct (Monetary)

- A sign on bonus (does not accrue for the employer or you—very popular way to make up a difference)
- A salary bump in the new fiscal year (gives time for the organization to budget in increases)
- A performance based salary bump in the new fiscal year (same as above but based on defined performance metrics)
- A performance-based bonus structure or increase in the existing percentage

Indirect (Non-Monetary)

- Additional vacation time
- A better job title (most future job transitions are based on the title you currently hold)
- Guaranteed Severance Package (if company might become insolvent, bankrupt or lays you off due to no fault of your own - more likely in startup or "turnaround" situations)
- An office or better office space
- Flexible scheduling (like four 10-hour shifts)
- Telecommute/remote work
- New laptop, computer, tablet, software, tools
- More or different duties and projects to ensure your continued professional development
- An earlier salary review than the typical 6 months or a year

Expense Allowance Items (depending on job):

- Phone bill subsidy (more likely when a person has to be on call, better than getting a company phone because they do not see calls)
- Transportation (especially if directly recruiting you and the new job is far from home - this may be temporary until a promised move)
- Housing costs (especially if directly recruiting you to a different city)
- Daycare reimbursement (especially if they are directly courting you out of "stay-at-home" status or If the job requires a move and loss of family support
- Wardrobe allowance (if meeting with high-powered clients in a forward-facing position)
- Moving expenses (warning- this is considered income and will be taxable)

- Pay for education and certification (need masters or specialized certification)
- A coach or consultant (speaking, selling, media, executive leadership, management, language...)
- Professional development (work-related conferences, workshops, classes, or membership in a professional association)

>Homework

The key to successful negotiations is to understand what value the employer has placed on the job and to use this information in salary quoting. Successfully getting to a job offer means being able to predict and quote this value. The amount has less to do with the highest earning possible in your field and more to do with the highest value of the range that the employer has placed on the position. The key to more money is to express gratitude, to state the value of the job, to state the value of your skills, and to be able to evaluate the whole compensation package.

Quiz 8: Salary Negotiations (T/F)

1.___ Desired Salary is how much you want to make.
2.___ Desired Salary is how much you are worth.
3.___ If the job asks for a Bachelor's Degree but you have a Master's Degree, the job will pay more due to your degree.
4.___ If you have a Bachelor's and the job only requires a High School diploma, it will pay more.
5.___ Salary negotiations are only about the base salary amount.
6.___ There are good ways to get more money that do not include a bump in salary.
7.___ There are two types of internal salary negotiations.
8.___ Salary negotiations are only based on the capabilities you bring to the job.
9.___ You can negotiate based on increased expenses.
10.___ A poorly done salary negotiation can end the job offer, and ability to negotiate is a final evaluation method.

Chapter 8: Answer Key (T/F)

1) False: If you want the interview and offer, desired salary is what the job is worth.
2) False: If you want the interview and offer, desired salary is what the job is worth.
3) False: The Master's is valued as a Bachelor's unless the job specifically asks for the higher level degree.
4) False: A job requiring a High School diploma will pay less no matter your degree level.
5) False: There are over 20 monetary and non-monetary items that can be negotiable.
6) True: There are many alternative salary negotiation items.

7) True: Salary adjustment (prevailing wage proof) and raise negotiations (merit-based)

8) False: Salary Negotiations are based on the person's skill value and experience, outside prevailing wage, the internal budget of the department, equity issues in the department, and the ability to find those skills.

9) False: Negotiate on strengths and prevailing wage. In general, the only time expense can be negotiated is with existing employee situations where the employer is dictating job changes that will incur expenses.

10) True: Yes, employers especially expect senior staff to be able to evaluate the entire value or a position as an indication of their ability to evaluate anything. If done poorly, an offer will be rescinded.

Chapter 9: Networking to Get a Job: Alternative Strategies

Once you have done the "Campaign Kickoff" and start getting interviews, there are additional steps to consider that will increase the number of interviews you get. Many candidates want to start with the methods presented in this chapter but the latest research suggests that "networking to get a job" is not the most prevalent method of getting hired. If you are leveraging your experience and degrees to make a step up, down, or laterally into a different industry, the campaign kickoff is the most reliable method to get great results. However, some candidates want to change their profession and industry into something completely different from their existing skills and education. In that case, the strategies discussed in this section are especially important, because a resume alone is not going to achieve your goals.

Many of us have heard two common phrases about hiring: 1) it's all who you know and 2) you have to network to get a job. A third common belief is that the Human Resource department is a gatekeeper that blocks great hires. This section explores the common myths and beliefs about networking to get a job and some of the newer methods to accomplish your career goals.

This chapter includes the following lessons:
9.1 – Networking Myths
9.2 – Making a List of Champions & Informational Interviews
9.3 – Volunteering

9.4 – Staffing Agencies, Freelance/Gigs, and Title & Reference Swap

9.1 Networking Myths

Myth 1: Hiring is all who you know.
This can sometimes be true depending on your age. LinkedIn recently performed a survey to report on "job seeker trends: why and how people change jobs." The results of the survey by generation is below.

Top Places People First Hear About Their New Job by Generation
- Millennials (18-35): Job Boards
- Gen X (36-50): Third Party Recruiter
- Baby Boomers (51+): Someone I know

This will not surprise most Millennials - you have to go out and look for a job. Since newspapers are not used much anymore, it is also not a surprise this generation sources their positions via online job boards. Third party recruiters, in general, are not targeting millennials due to lower income and lower commission on placement.

For the Gen X group, the third party recruiting industry is a critical tool in career progression. This is the largest labor pool for leadership positions due to age and experience. Recruiters tend to seek out candidates with the income earning power of $65,000, in part because their earnings are based on a percentage of the new hire's annual salary. The entire campaign kickoff is dedicated to tapping the recruiter's search for talent.

They do search for Millennials and Boomers, but their largest percentage of placement at this time are Gen-Xers.

The Baby Boomers are the only generation to report that they are primarily identifying their most recent position through "who they know." The success of this strategy for Boomers may be more indicative of the length of time it takes to build a strong network capable of helping someone get a career, rather than indicating this is a superior way to find a job. Boomers need more personal referrals to get work due to age and income issues, and are less inclined towards technology compared to previous generations.

For Millennials and Gen X, the methods taught in the preceding chapters directly match the primary ways that talent is being sourced for new positions. Boomers, the campaign kickoff can assist your professional contacts' ability to help you by presenting a job-market matched profile. For the B2W mom, there may be a source of re-entry work within your network that will help close the gap. So, we need to do everything in the preceding chapters along with networking.

Myth 2: Networking to get a job is easier.

Generally speaking, this is not true. For someone to want to help you, either 1) you are qualified for a position that they have influence over, 2) they have influence over any type of hiring, 3) they care and trust you will deliver if they refer you, and/or 4) they naturally like to develop and help people.

Myth 4: Networking to get a job is faster.

No, this is definitely not true. Networking to get a job can significantly extend your job search compared to the methods used in this book, in which a candidate's background is matched to open positions.

Myth 5. Networking can result in complete career changes.

This can be true. If a candidate wants or needs to change professions and industries, then this is not a "resume-fix." Even if you can technically do a job, that does not mean the market considers you qualified. In the situation where a job candidate does not have specific experience or does not want the open position that matches their experience and education, an employer will not view them as qualified. For instance, a candidate who has worked in journalism writing for a newspaper is not necessarily qualified for a social media marketing specialist, even though those two fields are related to each other. In certain circumstances, leveraging the people you know may be the only way to get a job.

Myth 6. If you have no experience to put on the resume, alternative methods are the only way.

This one is true. A resume cannot fix everything. Some career change candidates want to make total and complete career changes. For instance, I had a tenured Professor in Health Sciences that wanted to do water stream cleanups. There is not much you can do to a resume that is going to help with that career change. Volunteering and working a network can play a large part in these job moves.

Myth 7: Bypassing the gatekeeper is a great strategy.

Sometimes this is true, but there are complexities to this strategy. Bypassing the gatekeeper assumes that HR is blocking great candidates from the hiring manager. Remember that HR is supposed to be doing their job. Perhaps their reason for blocking a candidate is completely valid. However, most candidates have at least one experience where their resume was "quarterbacked" or taken directly to the hiring manager with great results.

LinkedIn offers a modern way to bypass the gatekeeper. Even if this seems desirable, the HR department does not take kindly to being subverted by a job candidate. A hiring manager has primary job duties that do not include hiring and may not want these types of interruptions to their day from a stranger. We will cover this more in the next section.

First, we will explore working a list of champions.

9.2 Making a List of Champions and Informational Interviews

When clients are asked to make a list of people who can help them with their job search, the response over 85% of the time is "I do not know anyone." However, the majority of the time, the candidate does in fact have valuable contacts. Often, the person who will ultimately help you is someone completely unexpected, not necessarily someone who is close to you. The person who helps generally fits one of three categories.

1. They are natural people developers.
2. They care about you personally.
3. They know about a job that fits your background and may even get extra pay for referring a qualified candidate.

The problem is there is no way to pre-identify those people easily. Do not discount anyone in your network and extended network, or even people that are not in your network yet.
This list below presents ideas about the type of people to put on your networking list:

• **People working in organizations that can really use your skill set:** These champions work somewhere that may really need your skills. So, in this case, think of employers and positions and work backwards to identify people you know.

• **People in Professional Organizations or Meetup.com Groups:** There are people meeting every day who you do not know with whom you can network to get valuable industry information and contacts. Look for these groups and start attending meetings.

• **People who are in a hiring capacity:** Do you know people who can make direct hiring decisions? The type of work they hire for may be completely unrelated to your skills and you will need to convince them of your fit or willingness to try something new.

• **People developers:** Do you know someone who has helped someone else get a job? Reach out to anyone you know who has the personality and who really enjoys this.

• **Mentors for informational interviews:** There may be people working in certain fields who you suspect might be a fit for your background. A great way to get feedback and also present yourself as a possible candidate without asking for their help to get a job is to alter your resume and set up a discussion to see if the resume fits the role.

• **People in your telephone, email, and LinkedIn list of contacts and their contacts:** Anyone in your contact lists and people they know may be an asset in your job search.

In the following exercise, a list of contacts will be made. You will then create a strategy on how to build a list and talk to the people you identify in your network. It is important to note again that expecting a job lead should be secondary in this approach. The goal is to send out signals of your skills and candidacy and to receive educational information about careers you may not have known about. It may result in a job lead later on.

Exercise 9.2a: Make a List of Champions

Start creating a list of people and where they work. Reach out via email, telephone, and LinkedIn emails. Use these ideas to start creating a list.

• People working at organizations that can use your skills.
• Professional organizations or meetup.com meetings you can attend.
• People that work in a hiring capacity no matter what the type of job.

• People that like to help people get jobs.
• People who can perform a resume review and provide an informational interview about a certain field.

Exercise 9.2b: Talk to Your Network

Before you make contact, find out the person's title, industry, and type of work. Be prepared to interview them with the following ideas in mind:

• If possible, locate a job in which you are qualified for positions or organizations that person can influence. Prepare your matching resume. Do normal interview preparation.
• People can support passion and concepts. If you have great soft skills, even if you are missing the "hard-skill" work experience, a good dose of reasonable passion can overcome missing technical abilities.

If this is more of a true "informational" interview, use the questions below to generate a conversation. Most likely this will not result in a job, but you can obtain career guidance.

• What does a day in your work life look like?
• What educational program or certification is typical for this field?
• What is a typical career path for this field?
• Are there nontraditional ways to obtain work experience in this field?
• What are the important keywords and skills to highlight on a resume?

- What are areas of job opportunities that are in demand that I might be able to fit into?

Based on their answers, say the following:
"I have done some of the work you are describing. For instance, I did _____, _____, _____." (List relevant experiences matching what they described). *Do you think an employer would be interested in my experiences as it applies to this position? If so, how do you recommend I highlight it?"*

9.3 Volunteering

If a job candidate has a goal to work in one type of position that is completely unrelated to their background, volunteering can be helpful in the following unexpected ways:

- Volunteer in exchange for a title and recommendation.
- Fill in gaps on the resume.
- Send the message that you are seeking work.
- If the volunteering is professional, and potentially for the desired organization, it offers a sample of your work.
- If you want to enter into the nonprofit field and can identify a professional level experience, volunteering can demonstrate your skills.
- Volunteering can make networking easier because you are actually doing something, versus cold-networking which is difficult for most people.
- This can be in the form of a leadership opportunity which looks good on the resume.

Here are a few examples of volunteer opportunities that ultimately resulted in job interviews or offers.

• A candidate with no formal work experience talked to friends who owned their own business, needed help, but could not afford to pay. The candidate worked for no money in exchange for a title, work experience, and a recommendation. This filled in a gap on the candidate's resume and taught him new skills.
• Another person volunteered to help at industry conferences. This was much easier than trying to network and she got to know the people who were active in the field, which resulted in a job.
• The candidate who wanted to leave her professor job to do stream clean up worked for a local environmental nonprofit. She volunteered doing grant-writing, fundraising, developing plans, and volunteer coordination, and was offered a position after about six months of volunteering.
• Sometimes a variety of candidates will get leads from volunteering with their hobbies, which makes them happy and promotes networking. Their happiness is infectious and it can open the door to people helping them with job leads.

Note: Organizations may use and abuse volunteers. It can be a real waste of time and very frustrating to spend too much effort in this area. One way to protect yourself is to focus on opportunities which demonstrate your level of professional abilities. Locate professional project opportunities to "try on" a new position with no expense to the employer. Set boundaries and well-defined limits to your contribution. Remember, the happier you are doing it, the more likely it is to result in an opportunity.

In the following exercise, you will brainstorm about different possible volunteer opportunities that can leverage your career change.

Exercise 9.3 Make a list of possible volunteer opportunities.

Exchange volunteer work for job title and a recommendation. Identify businesses needing free help that can offer you valuable experience, a title, and a reference to help get your career change moving.

If you desire to work in the nonprofit industry, seek out targeted volunteer experiences that demonstrate your abilities to the organization. (Be careful to not let the organization take advantage of you.)

Find professional conferences that allow you to attend for free in exchange for networking.

9.4 Staffing Agencies, Freelance/Gigs, and Title and Reference Swap

There are many opportunities for employers and candidates to work with each other first before making a long-term commitment. These short-term contract employment opportunities can facilitate powerful life-altering career changes. They can also help cover gaps. Yes, this is one of the core re-entry strategies for the B2W mom.

Staffing Agencies

If someone is currently employed, it may not make sense to leave a full-time job for a contract position. However, when someone is really ready to move on, or is unemployed, it is worth exploring these options. In this section, there is a differentiation between a staffing agency and a Third Party Recruiter.

One of the primary benefits of this method is that the interview process can be very short or nonexistent because the focus is on skill based questions. Because this may not be a "marriage for life" there is less interest in the long-term motivations of the candidate. Also, a staffing agency is more likely to consider a functional style resume and may use assessments to verify candidate requirements.

A staffing agency usually places for positions in office administration, accounting, and manufacturing opportunities. Not only can these opportunities be beneficial in making a career change but these staffing agencies are often used by employers for other opportunities that come up because they already have a recruiting agreement with the organization. Adecco and Kelly Services are well-known names in the staffing world for professional office work. These two organizations also have divisions that place science and engineering opportunities.

Positions with staffing agencies often have lower expectations of their placements, which allows candidates with large gaps in their resume to obtain work. These contract opportunities allow for job changes that would not otherwise be possible. Do not ignore the possibilities of obtaining work through these agencies.

In addition to staffing agencies, some industries like publishing have had freelance opportunities for decades. The freelance concept has become even more popular now, to the point that newspapers write about how our economy is changing into a "gig economy." Obtaining short term or one-project-at-a-time opportunities can build a portfolio of work and referrals that allow for a permanent career change. Gigs are typically found through a person's network of family, friends, colleagues or websites like Craigslist.com, Elance.com and Odesk.com. Like staffing agency contracts, this can be a powerful way to move careers.

Freelance/Gigs: Create Your Own Business and Select the Right Title

Freelancing or gigs is not just about seeking work experience. It is also about creating your own business. This can be a primary method of covering large employment gaps or of facilitating a complete career change by presenting recent history that matches your goal position. There are many professionals who freelance alongside their regular job. They may wish to create a business that will replace their income, make a side income, or they are dynamic individuals with many interests. It is possible to present your freelance and side gigs in a way that facilitates job acquisition.

With this strategy, candidates create a business name (one that does not currently exist) and creates a title for themselves as if they were working for someone else. It is important to title yourself with the likely title of your next position. For instance, don't say you are CEO of a marketing agency when the likely job for your skill level is Marketing Coordinator. Instead, make a business, title yourself Marketing Coordinator, and present yourself as an employee working for the self-owned company.

Title and Reference Swap: Work in Exchange for Learning, Title, and Reference (Internship Strategy)

This strategy is recommended when someone is really stuck or absolutely committed to heading in a new career direction. Find a small business in need of assistance related to what you want to do. Ask the business owner to exchange work, paid or not, for the ability to gain experience, receive a title, and have a strong reference. This is similar to an internship. For the older experienced candidate, it is better to call it a short-term contract than an internship.

This works for some fields better than for others. For instance, social media marketing has a large growth trajectory right now and there is a low supply of experienced workers. Someone interested in this work could do use this method to implement digital campaigns in exchange for a title and reference on their resume.

Creative temporary work arrangements from staffing agencies, freelance opportunities, and gigs are an additional angle in an overall strategy. They are not better or worse than full-time opportunities; they are different, and can be used to your advantage. If you have no experience in a certain field, this is sometimes the only way to make a move in a new direction because it provides proof of your ability to handle the new job duties. This can really work well for step downs or for a return to work after an extensive period of unemployment.

Exercise 9.4 Short-Term or Temporary Contracts Checklist

Use the checklist to become aware of and use short-term contract opportunities to earn money and change careers.

_____ **Staffing Agencies:** Look for contract or permanent-to-hire positions with staffing agencies In your field of interest. You can search on Indeed.com for this using the appropriate filter. It may be better to go straight to the agency's website to look for jobs or walk into a local office and talk to a staffing person.

_____ **Freelance Gigs:** Look for freelance work within your network to help fill in the gaps, get new types of work experience, and keep yourself busy and making money while you continue your search.

_____ **Title and Reference Swap:** Exchange work, paid or not, for the ability to gain experience, receive a title, and have a strong reference.

>Homework

If you are trying to go for a job for which you have absolutely no recent paid work experience, you will likely need to leverage your network, a staffing agency, or volunteering to make a shift. It is not a resume "fix" because a resume presents what you have done. You can search for roles that are different but will still need some background for the resume to do its job.

Quiz 9: Networking (T/F)
1.___ Hiring is "all who you know."
2.___ Alternative strategies are needed if work background is missing for the job.
3.___ People in hiring manager capacity make the most effective champions.
4.___ People of different ages get jobs in different ways.
5.___ HR acts as a Gatekeeper and blocks candidates the Hiring Manager would consider.
6.___ Volunteering can open doors.
7.___ Finding freelance gigs or short-term contracts can cover gaps and direct your search.
8.___ Staffing firms can overcome large gaps in work.
9.___ You can exchange work for title to assist in getting a job.
10.___ All gigs and volunteer opportunities offer the same level of opportunity

Chapter 9: Answer Key (T/F)
1) False: Recruiters search and hire complete "unknowns" every day.
2) True: This may be the only way to get a job if the candidate has no matching experience.
3) False: People who are people developers or that care about you tend to be more effective.
4) True: Millennial=Job Boards, GenXers=Recruiters, Baby Boomers=Network.
5) True: HR does act as a "Gatekeeper" and blocks for many reasons.
6) True: Volunteering can help but, when used for career be strategic about it.

7) True: Freelance gigs and short-term contracts can overcome gaps and shift careers.

8) True: Staffing firms' temp and temp-to-hire jobs can overcome gaps in work.

9) True: There are some fields that may permit work in exchange for title and reference.

10) False: The more targeted to your goal position, the better the opportunity.

Chapter 10: Advanced LinkedIn Strategies

Once you have done the "Campaign Kickoff" and have keyword-stacked your profile for your target position, there are advanced opportunities via LinkedIn to reach straight into an organization. This strategy can be a very powerful form of networking. In 2015, I added this unique strategy following a client that went from 24 connections to over 500 in a week's time resulting in four job interview requests without applying for a single job.

Advanced LinkedIn search is a unique networking strategy that is ideal for job candidates who meet the following criteria:
- Every working professional between 18-65 years of age,
- A one-company hyper-targeted focus,
- Highly-specialized professional field, and
- Low job supply.

Every working professional
Any professional that is 18-65 years old needs to be networking. In this section, we will learn that LinkedIn is programmed to function better for professionals with a high number of connections. This means that connecting with many people is not an exercise in popularity, it is maximizing the functionality of the system. At the time of this publication, this networking hack also means you can unlock the benefits of LinkedIn without paying for a costly LinkedIn Premium account.

This is also the easiest form of networking you will ever do in your lifetime. My introverted candidates will LOVE this form of connecting. With a few clicks you can offer a virtual handshake and send your electronic business card to thousands of targeted people. It is much quicker and effective than going to a cold in-person networking event.

When is it a good time to start networking? You intuitively know that it is better to have a network built BEFORE you need it. However, if you have not built it yet, and you need a job right now, you can still quickly leverage the benefits of LinkedIn advanced search to build and communicate with your network.

One-company hyper-targeted focus
There is a growing trend, particularly with job candidates under the age of 30, to become hyper-focused on working for one specific company like Google, Facebook, or other unique players. Highly desirable companies sometimes have a very long hire cycle and the entry-role is lower than what the professional could obtain with another company. There have been cases where a candidate was sourced and qualified for employment but had to wait a year or more for a position to open. That candidate may have been able to obtain a position with greater breadth, depth, and income with another organization. I advise you to run a general campaign and a hyper-targeted method at the same time to ensure the most job interviews. You need both quantity and quality to succeed.

Highly-specialized professional field
Some candidates work in very specialized fields and, over time, they will work with many of the same colleagues, creating a "very small world." This can be common in the science, research, and creative fields. In this instance, it is a good idea to constantly

expand and maintain a wide network of contacts through these advanced methods. This can offer protection from unemployment and stimulate advancement opportunities over time.

Low job supply
As in highly-specialized fields, there are certain professionals that either work in fields or locations with a low supply of jobs, or they have reached an executive level which automatically reduces the supply of positions. These methods may be necessary to maintain continued employment over the long-term.

Most candidates that are interested in an advanced LinkedIn strategy ask themselves one question: Should I pay for a LinkedIn Premium account? The following section offers advice and recommendations to that question along with advanced strategies that work.

* Note: The optimized LinkedIn profile taught in the Campaign Kickoff section is critical for success with this method because the first information a contact will see is your profile headline, location, and picture, not your resume. The profile has to be 100% direct-hit match to your goal to get results.

This chapter includes the following lessons:
10.1 – Advanced LinkedIn Strategy Myths
10.2 – LinkedIn Premium – To Buy or Not to Buy
10.3 – Networking 2.0 via a LinkedIn Connection Campaign

10.1 Advanced LinkedIn Strategy Myths

Myth 1: A LinkedIn Premium account is required to use advanced strategies.

No! At this moment, LinkedIn Premium is not required for the advanced strategies, which require search abilities which are available for free. The benefit structure of a Premium account is not well-designed to help someone "get a job" at this time. The following lesson will discuss the attributes of a Premium membership to assist in purchase decisions.

Myth 2: An advanced strategy requires specialized research skills.

No! I will teach you how to search for and communicate with the right individuals.

Myth 3: Advanced LinkedIn strategies are the best way to get a job.

No! The "Campaign Kickoff" taught in this book is the best way to get a job. However, once that method has been implemented, a job candidate will want to use advanced strategies to increase their interviews.

Myth 4: Advanced LinkedIn strategies are only for Executive-level positions.

No! This method can be used for any level of employment.

Myth 5: I have to know which company I want to work for to perform an Advanced LinkedIn strategy.

No! There are a multiple search parameters available including industry, location, and professional title.

Myth 6: The primary use of an advanced Linked strategy is to bypass the gatekeeper.

Yes and no. One goal is to use LinkedIn to network and bypass formal hiring procedures and the Human Resource department. However, in some cases it may be used to reach out and network with recruiters, hiring managers, and employees to "get on their radar."

Myth 7: Inmail and email are the same thing.

No. LinkedIn has an internal email system called Inmail. You can only Inmail 1st connections.

Let's dig in and explore the advanced strategies that can be used with LinkedIn. I cannot stress enough that you absolutely must have a keyword-stacked optimized profile for your goal position for these methods to work. Perform the Campaign Kickoff first.

10.2 LinkedIn Premium -To Buy or Not to Buy

The following lesson is used to help a candidate make a purchase decision in regards to LinkedIn Premium. At this time, purchase is not recommended or needed for an advanced LinkedIn strategy. However, this is a hot topic for job candidates right now which requires further explanation.

LinkedIn Premium is a paid account which professionals can use to access more features of the website. From a "double the interviews and leverage recruiters" perspective, the concept is to use LinkedIn to directly communicate with recruiters, or bypass the gatekeeper completely by contacting hiring managers or other employees personally. For this to work well, everything else taught in this book about matching your profile to job opportunities must be complete because the contact will primarily understand who you are through your LinkedIn profile.

With LinkedIn Premium, a professional can pay $30 a month or more for a LinkedIn Premium account. Below is a list of the attributes of the paid account.

LinkedIn Premium Attributes

1. LinkedIn Premium Badge
2. You surface higher in recruiter search
3. You can see who viewed your profile
4. Larger search parameters
5. At least three 'free' Inmails (LinkedIn's internal messaging system) per month

Let's review each benefit.

1. LinkedIn Premium Badge

There are some theories on the value of the LinkedIn Premium Badge. It can make a professional look more elite and established in their career but this is largely a perception. For someone seeking a job, it has a very limited impact because we know that the employer is looking for a direct-hit match to their needs, not someone who looks elite.

2. Surface higher in recruiter search

This is the only true "job getting" benefit of a Premium membership. Job candidates may be willing to pay for a Premium account if it will boost their chances of being found. The idea is that, if a recruiter is looking for a candidate with your qualifications, your Premium profile should surface higher in the rankings for their search terms. For instance, if there are 50 candidates, instead of being #45 perhaps you will be listed as #10. On paper this sounds good, but there is no way to verify if this works. To test the benefit, try one month of LinkedIn Premium. If there is an uptick in recruiter contacts, then this method is working for your background. If you receive no new reach outs, then this method will not be a good reason to maintain a paid LinkedIn Premium account.

3. See who looked at your profile

Some people want to know who is looking at them on LinkedIn. In hiring, this will have limited value. If a recruiter looks at your profile but does not reach out to you, contacting them is not going to help much. It might be deemed inappropriate to contact someone who viewed your profile but did not reach out (like calling an unidentified telephone number back after they called you but did not leave a message).

4. Larger search parameters

As reviewed in the beginning of this book, a recruiter can search for a job candidate among a variety of parameters; keyword, location, industry, and job title. Technically everyone can do this through the free advanced search option on LinkedIn, however when a recruiter or a job candidate pays more, they can search by a greater number of parameters. The parameter of interest to most recruiters is "rank" like Director, Manager, or Vice President. This has limited value to the job candidate. At this moment, the parameters needed by a job candidate are available for free.

5. *"Free Inmails"*

This is pitched as the biggest "job-getting" benefit for a Premium account. A Premium member can contact at least five non-connections per month and pay for at least ten more Inmails. These numbers can increase based on more expensive LinkedIn packages. There is a popular "free" way of doing the same thing so this has very limited value to a candidate.

The key to LinkedIn for most users is not a paid Premium membership. This will come as a relief for some job seekers who want to leverage LinkedIn to get more interviews, bypass the gatekeeper, or extend their professional network but do not want to pay $30 a month for questionable value. Refer back to chapter 4 which discusses online optimization and the free "Recruiter Push" function to get the maximum benefit from a LinkedIn.com account.

As we know, social media changes quickly and I will not be surprised if my recommendations about LinkedIn Premium change as the website develops. For now, LinkedIn Premium is not necessary. Let's review how to perform the advanced job search strategies that are available at no charge to the candidate.

10.3 Networking 2.0 via a LinkedIn Connection Campaign

The purpose of doing a LinkedIn advanced search connection campaign is to 1) capture low-hanging fruit, 2) offer another point of connection, and 3) become a 1st Degree Connection.

Low hanging fruit
A new connection may say *'oh, look at this person. They are perfect for that position I have coming open soon. I should talk to them.'* Yes, this does happen.

Offer another point of connection
Many large companies complain that they receive over 500 resumes for one position. An advanced LinkedIn campaign offers another point of introduction to the employer. It is a virtual handshake that passes them your electronic business card. An overwhelmed hiring manager may say *'this person is obviously interested in the role. I should consider them for my pool of candidates.'* Yes, this does happen.

Become a 1st Degree Connection
The hack I am about to teach you is far more effective than the paltry amount of Inmails you get with a LinkedIn Premium account. The reason you want to get connected is that you can Inmail a 1st degree connection for free as often as you like (within the confines of professionalism). If they are not a 1st degree connection, you have to pay to contact them.

As a professional that needs a job, you want to bypass the barriers placed in your way by connecting, networking, and contacting potential hiring managers in a friendly way. The following are the steps you need to take to maximize LinkedIn.

Exercise 9.3a 2nd Degree 'Quick Connect' Campaign

Initial Connections

If you have not connected with many LinkedIn members yet, it will be necessary to go to 'my network' and load up your email accounts and also seek out people that you know that may already be highly connected. For instance, a pastor of a large church, a friend that works in Human Resources, or an entrepreneur that is very networked in the community. Tapping your existing network opens up many initial 2nd degree 'quick connect' options.

2nd Degree 'Quick Connect' Steps

Click on the Advanced Search Feature on your LinkedIn profile which is the magnifying glass at the top of your home page.

The First Pass

Do a job search on LinkedIn and Indeed to see companies hiring for your various keywords and start making a list of the company names. Then take the company name that was hiring and do a general search and seek out 2nd level connections which allow the 'quick connect' feature. Send a 'quick connect.' A first pass can also be targeted by potential locations in a targeted industry and city.

The goal of the first pass is to connect with at least one person, literally any person, at each company. This connection can open up 'a universe' of 2nd connections at that company.

Second Pass

Now that you have gained one connection you will have the option for many more 2nd degree 'quick connects.' Sometimes this can be overwhelming. Just one new highly networked 1st degree connection can open up thousands of 2nd degree connections you did not have prior to the 'first pass.' Therefore, this may require a more targeted search for keywords or titles that are related to your professional skills. For instance, recruiter, human resource, VP of Marketing, Director of I.T, Help Desk Manager...etc.. You can also narrow down the target location, or remain open and do a broad 2nd degree 'quick connect' campaign with all your options at that company.

Select combinations of the following:
- Current company - enter the goal company name
- Title - enter job title
  - Title of peers (your title or titles from the Core-3$^{©}$)
  - Recruiter or human resources
  - Hiring manager title (your boss's title or similar)
- Location - leave blank or enter specific city
- Review results and click the "connect" button

Remember, this is softly handing out your virtual business card to more people at the company which will start raising awareness about you as a candidate and potentially capture low-hanging fruit. You are not necessarily saying anything – just clicking connect.

Repeat the first and second pass as often as necessary to target new companies, locations, industries, or professionals holding a certain title.

Exercise 9.3b Networking with your 1st Degree Connections

You now have many 1st degree connections that you can Inmail for free. This final step is optional in most cases. For instance, if your profile is optimized, online, and you are now well connected, you should already be the recipient of many job interviews. However, if you need or want to start reaching out on a more personal level to your 1st degree connections, use the following Inmail scripts.

Inmail Content to Peers

- *(Name), thanks for the connection. I have been interested in working for (company name) and would like to network with you to see what the job requirements are and if any openings may be coming up.*

Inmail to Recruiters

- Recruiter Email Content (No Advertisement):
(Name), thanks for the connection. I have been interested in working for (company name) and would like to network with you to see what the job requirements are and if any openings may be coming up.

- Recruiter Email Content (Advertised Job):

(Name), thanks for the connection. I have applied for (position title) and would like to network with you about the job. Based on my background in (previous titles, education, professional experience), I feel I would be a unique fit for the role.

Likely Hiring Manager Inmail Content

- Hiring Manager Inmail Content (No Advertised Job):

(Name), thanks for the connection. I am interested in working on your team and would like to network with you see if any openings may be coming up. Based on my background in (previous titles, education, professional experience), I feel I would be a unique fit for the team. Please review my profile and consider my background for your open role.

- Hiring Manager Inmail Content (Advertised Job):

(Name), thanks for the connection. I am interested in your team's (position title) position. I have applied for the position but have not heard back. Based on my background in (previous titles, education, professional experience), I feel I would be a unique fit for the role. Please review my profile and consider my background for your open role.

In recap, this final goal of the advanced connection campaign allows you to Inmail for free. You may never really have to use this stage but the option will be there for you which, if you had not done the connection campaign, would not exist without paying for LinkedIn Premium and, even with that, you get 10 Inmails per month. This is a much more elegant method of doing it for free and capturing low-hanging fruit in a 'nice' collegial way. Most LinkedIn members are still very click happy and non-protectionist towards connecting.

>Homework

It is much easier to learn how to do these campaigns via the online class. In addition, LinkedIn is always changing. Join the class to remain current on new campaigns and strategies. I use these methods every day for my clients. When I see a change or develop a winning campaign, I record a new video module and update the class.

Quiz 10: Advanced LinkedIn Strategies (T/F)
1. ___ A paid LinkedIn Premium membership is helpful in getting a job.
2. ___ The advanced strategy is really a free LinkedIn search function.
3. ___ Advanced LinkedIn strategies are the best way to get a job.
4. ___ All professional levels can use free advanced LinkedIn strategies.
5. ___ LinkedIn search can be by title, profession, or company.
6. ___ A popular use for advanced search is to bypass the HR gatekeeper.
7. ___ Just connecting can result in job interviews.
8. ___ A paid Premium membership is necessary to communicate with non-connections.
9. ___ A 2nd Degree connection can be personalized or just a quick handshake and electronic business card pass.
10. ___ The only way networking with LinkedIn can be productive is if I personally reach out to all connections.

Chapter 10: Answer Key (T/F)
1) False: Premium offers little or no help in getting a job (right now).
2) True: The advanced method is a free search function.
3) False: This is one step following the Campaign Kickoff.
4) True: Any professional level can use and benefit from these free techniques.
5) True: LinkedIn search allows a number of search parameters.

6) True: Getting around HR is a popular reason to use advanced search.
7) True: The act of connecting itself can result in 'low hanging fruit.'
8) False: The 2nd Degree 'quick connect' allows you the potential to communicate for free.
9) True: Yes- you can write a personalized note on your 'quick connect' or perform a quantity campaign.
10) False: The act of connecting, when your profile is optimized, can result in job interviews. The option will be there later to do personalized networking.

Chapter 11: Unique Career Change Types and Strategies

The beginning of the B2W mom book teaches the strategy necessary to overcome the gap on your resume. The overall Stacked strategy is a campaign kickoff that teaches you how to keyword-stack your resume and online job board profiles to leverage recruiters. This section is dedicated to special issues that do not apply to every single candidate and therefore have been divided into different lessons. There are about 10 unique career changes you could make in a lifetime. Let's take a look at some myths and common beliefs about career changes and then dive into job search, resume, and interview strategies that are common with each unique type.

This chapter includes the following lessons:
11.1 – Career change common myths
11.2 – Lateral career moves
11.3 – Overqualified-step down
11.4 – Move for promotion
11.5 – Return to a prior profession
11.6 – New graduate or entry-level
11.7 – New industry
11.8 – New profession (complete career change)
11.9 – Gaps on resume
11.10 – Geographic relocations

11.1 Career Change Common Myths

Myth 1. There are no resume or interview challenges when making a lateral move.

A lateral move typically is a job change into a position that is virtually the same title and industry. However, at this point in the course you know that candidates can reposition themselves for market opportunities by highlighting skills that match the job advertisement so that recruiters can identify you as qualified for the role. Whether the most recent title matches the future position or not, this process essentially mimics the look and feel of a lateral move.

Even though the lateral move is the easiest career change to make, it can still be difficult to explain your job transition goals. An employer will wonder why you would want to leave one job for the next if the work is that similar, and this is a key reason candidates often get overlooked for positions even when they are a "shoe-in." Lesson 10.2 discusses strategies for "lateral moves."

Myth 2: Being over-qualified is a good thing in the job market.

It would seem that in a market hungry for skills, no candidate can be too "over-qualified." This unfortunately is not the case. When a candidate hears that they are over-qualified, the employer is essentially saying "I do not think you will be happy or that you will stay in this job." The hiring manager may also feel threatened if they hire someone with the same or higher level of experience. The goal is to make the resume and interview look like a lateral move but this can be especially difficult when a candidate has had upper-level titles. Because there are so many reasons a candidate could be tagged as overqualified, this will receive special treatment in lesson 10.3.

Myth 3. You can't achieve a promotion through a new position.

Actually, this is sometimes the *only* way to get a promotion because employees tend to be pigeon-holed by their employers. The key to achieving a promotion through a new job is to capture and communicate upper-level accomplishments for targeted skills required by the new job. This creates a lateral move even if your most recent title is at a lower or different level. Move-for-Promotion strategies are discussed in lesson 10.4.

Myth 4. You can't move back to a prior profession.

This is one of the most popular job moves to make and it is even easier if skills from the current position can be mixed with previous positions and industries. The challenge with this move is that the employer may perceive skills as stale if the candidate held the previous role a long time ago. In addition, explaining job transitions in a way that makes sense to the interviewer can take persistence. However, many incredible career changes can be made by leveraging previous roles. These strategies are covered in Lesson 10.5.

Myth 5. New graduates have no skills to leverage in the job market.

It is actually very rare for a new graduate to have no skills. There are ways to use classwork and even side jobs to locate new work. New graduates can also be attentive to ways to take on management roles in their pre-professional jobs or to seek temporary or contract work that can be leveraged later. New graduate strategies are covered in Lesson 10.6.

Myth 6. Switching industries is not possible.

This is often one of the easier career changes to make for a professional. A job candidate can neutralize or remove industry information and focus on professional category information to help make moves between industries. For instance, if an accountant is working in manufacturing and is seeking to move into a bank, the resume can remove all of the targeted manufacturing industry information and leave just accounting details. This strategy is covered in Lesson 10.7.

Myth 7. Switching both industries and professional categories is not possible.

This is where things can get tricky; next to being "overqualified" this is the most difficult career change. It is possible if you have an unusual mix of transferable skills, however these can often be lengthy career transitions, or, require a job candidate to angle in through alternative methods like a volunteer opportunity or short-term contract. Lesson 10.8 covers special strategies.

Myth 8. Years of experience, education, and level of responsibility are not that important.

The very first lesson in this book on how a recruiter uses LinkedIn should convince you that managing this information is a critical component of career change. A matching education is more important in quantitative fields like science, technology, engineering, accounting, finance, and math. Many other professional categories are tolerant of different educational backgrounds if the same level of education is present. Specific strategies on how to manage these issues are covered in lesson 10.9.

Myth 9. A history of many different types of jobs shows how flexible and adaptive I am.

That is not what the employer values. An employer wants to see a strong commitment to one path by the candidate. A candidate who changes professions, industries, and jobs often is usually perceived by the employer as someone who does not know what they want, is wishy-washy, lost, and (if the jobs were short-term) unreliable. Lesson 10.10 covers the creation of a cohesive storyline of a stable and happy employee.

Myth 10. Gaps between employment periods are the worst thing on the resume.

If a gap in employment is in the past and there is a more recent stable work history, the gap is practically irrelevant. The job market is accustomed to people losing jobs due to reorganizations, closures, and relocations, therefore a gap on the resume for those reasons is almost expected. If the gaps are current, you have to be very thoughtful in how you present your reason for leaving the last position. Lesson 10.11 presents a special section for assisting on this matter.

Myth 11. Relocating to a new city is no problem.

Actually, this can be a big problem. The employers know there is a large statistical link between how close a person lives to their job and the likelihood that they will stay. Applicant tracking systems are pre-programmed to search for distance to your zip code. If it is too far, you will be eliminated. Also, job candidates who relocate tend to have no support system and are very likely to return back to their home town or move somewhere else. There is an exception to this rule. Some professions have relocation built right into the work. Executives, professors, new doctors, and certain professionals virtually require a geographic relocation at some point in their career. For everyone else, lesson 10.12 offers different strategies.

Move to the lesson that most closely matches your job search goal at this point in your career.

11.2 Lateral Move Lesson

When a candidate is making a lateral career move, it typically means they are applying for positions that have the same title, and often with the same years of experience, level of responsibility, and industry experience. Let's explore some myths and beliefs about this type of career change.

11.2.1 Lateral Change Common Myths
Myth 1: There is only **one** basic lateral move for each person at any given time.

This is not true. Most candidates have at least three lateral moves possible at any given time in their career because jobs are multifaceted. Even if you feel that you do not want to be in the same field, there is a high degree of likelihood that one of your available lateral moves would match your career goals. The Core-3© helps identify these moves.

Myth 2: A candidate who is making a lateral move tends to have a higher degree of success in receiving calls on their resume because the profile has the keywords and stylistic appearance that recruiters identify as a good match for the position.

Yes, this statement is true. Lateral moves tend to be successful because the job candidate naturally understands how to present their background to match a direct market need. The job market can provide the profile information necessary for a candidate to build a lateral shift profile that represents a different work or lifestyle even though the market perceives the move as lateral. There are other types of career changes but this method produces the fastest and most profitable results.

Myth 3: Lateral career changers face no challenges on their resume or in the interview.

Even though this is the easiest career change to make there are still challenges. The Market-Based Resume Profile© recommendations are all designed to facilitate this career change, however there are more tips for aligning directly for a lateral move, which we will cover below.

Candidates making lateral moves often face unique challenges during the interview. If the person is currently employed and applying for the same position that they currently hold, the big question in the mind in the recruiter is, "Why would this candidate want to move into the same basic position that they currently have?" If the job candidate is currently unemployed, the recruiter may also ask themselves, "Is this a problem employee that created a bad situation at their previous employer and got fired or quit?"

Myth 4: A Lateral Move cannot be a "Move for Promotion."

A lateral move can also be a promotion if the candidate can verify that they have been performing work at a higher level than their title.

Myth 5: Moving for money or anger is a successful "reason for leaving" answer.

Another common issue with "lateral move" job candidates is that they are angry or extremely frustrated by their current career situation. Common sources of anger are pay, job conditions, or lack of promotions. Employers do not like to hire people that state these answers. Job candidates may feel frustrated because they feel they are being asked to lie in order to get a job offer and improve their life. The recommendation in both cases is to restate and find another truth that is more attractive to the employer.

The following exercises assist in lateral move resume changes and interview answers specific to a lateral move.

Exercise 11.2a: General "Lateral Move" Resume Tips

The following resume tips will help with lateral moves. Check them off to make sure you have done them.
1.____ Follow the Market-Based Resume Profile© techniques.
2.____ Match the skill need of the job advertisement -- line item by line item.
3.____ Do not oversell experiences.
4.____ Prepare accomplishments at the level of the new job - not over and not under.

Exercise 11.2b: Scripts and Explanations for Making a Lateral Move

The most important question that an interviewer has for a candidate making a lateral move is, "Why are you leaving your current position?" This information is sometimes asked on the job application under the section "reason for leaving" but it is most common during a phone screen and later while performing the in-person interviews. A candidate must select the answer that fits the new job they are applying for. Answers can be combined if there is more than one that applies. Money can be mentioned but typically not as the only answer.

Scripts and Explanations Based on Scenario

Situation 1: If the new job is closer to your house than the old job:
"This position is closer to home which will allow me to dedicate more time to work and less to commuting."

Situation 2: If the organization is dramatically smaller than the current organization:
"I prefer a smaller organization that is more personable than the large company I currently work for."

Situation 3: If the organization is dramatically larger than the current organization:
"I prefer a larger organization that offers growth opportunities."

Situation 4: If the organization offers a better schedule than the current position:
"This company offers a better schedule."

Situation 5: If the new organization pays better:
"This organization offers a better combined compensation package."

Situation 6: If your previous organization is closing or relocating:
"The organization I work for is _____ (closing, relocating, or there are funding changes)"

Situation 7: If your previous/current work environment is terrible for whatever reason and the above previous answers do not fit:
"The business I work for has re-organized and my work has dramatically changed. I enjoy doing the work that I have been doing _____ (state the skills the new job has)."

Situation 8: If there is growth or a better use of skills at the new organization.
"The business I work for has re-organized and my work has dramatically changed. I enjoy doing the work that I have been doing _____ (state the skills the new job has)."

Situation 9: If you are losing your job and the previous answers do not fit:
"Due to industry changes, the organization I work for has re-organized and my position is being eliminated."

11.3 Overqualified - Step Down Lesson

Many candidates in today's market are hearing that they are overqualified. This section explores myths and beliefs related to this career change.

11.3.1 Overqualified Common Myths

Myth 1: The only people that seek to take a "step down" are desperate unemployed people.

This is not true. There are five common reasons that candidates move on to positions that are technically a lower level of responsibility, title, or pay than their most recent position.

Step Down Assessment

Select any option that applies:
____ You are unemployed and need to find a job, any job, regardless of title or pay level.
____ You are tired of supervising people and want a non-supervisory role.
____ You have many skills and want to work in one functional area.
____ You are burned out from your current level of responsibility.
____ You are primarily motivated by priorities other than money.

Myth 2: The candidate determines if they are taking a "step-back" or "step down."

Sometimes a candidate will understand that the role is a step back; in other cases, the employer will surprise a candidate by telling them that the role is a "step down." Even when the job candidate feels the move is acceptable or desirable, the employer may fear the prospective employee will not be happy or will not stay in the position. Therefore, this can both be a conscious decision by the candidate or an unexpected, and unwelcome, employer announcement.

Myth 3: Candidates always know that they are applying for jobs that they are overqualified for.

As we just discussed, no, this is not true. There are instances where being "overqualified" comes as a surprise when the candidate feels they are perfectly suited for the position. Hearing the proclamation of "overqualified" is an indicator that the job is either below your skill level, below your expected pay level, or the new boss feels threatened by you. The resume either needs to be re-aligned more or you need to apply for positions that are at a higher level.

Myth 4: Having more skills should make it easier to move jobs.

That is not always true. Remember, making an exact match on many different factors, including skill and level of responsibility, is critical to avoid this issue. Of all the career changes, this is one of the most difficult to perform because employers do not trust that the candidate will be happy or that they will stay in a position that makes significantly less, or that has less responsibilities, than their most recent position.

<u>Myth 5: When the employer says overqualified it means just that - overqualified.</u>

This is not necessarily true. What the recruiter is really trying to tell the job candidate is the following:

"Although you may be qualified, I do not think you will be happy or stay in the position. I would rather seek someone with lesser skills than take the chance you will destabilize the team or force me into the hiring process again in a few months because you quit when you find something better."

Or ...

"You could easily do my job or my boss's job. I am not going to hire someone with the same level of skills or greater than mine and face competition or confrontation."

<u>Myth 6: I will get hired in a step-down position if I just tell the employer I need the job because of unemployment, burnout, personal preference, or passion.</u>

Although passionate commitment can sometimes get you a job, it typically does not work if your work experience is not there to back it up. These answers do not tell the recruiter that you will be a capable, happy, and stable employee. To manage this issue, you must re-position your image to match the level of responsibility of the position that you are applying for and tell the recruiter "I want this job." In addition, you must convince yourself that you want to make a step down. This is important because most people are not great actors. The recruiter can usually feel if a candidate is planning on quitting quickly. The most powerful statement a job candidate can tell a recruiter, both on the resume and in the interview, is that "this is the exact work I have done and I want this job." Saying it is not enough. You have to feel it too.

Myth 7: I can get a management position or lower once I have been a Director, Vice President, or some upper-level title.

Unfortunately, if you have upper level titles on your resume, it will be very challenging to take a step down. The advice throughout this program and in this section should be sufficient for a candidate who has not reached an executive level of employment. Most candidates can tailor their resume and their answers to present a customized "lateral" fit image for the position, even for a step-down.

If you have reached a title of Director or higher, you may need to consider moving for a new job, traveling for work, consulting, or becoming entrepreneurial to maintain employment. Unless you lie, your title is a giveaway of your level of responsibility. This is one of the reasons that candidates over fifty years of age can face challenges in the job market. Once an applicant has reached a high-level of employment, there simply may not be many jobs in one geographic location at that title.

Myth 8. Only older "upper-level" candidates are told they are overqualified.

This is absolutely not true. A candidate can be between ages 20 and 80 and still hear they are overqualified if the employer feels that the applicant has more skills than the job requires.

Myth 9. I can get the same pay rate as my highest responsibility position at a lower level job.

If you have reviewed the salary negotiations lessons, you will now know that every job has a pay range assigned to it by the employer. No matter how much you have made in previous positions, the assigned rate for that role will not change. Your skills will determine where you fall within the range of pay or if you even qualify for the range. The average Bachelor-degreed American makes $65,000 per year. If you have worked above that pay rate, you may be surprised that a large amount of available jobs you will be interested in, with some exceptions, sit between $65,000 and $75,000. The pay rate is based on the value the employer has placed on the job, not necessarily on your highest salary.

The next exercise offers specific resume changes that can set the stage to get calls and to perform a successful "step down" interview.

Exercise 11.3a: Resume Tips for Step-Down Career Transitions
The following resume tips will help with a step down. Mark the checklist to refine this resume type:
1.____ Follow the Market-Based Resume Profile© techniques.
2.____ Create simple statements and use the skills and abilities at the same level of responsibility as the new job.

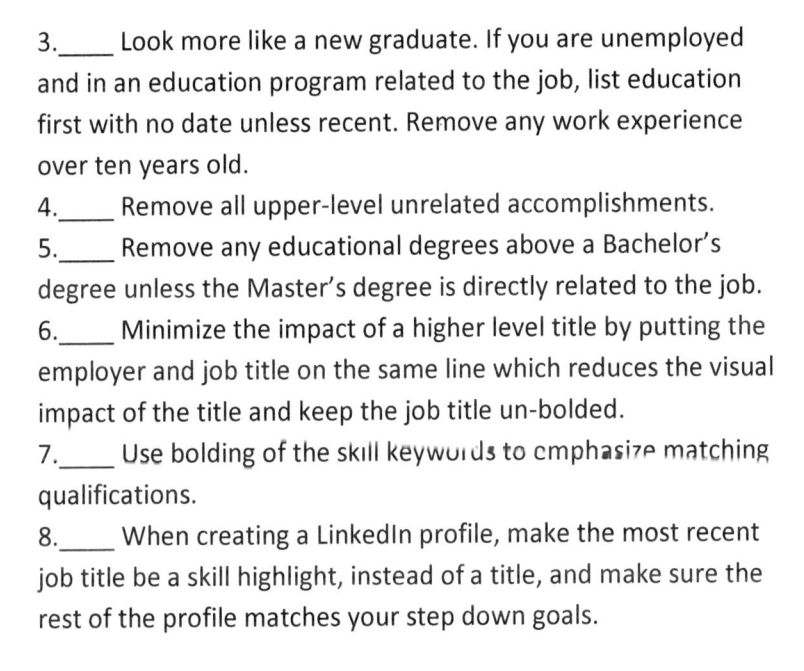

3.____ Look more like a new graduate. If you are unemployed and in an education program related to the job, list education first with no date unless recent. Remove any work experience over ten years old.

4.____ Remove all upper-level unrelated accomplishments.

5.____ Remove any educational degrees above a Bachelor's degree unless the Master's degree is directly related to the job.

6.____ Minimize the impact of a higher level title by putting the employer and job title on the same line which reduces the visual impact of the title and keep the job title un-bolded.

7.____ Use bolding of the skill keywords to emphasize matching qualifications.

8.____ When creating a LinkedIn profile, make the most recent job title be a skill highlight, instead of a title, and make sure the rest of the profile matches your step down goals.

The next step is to create explanations that can ease the recruiter's concerns.

Exercise 11.3b: Interview Scripts and Explanations for Making a Step Down

If the resume is done well and sufficiently minimizes the impact of previous upper level titles, the conversation about having had a higher level of responsibility may be entirely avoided. However, assuming the recruiter sees the upper level titles and still calls on the resume, the following scripts are offered in order of preference when answering the interview question "Why are you seeking to take a step down in your career?"

Situation 1: The job candidate may need to find a job, any job, regardless of title or pay level, due to a period of unemployment.
"This work is the exact work I have done every day. Regardless of title, my daily duties were _____, _____, _____ (name the skills from the job ad). This is the type of work I want to be doing."

Situation 2: The job candidate finds themselves "burned out" or stressed out at their current title or industry.
"This is the exact type of work that I have done even though my title and industry says that it is different. Regardless of title, my daily duties were _____, _____, _____ (name the skills from the job ad). This is the type of work I want to be doing."

Situation 3: The job candidate prefers to do one aspect of a job that happens to be a lower title or pay level.
"I know that my previous title suggests that I am overqualified for this position. Regardless of title, this is the exact type of work I have done and prefer to do. My daily duties in my previous position include _____, _____, _____ (name the skills from the job ad). This is the type of work I want to be doing."

Situation 4: Some candidates want to change into a new industry and are willing to accept a lesser position to make the move.
"This is the exact type of work I have done even though it is not reflected in my previous titles. Regardless of title, I have experience in the following _____, _____, _____ (name the skills from the job ad) *while working at* _____ (name the employer from the resume) *or volunteering with* _____ (name

the organization). *This is the type of work I want to be doing for this organization and in this industry."*

11.4 Move for Promotion Lesson

This career change is for candidates who have the skills necessary to perform at a higher level title or for more money.

11.4.1 Move for Promotion Myths

Myth 1: Getting a job at a higher level than the title I currently hold is difficult.

Strategically, seeking a promotion in a career change is often the only way you can grow quickly in your field. Most employers do not have the level of organizational growth possible to move an employee quickly up through the ranks, nor do they like to give large salary increases and promotions. Therefore, a move for promotion will be necessary if you are seeking growth in responsibility or income.

Myth 2: I can only move up in the same industry.

These jobs are usually in the same professional category and sometimes in the same industry. A job move for promotion may include an increase in pay or it may be a step to gain additional experience and a better title that can be leveraged later in the career for salary increase. If the candidate has a mix of desirable skills, a move for promotion may include a change in professional category and industry.

Myth 3: Employers fear overly-ambitious candidates.

Sometimes this is true. The unique challenge with this career change is that recruiters may fear that ambitious candidates will take the job and leave quickly when another higher-level position or more money presents itself. In addition, a frequent job jumper may appear unstable if they are not maintaining a certain amount of time at each employer. A job candidate can pull off frequent moves for promotion if the career changes add skill mixes that are in hot demand. However, in many fields, a job candidate has about a 10-year window of time when they can jump about once every two years. Remember, your previous history allows the employer to predict your behavior. If you jump at regular intervals, there will be a point where an employer is concerned about hiring you.

Myth 4: The recruiter may be concerned that a job candidate with a lower level title does not have the skills and abilities for the higher level position.

An applicant can use skills and accomplishment statements to combat the lack of job title for the upper level positions the candidate is seeking to grow into.

Myth 5: Anyone can make a move for promotion.

Technically, anyone can attempt to make a move for promotion but it is easier if the candidate meets these basic characteristics.

Select one or more of the following:
1.____ I have been doing the job of a higher-level title but I have not been given the money or title that match my unique skills and accomplishments.

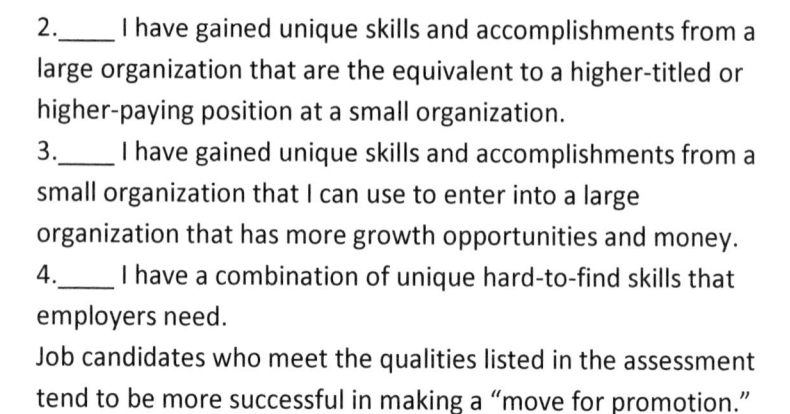

2.____ I have gained unique skills and accomplishments from a large organization that are the equivalent to a higher-titled or higher-paying position at a small organization.

3.____ I have gained unique skills and accomplishments from a small organization that I can use to enter into a large organization that has more growth opportunities and money.

4.____ I have a combination of unique hard-to-find skills that employers need.

Job candidates who meet the qualities listed in the assessment tend to be more successful in making a "move for promotion."

A candidate can make a move for promotion by taking experience gained in a large organization and applying it to a smaller one with the goal of obtaining a better title and potentially more money. An example of this might be an accountant for a larger manufacturer seeking to become the controller for a small manufacturer. Even though the candidate held a much lower title at the larger organization, the breadth and depth of skills gained at the large manufacturer may qualify the candidate for a controller-level position within a smaller company.

Smaller organizations sometimes offer deep, rich experiences that do not pay well or have the high-growth path desired by the job candidate. However, these rich experiences may be used to enter into a larger organization offering the potential for growth, higher income, or performance incentives.

It may become evident to the job candidate that they are doing the work of a higher-level title or pay rank. In addition, the candidate may find a skill mix that can create a unique advantage that leads to a higher-level title or income. For instance, an accountant who is moving to a controller-level position may be able to leverage the employer's need for an industry-specific skill, a second language, or knowledge of articular software.

Myth 6: I can make a move for promotion without capturing, quantifying, and communicating my accomplishments.

A job candidate who wants to climb quickly will have to learn how to capture, quantify, and communicate accomplishments as soon as possible. This job candidate needs to make an extensive effort to move away from a duty-based resume and into an accomplishment-based profile.

Myth 7: The recruiter will wonder why an exceptional candidate has not been promoted by the current employer.

This can be an issue for this career change type. The recruiter may wonder why an accomplished candidate has not been previously promoted or, if the applicant is unemployed, why they were let go if they were skilled. The solution is to create an irresistible "exact fit" resume profile and interview answers.

Myth 8: Telling the employer that I want to move for more money is appropriate in this case.

An explanation for a move for promotion should not only be about better compensation or benefits because the employer may be concerned that you will quit your job later for more pay.

The next exercise offers specific resume tips and interview scripts to help the process flow smoothly.

Exercise 11.4a: Resume Tips for Promotion Career Transitions

The following resume tips will help with a job transition for promotion.
Mark the checklist to refine this resume type:
1.____ Follow the Market-Based Resume Profile© techniques.
2.____ Upsell experience with accomplishments at the level of the next job.
3.____ Quantify accomplishments that match the job level.
4.____ Move from a duty-based resume.

Exercise 11.4b: Interview Scripts and Explanations for a Move for Promotion

If the resume is done well, it will sufficiently demonstrate that the candidate has the skills to do the position. The following scripts help you explain to the employer that you want "this job" and that you will not leave quickly to move on for more growth and additional money. Combine this with the answers that describe the reason for leaving a job (listed below) for a powerful explanation.

Situation 1: The job candidate is seeking to take experiences gained in a larger organization to a smaller organization with a higher level of title and responsibility.

"*While working at* _____ (state the name of the larger organization), *I gained upper level experiences in* _____, _____, _____ (state the desired accomplishments). *But, I* am just a cog in a machine. I prefer a smaller organization that can really use these skills to make a difference."

Situation 2: A job candidate who worked in a smaller organization and gained many skills but no title is now seeking growth with a larger organization.
"At my current smaller employer, I am required to be a "jack of all trades" without being given the title. On the positive side, I have developed a wide breadth of skills that you can use. I feel the larger organization is a better fit for me."

Situation 3: The job candidate has performed the work but has not been given the title.
"I have done this exact work and gained many skills and experiences as evidenced by my accomplishments, but my current employer is not in a position to offer me the next step due to business or industry conditions. For this reason, I am seeking a role that can use these skills and offer me the title that goes with them."

**Situation 4: The job candidate has a number of key skills for this position which
are difficult to locate in the job market right now.**
"I have done this exact work and I am seeking a position that can use the following skills _____, _____, _____ (state at least two to three hard-to-locate skills), and accomplishments _____, _____, _____ (state one to three desirable accomplishments).

Combine the responses above with answers to "Common Interview Question #2": Why did you transition from one job to another? and/or Why are you looking to leave where you are?

Use the following script to answer the question:

"I moved from my employer because _____ (select one or a combination of the following options)."

- the next position was the next step in my career path of _____ (a skill that the next job has) or,
- I enjoy doing _____ (a skill that the next job has) or
- this is a better use of _____ (a skill that the next job has) or,
- this is a return to an industry or,
- this is closer to home or,
- this has better hours or,
- _____. (some unique aspect that I like that the old place did not have.)

11.5 Return to Prior Profession Lesson

Most people have worked in multiple professional categories or industries. Any time the most recent work experience is different than the job you are applying for, yet matches a previous work experience, it falls within the category of retuning to an old profession.

11.5.1 Return to Prior Profession Myths

Myth 1: This is one of the hardest job moves to make especially with modern hiring systems.

This answer is both true and not true. In one way, this is not difficult because the resume's Title Bar, Summary of Skills, and Skill Highlights can all point towards the old professional accomplishments. However, recruiters and ATS programs stress the use of the reverse chronology resume which focuses on the most recent work experience first. Even with LinkedIn, the recruiters focus on searching the most recent job title to identify candidates. However, these job moves can be very successful if the skills gained from the most recent position can complement the previous profession.

Myth 2: Employers will not be concerned about when I did the work.

This is not true. If the resume makes it through the software or online search, the recruiter will have a variety of red flags: "Why did you move from this type of work in the first place? Why do you want to return to this type of work? If you have not been doing this work lately maybe you are rusty."

In the past, the solution to this resume problem was to use the functional style that stresses skills over title, employers, and dates of employment. However, the ATS program is diminishing the use of the functional resume. The best solution is to create a combination of the reverse chronology and the functional resume using the Market-Based Resume Profile© techniques.

Myth 3: The biggest issue I will face is proving I can still do the work.

Actually, the biggest issue is explaining your job transitions in a way that makes the employer believe that this is something you really want to do. An employer may not be excited about hiring an employee that abandoned the profession. The interviewer will dig deep to uncover what happened until they are satisfied with the response. This can be a challenging process that requires repeating the same answer over and over again.
The next exercise offers specific resume, applicant tracking and online profile tips, and interview scripts to help the process flow smoothly.

Exercise 11.5a: Resume Tips for Career Change Back to Recent Prior Profession -Recent Job Has Some Matching Skills

The following resume tips will help with a job transition back to a prior profession.
Mark the checklist to refine this resume type in the order presented:
1.____ Follow the Market-Based Resume Profile© techniques.

2.____ Create a larger Skill Summary area at the top of the page.

3.____ Highlight related skills at the current employer and leave unrelated skills off.

4.____ Put the employer, title, and years of employment on the same line to minimize the impact of an unrelated title. Do not bold the employer/title/dates of the employment line.

5. ____ Create a skill statement that directly matches the job. Bold the statement to take the eye away from the employer and on to the skill statement.

6.____ Make sure the previous matching job title is on the first page.

7.____ In the ATS, use the correct title but paste in all the functional related skills into the job description box.

8.____ In LinkedIn, use a summary and headline that focuses on the previous profession.

Exercise 11.5b: Interview Scripts and Explanations for a Career Transition Back to a Prior Profession

If the resume is done well and sufficiently presents accomplishments at the level of responsibility of the next position the conversation regarding any concerns about returning to a prior profession should be easier, but will not be avoided. The following script assists in the conversation.

"While I was working in my most recent profession, I really came to realize how much I missed _____, _____, _____ (fill in the blanks with skills or experiences that match the prior profession that are not a part of the most recent profession). Now I am seeking to return to my prior profession because that is the work I prefer to do. I particularly miss _____, _____,

_____ (state skills and work environment descriptions that match the job)."

11.6 New Graduate or Entry-level Lesson

A new graduate resume puts the job candidate's education before the work experience section. The next section reviews common myths and beliefs about this resume style.

11.6.1 New Graduate Common Myths

Myth 1: If I am a new graduate I should put my education first.

No, not always. This strategy should be used only in certain circumstances because relevant practical current work experience is always more important than education. Although new graduates feel that they do not have professional experience, in most cases they do and it should be presented first when it relates to the job application.

The following examples present the common scenarios in which the new graduate resume is the expected and necessary choice.

Select one or more of the following:
1. ____ I am applying for internships.
2. ____ I am a new graduate with no internship, work study, or professional work experience.
3. ____ I am applying for a job in which the degree is a prerequisite to work in the field.

If you selected any of the options above, then you should put education first on your resume. Internships are usually for younger new graduates or those still in school. It is less common for an older and more experienced job candidate to obtain an internship. An older candidate (over 40 years of age) will need to highlight academic accomplishments and recent matching professional work experience. New graduates who have absolutely no internships, work-study jobs, or professional work experience should use this format. There are certain scientific, medical, and quantitative fields that require a specific education; it often makes sense to state that information at the top of the resume.

Myth 2: If I have many years of work experience, I should not use this resume style.

There are a few instances when a candidate may want to use a New Graduate or Entry-level resume as a strategic choice.

New Graduate Resume Style Selection
• I need to make a "step down" so I want to appear younger and less experienced.
• I have been unemployed for over a year and I am currently in school or have recently graduated.
• I have had many jobs with less than a year or two of experience.

This type of resume helps "step downs" by presenting an image of a candidate with less skills, accomplishments, and work history; it can assist someone who is "overqualified" to make a career change in a new direction. In addition, going back to school can be used strategically to help a candidate cover a period of unemployment or to change professional categories. School can be used as a "reset" button for applicants who are having trouble getting a job due to many periods of unemployment, job jumping, or erratic employment.

If a job candidate is unemployed and in school, this is an excellent opportunity to cover an employment gap. Putting education first is useful if the candidate is in school and seeking to return to an earlier profession, particularly a job related to the education. There are some academic, science, and math degrees where the proper education and licensure are mandatory prerequisites to employment.

Some candidates just cannot or do not remain in a job for very long, which tells the employer two things: the job candidate will not be happy and will not stay in the new job. Since those are the two qualities that employers value the most, even above skills, it may be important to use school as a "reset button." Use the following assessment to determine if you have a job transition history that allows employers to predict if you will leave quickly.

Job Jumper Identification: Check the items that apply.
___ I have had a different job every year for the past five years.
___ I have had a job every two years for the past ten years.
___ I held a job for over three years in my past but recently, I have had two jobs that lasted no more than two years each.
If you were able to check any of the above, consider going back to school and presenting your education first on your resume. After education, present those different jobs as "school-time" or "pre-professional" employment. If you are under 40 years of age, consider shaving off a tremendous amount of past history to present that new-graduate image. There is one more thing to note here: employers do not value a person's ability to job jump. Job jumpers sometimes feel that their ability to do many different things (as reflected by many different jobs)

demonstrates their flexibility, adaptability, and teach-ability. Although this may be true, it also tells the employer you will not stay and be happy.

Some job jumping at the beginning of your career or after a period of unexpected unemployment is acceptable to the job market. Beyond that, from a job market perspective you are expected to "find yourself" and commit to an employer and a career.

The biggest challenge with a new graduate or entry-level professional is whether you have the skills to do the job, if it is what you really want to be doing, and if you will stay with the organization once you have the work experience. The next exercise offers specific resume tips and interview scripts to help the process flow smoothly.

Exercise 11.6a: Resume Tips for New Graduate and Entry-Level Career Transitions

The following resume tips will help with new graduate and entry-level career transitions. The items in CAPS denote a written resume header section.

I am applying for internships.

Resume Tip Checklist: Internship Application
Mark the checklist to refine this resume type:
1.___ Appear like a younger person with no more than 10 years of experience, if any.

2.___ Follow the Market-Based Resume Profile© techniques but do not use the classic reverse chronology format; instead use the recommendations below:
3.___ Place the current EDUCATION section at the top.
4.___ Detail classroom projects as if they were work experiences.
5.___ List other internship experience if available.
6.___ Follow with WORK EXPERIENCE.
7.___ Present unrelated education at the bottom ADDITIONAL EDUCATION.
8.___ Add SCHOLARSHIPS AND ACADEMIC AWARDS.
9.___ Add a section for VOLUNTEER AND LEADERSHIP EXPERIENCE.
10.___ Professionalize work experience by speaking about the volume of customers, special projects, and working extra shifts.

I am a new graduate with no internship, work study, or professional work experience.

Resume Tip Checklist: New Graduate - Absolutely No Work Experience
Mark the checklist to refine this resume type:
1.___ Follow the Market Based Resume Profile© techniques but do not use classic reverse chronology format using the recommendations below.
2.___ Place the current EDUCATION section at the top.
3.___ Detail classroom projects as if they were work experiences.
4.___ List other internship experience if available.
5.___ Follow with WORK EXPERIENCE.

6.___ Present unrelated education at the bottom as ADDITIONAL EDUCATION.
7.___ Add SCHOLARSHIPS AND ACADEMIC AWARDS.
8.___ VOLUNTEER AND LEADERSHIP EXPERIENCE.
9.___ Professionalize work experience by speaking about the volume of customers, special projects, and working extra shifts.

I have been unemployed for over a year and I am currently in school or have recently graduated.

Resume Tip Checklist: New Graduate - Unemployed
Mark the checklist to refine this resume type:
1.___ Follow the Market-Based Resume Profile© techniques but do not use classic reverse chronology format. Use the recommendations below:
2.___ Put EDUCATION first after the summary of skills and list the dates as if it were a job to visually cover the gap.
3.___ Match previous work experience to the job and present no more than 10 years of experience, preferably much less.
4.___ List other internship experience if available.
5.___ Follow with WORK EXPERIENCE.
6.___ Present unrelated at the bottom as ADDITIONAL EDUCATION.
7.___ Add SCHOLARSHIPS AND ACADEMIC AWARDS.
8.___ Add VOLUNTEER AND LEADERSHIP EXPERIENCE.

I need to make a "step down" so I want to appear younger and less experienced.

Resume Tip Checklist: Step-Down/Appear Younger
Mark the checklist to refine this resume type:

1.___ Appear like a younger person with no more than 10 years of experience if any.
2.___ Follow the Market-Based Resume Profile© techniques but do not use the classic reverse chronology format. Use the recommendations below:
3.___ Place the current EDUCATION section at the top.
4.___ Detail classroom projects as if they were work experiences.
5.___ List other internship experience if available.
6.___ Follow with WORK EXPERIENCE but shave off years of work and upper level titles.
7.___ Present unrelated education at the bottom as ADDITIONAL EDUCATION.
8.___ Add SCHOLARSHIPS AND ACADEMIC AWARDS.
9.___ Add a section for VOLUNTEER AND LEADERSHIP EXPERIENCE.
10.___ Professionalize work experience by speaking about the volume of customers, special projects, and working extra shifts.

I have had many jobs with less than a year or two years of experience.

Resume Tip Checklist: Job Jumper Using Education as Reset
Mark the checklist to refine this resume type:
1.___ Follow the Market-Based Resume Profile© techniques but do not use classic reverse chronology format. Use the recommendations below:
2.___ Put EDUCATION first after the summary of skill and list the dates as if it were a job to visually cover the gap.
3.___ Match previous work experience to the job.

4.___ List WORK EXPERIENCE that was during school or five years before school, for a total of about ten years of work history.
5.___ Present unrelated education at the bottom as ADDITIONAL EDUCATION.
6.___ Add SCHOLARSHIPS AND ACADEMIC AWARDS.
7.___ Add VOLUNTEER AND LEADERSHIP EXPERIENCE.

Exercise 11.6b: Interview Scripts and Explanations for a New Graduate and Entry-Level Career Transitions with Little Professional Experience

The following scripts help to answer recruiters' concerns when they ask themselves, "Does this person have the abilities to do the job? Is this really the job the candidate wants to be doing? Will they stay after the organization invests in their development?"

The Script:
"As a new graduate or entry-level candidate in this field I bring with me a host of experience that demonstrates my interest and dedication to my growth in this field. These include_____ (a list of school, leadership, or volunteer activities that match the job). This is the position I want and this is the organization I want to grow with because _____ (fill in the blank with a background research about the organization or job).

11.7 New Industry but Same Profession Lesson

A career change into a new industry but same profession means that the job candidate is doing the same type of work but in a different type of business.

11.7.1 Changing to New Industry Myths

Myth1: Industry should not matter if you know how to do the work.

The biggest challenge with this transition is that industries use different systems, methods, rules, and regulations, and have different environments. An employer may ask why a candidate would want to change industries, or may have concerns about their adjusting to differences. Changing industry is one of the easier career changes to make but it is important to present an industry neutral profile.

The next exercise offers specific resume tips and interview scripts to help the process flow more smoothly.

Exercise 11.7a: Resume Tips for a Career Change into a New Industry

The following resume tips will help with a new industry job transition.

Resume Tip Checklist: New Industry
Mark the checklist to refine this resume type:
1.____ Follow the Market-Based Resume Profile© techniques.

2.____ Only present industry neutral information that applies to the professional category.

3.____ Present the professional title before the employer.

4.____ Bold the professional title and related skills and un-bold the employer to keep the focus on the matching professional category.

Exercise 11.7b: Interview Scripts and Explanations for a Career Change into a New Industry

The following scripts help to answer an employer's concerns when they ask themselves or the candidate, "Why are you interested in changing industries?" and "How do you think you will adjust to this new industry?"

The Script:
"This is the exact work that I have done. Although I have been working in _____ *(fill in the blank by naming the most current industry) the work is the same or similar. I may need to learn some new systems but from starting and learning the previous system from scratch, I do not foresee a problem. In addition, any rules or regulations will take limited time to learn. I believe my previous work environment and this work environment and job have the following in common* _____ *(list the items that they might have in common). I believe this business can gain from what I learned in the last one. For instance, in the areas of* ____, _____, *and* ____ *(state the possible areas that will could be positive).*

11.8 Complete Career Change into a New Profession and Industry Lesson

A complete career change into a new industry and professional category suggests that the desired job move has absolutely nothing to do with the most recent or previous work experience. In other words, the professional is seeking a new experience that does not leverage their background. It is important to examine motivations behind these changes because the Core-3© exercise and job search will often identify new career trajectories, work environments, and lifestyle opportunities (new city, part-time, work-from-home, contractor) for existing skill sets. Lets explore myths related to a complete career change.

11.8.1 Changing Profession and Industry 'Complete Career Change' Myths

Myth 1: Getting into a new profession and industry is the hardest career change to make.

Believe it or not, taking a step-down can be more difficult than a complete career change but yes, this is a difficult move. The primary issue in this situation is that there is no pattern recognition basis for the recruiter to call the job candidate based on resume alone. The candidate cannot produce a 'direct-hit' match. You can achieve the career you want, in most cases, without making such a drastic move, but if your heart is set on this path, there are options.

Myth 2: A resume will help me make this transition.

A resume will probably not help unless you can figure out a way to leverage your previous work experience and education to the benefit of the new industry and profession. For this reason, these types of career changes are often facilitated by volunteer experience, informational interviews, referrals, or returning to school to obtain an education that moves a career in a completely new direction.

Myth 3: I can make this move in a few months.

Be prepared for this career change to take well over six months to a year unless you have a strong personal network that can communicate your abilities to the employer, since there will be no matching education and work experience. These career changes do happen every day with the help of an applicant's personal network, with luck, or through experiences gained outside of the work environment.

The next exercise offers specific resume tips and interview scripts to help the process flow more smoothly.

Exercise 11.8a: Resume Tips for a Complete Career Change into a New Industry and Professional Category

The following resume tips will help with a career change into a new industry and professional category.

Resume Tip Checklist: Complete Career Change New Industry & Profession
Mark the checklist to refine this resume type:

1. ____ Follow the Market-Based Resume Profile© techniques.
2. ____ Remove or minimize information that does not apply to the new industry and professional category, and replace with a heavy focus on general skills that can be used across different industries and professional categories.
3. ____ Attempt to describe experience in a way that the new job can use. This may require the help of someone working in that industry who also knows your background.
4. ____ Use volunteer and leadership experience if it applies.

Exercise 10.8b: Interview Scripts and Explanations for a Complete Career Change into a New Industry and Professional Category

The following script helps to answer employers' concerns when they ask themselves or the candidate, "Is this person qualified to do or even learn this job?"

The Script:
"Although I have been working in _____ (name the various professional categories) I have been interested in this work for a long time. I believe my background in ____ (list any experiences or skills that may apply) can make up for my lack of experience in the following areas ____ (name the skills they are seeking). I may need to learn some new systems but from starting and learning the previous systems from scratch, I do not foresee a problem. I believe my previous work environment and this work environment and job have the following in common _____ (list the items that they might have in common). I also have previous volunteer and leadership background that applies to this position."

11.9 Gaps in Employment Lesson
A gap in employment could be due to a termination or quitting a job.

11.9.1 Gaps in Employment Myths

<u>Myth 1: Gaps in employment are the worst red flag on the resume.</u>

Gaps on a resume differ in the severity of their impact depending on the length of time and when they happened in a job candidate's work history. Some gaps are more severe than others. Use the following assessment to determine how challenging your gaps are to your career change.

Gaps in Employment Assessment
Select which option applies to your situation:
Less Severe:
____ I am currently employed but have had one or two gaps under a year in length in the past.
____ I am currently employed and had one large gap over two years long.

More Severe:
____ I am currently employed but have had more than two gaps in the past.
____ I am currently unemployed for over a year.
____ I am current unemployed and I have gaps in the past.

In the past, gaps in employment were the worst red flag. The recruiter used to have immediate concerns about the candidate being an unmotivated low-producing employee that either could not do the job or created problems for the organization resulting in their termination. With today's economy, it is much more common to see job gaps on the resume and they no longer hold the immediate stigma that they did in previous years.

Myth 2: The employer only cares whether I was terminated or quit - not why it happened.

Why a person left a job, or the "reason for leaving," is one of the most important indicators of a job candidate's ability to stay on the job and be happy with their work. The recruiter will continue asking about this until they are satisfied that the employee truly wants the job, that they will stay, and that they will be happy.

Myth 3: I should cover my gaps in employment, no matter how short-term the work experience was that filled the gap.

In some cases, it is better to have a gap on the resume than many brief work engagements or a recent short-term job that did not work out. A job candidate does not want to explain many job transitions. It may be better to say "I was looking for work" than to say "This job did not work out because of ___."

Because job transitions are so important in determining your future success, you want to explain as few of them as possible. Do not create more problems for yourself by explaining additional career changes if you do not have to. A gap, especially one under a year long, may be better than having to tell the employer why you moved from job to job over short periods of time.

The next exercise offers specific resume tips and interview scripts to help the process flow more smoothly.

Exercise 11.9a: Resume Tips for Career Changes with Gaps in Employment

The following resume tips will help with a career change when there are gaps in employment. The options depend upon the scenario.

Resume Tip Checklist: Gaps in Employment
Mark the checklist to refine this resume type depending on scenarios.

Scenario 1 & 2: Currently employed, one or two gaps under a year in length in the past, or currently employed and had one large gap over two years long.
1.____ Follow the Market-Based Resume Profile© techniques.
2.____ Use year-to-year dates on the resume to minimize the impact of gaps under a year in duration. For instance, 2013-2014 or 2013 to 2014.

Scenario 3: Currently employed but with a gap over two years in the past.
1.____ Follow the Market-Based Resume Profile© techniques.
2.____ Use year-to-year dates on the resume to minimize the impact of gaps under a year in duration. For instance, 2013-2014 or 2013 to 2014.

3.____ Take up the entire first page with the summary of skill, skill highlights, and the current position accomplishments if there is enough material.
4.____ Move the employment gap to the second page.
5.____ On the second page, list each employer in a single line in the following order: employer name, title, and then years of employment. Leave un-bolded. Bold the skill highlights or;
6. ____ If the current job is highly related, create a section called TITLES AND POSITIONS and list employer, title, and years in one line with no detail, un-bolded.

Scenario 4: Currently unemployed, or currently unemployed with previous gaps.
1.____ Follow the Market-Based Resume Profile© techniques.
2.____ Use year-to-year dates on the resume to minimize the impact of gaps under a year in duration. For instance, 2013-2014 or 2013 to 2014.
3.____ If in school, do a new graduate resume to cover the gap.
4 ____ If working on the side or freelancing, create a business name and have the information as your current employment.
5.____ Seek out unpaid work experiences in exchange for a title and reference and put the information in the current employment section.
6.____ Move previous employment gaps to the second page. If during an educational period, consider removing and letting school take up the time period.

Exercise 11.9b: Interview Scripts for Career Changes with Gaps in Employment

If the resume has properly managed a gap, this issue should be minimized. In the interview, this commonly appears as two questions: 1) "Why did you leave each job?" and 2) "Were you ever terminated from a position?" The following interview scripts will help with a career change where there are gaps in employment. Select the response based on the different scenarios.

Choose from the list of answers which are ordered from the most preferable to the least.

Script 1: "I left each position before having a new job for the following reason ___ (choose from the following options but not use the same one twice)."
- I decided to go back to school.
- I moved cities.
- The employer closed.
- The job, department, or business was moved to another location..
- The market and industry for this position fell apart.
- There was not enough work.
- I left this position to take another one but it did not work out leaving me unemployed for a period of time.
- There were changes in management and they restructured the department.

11.10 Geographic Relocation Lesson

Many candidates seek to move geographic regions for personal reasons or for new career opportunities.

11.10.1 Geographic Relocation Myths

Myth 1: People move to different cities for work all the time.

Although the United States has one of the most geographically mobile labor forces in the world, only about two percent of people actually move out of their town or state for a job each year.

Myth 2: An employer should not be worried that I will stay on the job.

Employers report that 60% to 80% of their relocating new hires quit within two years. This strong statistical correlation between relocation and attrition cause employers to program their Applicant Tracking Systems (ATS) to look for only local job candidates in a certain set of local zip codes. A relocating candidate may be skilled enough to do the job but they may not be happy or stable enough to remain in the position. One reason this occurs is that it can be quite difficult for a job candidate to focus on work when their entire support system is in another location. This is especially true as the job candidates gets older.

Myth 3: All professions are the same when it comes to problems with changing cities.

Some positions have relocation built in to the professional category, such as in construction, professors, and executives. There is an expectation that these employees will relocate for work one to three times (or more) in their career. However, the vast majority of job types and people will remain in one area for their whole life.

The following exercise presents a checklist to help with the relocation resume and interview.

Exercise 11.10a: Relocation Resume Tips

Use the following resume tip checklist to assist with the visual impact of relocations.

Resume Tip Checklist: Relocations
Mark the checklist to refine this resume type:
1.____ Follow the Market-Based Resume Profile© techniques.
2.____ Use a local address and zip code on the resume even if you are not there yet.
3.____ Consider a local telephone number through google voice and list it on your resume.
4.____ Remove employer locations from the resume.

Exercise 11.10b: Relocation Interview Scripts

If you have stated a local address and telephone number, the issues about relocation should be minimized from the perspective of the recruiter. However, assuming they know that you are a relocation candidate, or if you do not have an address to use, the following scripts will help to answer the recruiters' concerns when they ask themselves "Will this person stay in this job?" A job candidate wants to express stability by saying there is a friend or family support system in the area.

Scenario 1: Moving Away from Hometown or Long-term Location
- "I moved to this location because my spouse found (or was relocated) for a job here."
- "I moved to this location for better opportunities, and I have always wanted to live here because I have family or friends that live here."

Scenario 2: Moving Back to Hometown or Long-term Location
- "I had wanted to move back home to be near my family, so I did it."

>Homework
Keep in mind that every recruiter is seeking someone who can do the job and will stay with the organization. When presenting your resume and speaking in an interview, build a cohesive story that shows you are a stable, happy, non-disruptive team member.

Quiz 11: Career & Job Change Types (T/F)
1.___ There are no resume or interview challenges when making a lateral move.
2.___ Being over-qualified is a good thing in the job market.
3.___ You can achieve a promotion through a new position.
4.___ You can move back to an old profession.
5.___ New graduates have no job skills.
6.___ Switching both industries and professional categories is difficult.
7.___ The years of experience, education, and level of responsibility are not that important.
8.___ A history of many different types of jobs shows how flexible and adaptive I am.
9.___ Gaps between employment are the worst thing on the resume.
10.___ Relocating to a new city is no problem.

Chapter 11: Answer Key (T/F)
1) False: Lateral career moves face unique resume and interview issues.
2) False: The employer fears an over-qualified candidate.
3) True: It is easier to get promoted through a new job than your current employer.
4) True: A return to a previous profession is one of the easier career changes.
5) False: Most new graduates have job skills to leverage.
6) True: Switching both industries and professions is one of the most difficult moves.
7) False: Matching years of experience, education, and level of responsibility are critical.

8) True: A history of many different types of jobs shows how flexible and adaptive I am.

9) False: Gaps between employment are almost expected and old ones are barely relevant.

10) False: This is truly becoming a chronic issue requiring an advanced strategy.

Chapter 12: Timing and Troubleshooting the Job Search Campaign

The first part of this section includes my nitty-gritty comprehensive Stacked Strategy for doubling your interviews, leveraging recruiters, and unlocking LinkedIn. If you have read the previous chapters and passed the quizzes, you can skip the recap and jump straight to the checklists that offer a quick strategy recap, troubleshooting issues that may arise, and common questions about 'how long things take' in hiring.

B2W Mom & Stacked Campaign Kickoff Steps Recap

Step 1: B2W Mom Strategy Selection

Determine which of the six strategies, or combination of options, you are going to use to close the gap, perform the re-entry period, or leverage existing re-entry work that you have been doing to achieve full-employment.

Step 2: Use the Market: Identify Skills and Search for Demand – The Core-3©

The **Stacked Strategy** is built on the concept that writing your resume and online profiles using keywords sourced from job advertisements allows recruiters to find and identify you as a qualified professional. This begins with an inventory of skills, a gathering of keywords, and then using the market to tell you where those skills are needed. This method doubles interviews, reduces transition time, and can often result in a higher income and more career growth by matching your abilities with demand in the market.

Step 3: Perform a Search on Indeed.com

When searching for jobs based on key skills, titles will come up that you may never have considered. Use the market at all times in building your career. Indeed.com aggregates from multiple job boards, making it one of the best sources for identifying jobs.

Step 4: Refine Search Based on Additional Information Derived from Job Ads

The job advertisements will offer a wealth of information on additional keywords, titles, and industry players that you may not have considered. Add those qualifying skills to refine the search.

Step 5: Create Job Alerts on Indeed.com to Receive Daily Pre-Qualified Job Ads

Job alerts can assist in your job hunt by dropping pre-qualified job ads into your email inbox on a daily basis.

Step 6: Create Resume Profiles that Match the Job Ads

Most candidates have three potential lateral moves matching a certain profession, in addition to multiple non-lateral career changes. Use the keywords and duties listed in job ads to help build a Market-Based Resume Profile© so that the resume looks like the job listed.

Step 7: Create a Line-item Accomplishment Inventory

Accomplishments increase the chances of getting a call for a job, getting a job offer from an interview, and getting more money from salary negotiations.

Step 8: Post Resume to Job Boards

Use the resume to build a robust online presence that will bring recruiters straight to you for the jobs you want. The job boards include Indeed.com, Monster.com, niche professional or recruiter websites.

Step 9: Perform an Indeed.com Quality Check

Search for your own resume and use the competition on indeed.com to identify how many times your keywords need to appear to boost your rankings. Improve on missing content by reviewing other people's resumes and optimizing your profile.

Step 10: Adjust the LinkedIn Profile

Ensure that LinkedIn is also keyword-stacked and matches the likely recruiter search for your background based on the job ads and new resume built for those positions.

Step 11: Submit 10 Applications Matching the First Goal Campaign.

Recruiters search online resumes to hunt down qualified applicants. Since this requires little effort, a passive search is an important additional component of a job search. Use multiple websites like Monster.com, Indeed.com, and local job websites because a recruiter may only search one. In addition, many job boards offer "quick apply" options that can allow a professional to do a large quantity of applications quickly.

Step 12: Receive Unexpected Phone Screens from Recruiters Who Find You

With this method you will receive calls for jobs that you both applied for and did not apply for. Sometimes candidates are upset that they get unsolicited calls, but these calls indicate that the campaign is working efficiently. You need to be proactive and take control of these interviews. To manage the phone screen for a job you did not apply for, take a message, ask for the job ad, and set a time to interview in a way that gives you time to prepare. These phone screens can come as a surprise and you cannot interview well in a caught-off-guard position, so control the engagement.

Step 13: Receive Phone Screens for Direct Applications

Phone screens will also come in for jobs that you applied for. In this case, you still need to manage the call by taking a message or letting the call go to voicemail. Find the job advertisement and resume you sent. Prepare the phone screen questions. An alternative strategy is to say "yes" to everything and keep the "ball in the air" as long as possible, resulting in better overall decision-making about new possibilities.

Step 14: Do Not Do On-the-Spot Phone Screens

Can I say much more about this? It is that important that you not treat these calls casually - learn how to answer the questions that come with the phone screen. However, at some point you will become a pro at saying "yes" and getting the recruiter excited about your potential. You can always decline a future interview later.

The campaign kickoff is the heartbeat of the "Double Your Interviews" strategy. If these actions do not double your interviews, use the troubleshooting checklist (Section 11.2) to get your job search moving.

12.1 The 3-Month Stacked Job Search Checklist

Post this schedule to stay on track with your job search for re-entry or full employment transition.

FIRST TWO WEEKS
____ Determine your B2W mom strategy.
____ Identify keywords, core skills, and skill mixes using the Core-3© exercise.
____ Perform a search on Indeed.com.
____ Refine your search based on additional information derived from job ads.

____ Create job alerts on Indeed.com to receive daily pre-qualified job ads.
____ Create Market-Based Resume Profile© that matches the job ads.
____ Create a line-item accomplishment inventory that matches the job ads.
____ Post resume on the job boards.
____ Revise your LinkedIn.com account.
____ Submit at least 10 applications matching to first goal campaign.
____ Receive unexpected phone screens from recruiters who find you.
____ Receive phone screens for direct applications.
____ Do not do "on-the-spot" phone screens! Prepare for each one before answering.

If there are no calls on the resume within two weeks, proceed to the next strategy.

THIRD WEEK
____ Perform a campaign kickoff on the second set of jobs identified in the Core-3© exercise.
____ Rotate the resume on the job boards.
____ Revise LinkedIn.com account for current strategy.
____ Submit 10 resumes.
____ Receive unexpected phone screens from recruiters who find you.
____ Receive phone screens for direct applications.
____ Careful with phone screens! Multiple campaigns = different conversations. Be ready!

If there are no calls on the resume in three weeks, proceed to the next strategy

FOURTH WEEK
____ Perform a campaign kickoff on the third set of jobs identified in the Core-3© exercise.
____ Rotate the resume on the job boards.
____ Revise your LinkedIn.com account for current strategy.
____ Submit 10 resumes.
____ Receive unexpected phone screens from recruiters who find you.
____ Receive phone screens for direct applications.
____ Careful with phone screens! Multiple campaigns = different conversations. Be ready!

If there are no calls on the resume in four weeks, proceed to the next strategy. Perform some troubleshooting using the following section.

12.2 Troubleshooting Checklists

Sometimes a job candidate will think their entire search is ineffective when actually only a specific area needs their attention. There are four main areas to focus on:
1. No Calls
2. No in-person interview invites
3. No offers
4. Dreamy change

1. RESUME & APPLICATION TROUBLESHOOTING: NO CALLS

You are submitting your resume but not getting calls for interviews.
____ I have created a keyword-optimized resume matching a stream of jobs.
____ I periodically change the top third of the resume to match jobs.
____ I have my online profiles optimized and running.
____ I do not talk myself out of applying for jobs.
____ I have done "quick applies" and direct applications.
____ I have submitted at least 10 resumes per job stream in the first month.
____ I am focused on getting calls, not on a "dream-employer/dreamy-job" scenario.
____ I have at least 75% of the requested qualifications on jobs I apply for.
____ I say "yes" to skill based questions so that I get through the ATS.
____ I did not start my search during the "slow hiring season" November 15th through January 15th.
____ If I want a job I have never done before, I know my search is not a "resume" solution.

2. PHONE SCREEN TROUBLESHOOTING: NO IN-PERSON INTERVIEWS

You are getting phone screens but are not invited for an in-person interview.
____ I let unidentified calls go to voicemail or take a message.
____ I use the job advertisement to prepare for phone screens.
____ I have learned how to quote different desired salary expectations per job.

____ I know how to explain my job transitions and goals to match the job.
____ If no job ad, I ask questions to uncover the requirements and say "I have done it."
____ I treat every job as my dream job until I get an offer.
____ I respond to emails and phone calls within 24 hours.
____ I love unexpected calls by recruiters and know how to manage these calls.
____ I know that third party recruiters are sales people and I manage these relationships.
____ I do not show I am upset when HR departments miss phone screens.
____ I know the only time I am in a power position is once I receive an offer.
____ I know my whole job during a job search is to get job offers.
____ I adjust my answers for each job, including desired salary so that I get job offers.

3. INTERVIEWING TROUBLESHOOTING: NO OFFERS
You have been through the full interview process multiple times but did not get an offer.
____ I send thank-you emails every week until I receive a final determination.
____ I know that it can take weeks to get a final offer or next call after my last interview.
____ I have updated my clothes, hair, and shoes for interviewing.
____ I have developed solid behavioral interview examples for each job.

____ I prepare for every single interview even if it is the fifth one.
____ I use the "Questions for Them" strategy.
____ I have performed a mock interview and received constructive feedback.

4. "DREAMY JOB" TROUBLESHOOTING

You are not getting calls, interviews, or offers, which significantly delays transition time:
____ I only pursue dream scenarios.
____ I only apply for jobs for which I am missing over 25% of the qualifications.
____ I apply for only one job a month.

Strategies for "Dreamy Job" goals:
____ Consult with a career strategist to find the right method.
____ Seek jobs across the nation (geographic move) which takes longer.
____ Create a list of champions for informational interviews (leveraging who you know).
____ Locate and perform the right volunteer opportunity (creating more connections).
____ Target staffing agencies and freelance/gig opportunities (get experience).
____ Identify hot degrees or certifications that the market wants (re-education).

12.3 Job Search Timing Checklist

Use the checklist to maintain awareness of the different timing that can occur in career changes:

Milestone 1: Campaign Kickoff (5-10 hours)
• Identify jobs, write matching resume, align online profiles, and 10 combined quick-apply and direct applications.

Milestone 2: Phone Screens - Calls on Resume (2 weeks)
• Following a Campaign Kickoff, first phone screens come in between 3 days and 2 weeks. A fast result indicates a well-optimized campaign and/or a hot area for hiring.
• No phone screens indicate a campaign poorly aligned to job market need.
• Attempt alternative campaigns to get calls if there is nothing in 2 weeks.

Milestone 3: Phone Screen to In-Person Interview Request (3 weeks from call)
• If the phone screen is a Third Party Recruiter you can communicate regularly, but they have limited control over the employer. This can take one to three weeks on average and you can call the recruiter weekly to get status reports.
• If the phone screen was an internal HR recruiter or hiring manager, they will do one of the following: 1) If they are interested in proceeding they typically schedule an in-person interview within two weeks of your phone screen, 2) if they are not interested, they will send an email or, unfortunately, they may say nothing and just avoid the issue, 3) if something

happens to the position that delays the process, they may say nothing.

The HR department often have their hands tied by the hiring managers and they typically have multiple duties.
Communicating with job candidates is often the bottom of their list. In the best scenarios, they will proceed with in-person interviews within two weeks of the phone screen or indicate if they are not moving forward. If there is no response that does not mean much except to proceed with your job search until you hear a yes or a no about your candidacy.

Milestone 4: 2nd, 3rd, 4th, and 5th Interviews (3 to 6 months from phone screen)
After the phone screen, it may take two to three weeks to hear back about scheduling another interview. On average it takes 3 to 6 months for non-executive roles and 6 months to 2 years for executive roles.
_____ There may be three weeks between the first in-person interview and the next round.
_____ It is common for there to be up to four rounds of interviews.
_____ It is common to wait months before receiving a rejection on a job (if ever).
_____ By the third or fourth interview you should be close to a job offer or rejection.

Milestone 5: Negotiation (48-Hours from offer)
_____ Once a job offer is made you have no more than 48 hours to make a decision on the final negotiated offer. At this time,

you are still interviewing. How you handle this time period is critical to maintaining a job offer.

Repeat this strategy about two years after your re-entry period to achieve full employment.

>Homework

Getting the job offer, especially under three months, is like training for a marathon. To win the big cash prize takes practice, apply for a variety of jobs, even ones you are not sure about, to get practice at getting interviews and job offers. You may just uncover an amazing opportunity that you would have talked yourself out of if you did not take this approach.

Quiz 12: Job Search Strategy (T/F)
1.___ My first job back to work has to be perfect!
2.___ If I talk myself out of applying for jobs, I will not get as many calls.
3.___ Phone screens are ultra-serious and not casual.
4.___ Every job is my dream job until I get the offer!
5.___ The only time I am in a power position is once I get a job offer.
6.___ My whole job in my job search is getting offers.
7.___ If I have no experience with the job I want, I need to take alternative steps.
8.___ Getting unexpected calls is a good thing.
9.___ Most active job hunts take 3 to 6 months.
10.___ I will need to repeat this strategy in a few years' time to achieve full employment.

Chapter 12: Answer Key (T/F)
1) False: Your first job back to work needs to cover your gap and lay the foundation for full employment in approximately two years time.
2) True: The first step to a great strategy is to actually apply for jobs!!
3) True: The phone screen questions address all the reasons they are concerned about your candidacy.
4) True: Employers want to hire people that want the actual job they are hiring for! Therefore, every respective job you interview for has to be your "dream job" to get an offer.
5) True: Once the employer commits to you, you are in power; until then, they are in control. Your power is only subtle in that you understand how to respond and what to present.

6) True: Yes, Yes, Yes. This program teaches you how to get to the offer.
7) True: Resumes present matching experience. If you have none, alternative measures are required.
8) True: Getting unexpected calls means your campaign is optimized for the in-demand jobs you are qualified for.
9) True: Yes, in most cases it takes about 3 months of interviewing alone from first contact to transition..
10) True: You probably will not achieve full employment without first doing a re-entry strategy.

~•~

You have reached the end of the strategy I use for my B2W mom candidates. This strategy:
- Gets moms back to work
- Gets moms back to full professional rate (as if you had not left)
- Offers reliable strategy that provides more certainty to your career change goals
- Quickly and happily overcomes a gaping hole on your resume
- Brings recruiters to you for the jobs you want
- Allows you to perform a passive and active job search
- Enables cutting edge interviews
- Achieves salary increases
- Decreases unemployment time

This book also came with a bonus link to the free video course (www.karengurney.com/mom) with downloads and the ability to ask me specific questions. I look forward to helping you achieve your career goals!

About the Author

Dr. Karen Gurney was born, raised, and lives in Cleveland Ohio with her husband, two Goldendoodles, and a Papillon. As a Clevelander, she grew up living 'the death of a city.' This fostered her interest in urban economic development and why places grow, die, and are re-born and what the people that live there can do about it.

Your author loves economies. One of the greatest joys of coaching across the nation (and even the world) is to understand the job market that creates the demand for her clients' background. For instance, there has been a huge outmigration of jobs from the expensive Northern California market to places like Chicago or Houston where the labor pool is highly trained, less expensive, and more central to serving the country. This background has created her unique market-based strategy for career coaching.

Karen has 20 years of combined experience in executive search consulting, career coaching, and human resources. As the Director of Strategic Development of Career IQ, she leverages a Doctorate in Economic and Workforce Development and a Masters in Business Administration. Dr. Gurney's work has been featured on major U.S. news networks and she currently has eight online classes that teach career and business strategies in over 100 countries assisting over 8,000 students in their career pursuits.

I have a variety of specialized career books in the works so do not miss out! Join my class to stay current with releases at www.karengurney.com/mom.

Want to work with Karen one-on-one visit wwww.karengurney.com/consult.

One Last Thing

If you liked this book and found it useful I would be very grateful if you would post a short review on Amazon. Your support really does make a difference to me and other readers that need this information.

If you have other feedback or requests for me please connect on https://www.linkedIn.com/in/karengurney.

I respond to each and every comment personally.

Thanks again for your support.

Dr. Karen Gurney